HOPE

the heartbeat of mission

Together in word and action

contents

Introduction

Prayer

Proclaiming the word

Calendar

Festivals & fun days

Autumn: HOPE explored

Harvest

Work

Community

Final thoughts

introduction

'It has been a privilege for us at HOPE to play even a small part in what God has been doing and we're thrilled to be providing you with this resource in the hope that we can all do more to see God's kingdom come on earth.'

Dear friends...

This is an exciting time for the people of God. We're seeing more churches reach out into their communities than ever before, demonstrating the good news through their words and actions. Churches are partnering together to be able to do more, showing their cross-cultural unity, and seeing their communities changed as a result.

It has been a privilege for us at HOPE to play even a small part in what God has been doing and we're thrilled to be providing you with this resource in the hope that we can all do more to see God's kingdom come on earth.

Within the pages of this book, we have gathered together some of the best and most innovative ideas to enable churches to work together to communicate the gospel in both words and actions. There are ideas for everyone from small groups to large multi-church initiatives. Of course the intention of this resource is not that you would attempt to do everything, but that you would see what fits with your church, your resources and your community, and you would pick the best ideas that work for you. Our dream is that this resource would be a tool in your hands to bring change to individual lives and to keep your church at the heart of the community being good news.

We are praying that 2014 would be a catalytic year where churches will work together around the Christian calendar, festivals and new mission initiatives to bring good news to a lost and broken world. The fruit of this could be thousands of changed lives and a great harvest for the kingdom of God. As you plan your mission activities it is vital to keep in mind that any new Christians will need to be discipled into the faith, in order for them to keep walking with God and lead changed lives. Whilst this resource focuses strongly on mission, we recommend you also plan discipleship activities as a follow up to your community action.

WE HAVE GATHERED TOGETHER SOME OF THE BEST AND MOST INNOVATIVE IDEAS TO ENABLE CHURCHES TO WORK TOGETHER TO COMMUNICATE THE GOSPEL IN BOTH WORDS AND ACTIONS.

We have been really excited to see the breadth of ideas within the body of Christ, meeting critical needs in the community and reaching out with the good news in creative and relevant ways. In fact we have gathered so many ideas, articles and pieces of advice that we couldn't fit everything in here, so please do go to our website **www.hopetogether.org.uk** for further resources that will help you build and maintain a rhythm of mission for 2014 and far beyond.

God bless you,

Roy Crowne
on behalf of the HOPE team

Background to HOPE

HOPE came from a vision and conversation between Roy Crowne, Mike Pilavachi and Andy Hawthorne who were all passionate about churches in the UK reaching their communities with the good news of Jesus. HOPE focused initially on equipping and encouraging churches to take part in a year of mission in 2008. In that year churches were re-envisioned to get involved in their communities and saw many come to faith as a result. With this momentum gained, it was clear HOPE should continue and find new ways to resource and encourage churches in the amazing work they were doing. You can read more about the story of HOPE on our website www.hopetogether.org.uk.

Contact HOPE, 8a Market Place,
Rugby, Warwickshire CV21 3DU
T: 01788 542782
E: info@hopetogether.org.uk

The Importance of Word and Action

Over the centuries, Christians have asked what our priorities should be - unashamed gospel proclamation or serving the most vulnerable and marginalised. It's exciting to be part of the generation that's discovered the answer is both.

Andy Hawthorne, Message Trust

Our faith and mission will only become authentic at the junction where our love for God is expressed in our love to our neighbours, without compromising the commission to proclaim the gospel unashamedly.

Agu Irukwu, Chair of the Executive Council RCCG UK and Senior Pastor, Jesus House UK

Sharing our faith in Jesus Christ means living in such a way that our actions demonstrate the rule of Christ in our lives and that, wherever we can, we offer testimony to the difference following Jesus Christ makes. We need to be people of word and action.

When we work together as churches in mission these two things go seamlessly together. As Christian communities we should demonstrate the love of Jesus Christ to our wider community by our actions and faithfully explain our faith, the story of Jesus, offering others a clear way to join us as fellow disciples. We need to be people who know how to both act out and explain the Christian story in the 21st century in which we live.

Rachel Jordan, National Mission and Evangelism Adviser, Church of England

As Christians, we are called to share the life-changing news of Jesus – both speaking about our faith as well as demonstrating his love through acts of service.

Nicky Gumbel, Vicar of Holy Trinity Brompton

BELIEF AND BEHAVIOUR ARE INSEPARABLE FOR OUR CHRISTIAN WITNESS TO BE AUTHENTIC AND REAL.

Jesus modelled word and deed mission and so we follow his example; the good news needs to be experienced as well as heard.

Steve Clifford, General Director, Evangelical Alliance

Many may not want to hear what we say, but very few will deny an act of love that affirms the confession of our faith.

Yemi Adedeji, Director of One People Commission and Associate Director of HOPE

Belief and behaviour are inseparable for our Christian witness to be authentic and real. The true measure of Christian witness is to pass the test of credibility.

André Cox, Territorial Leader, The Salvation Army in the UK and Ireland

In the Vineyard we have always placed an emphasis on not just being biblically literate, but being biblically obedient too. Because of this we are intentional about reaching our communities and being missional in our activity. This is a worthy pursuit and it is our hope that both individuals and their churches would be inspired as they read this book, to go out, introduce people to Jesus and change the world in the process!

John Mumford, National Director, Vineyard Churches UK and Ireland

'When people see the difference the church makes on a local level, they're much more receptive to hear about how Jesus makes a difference on a personal level.'

Rachel Gardner, Romance Academy

'The Word became flesh'. Being like Jesus means we can no longer separate word and action. They are more than two sides of the same coin; they are the copper and nickel that create the coin. They are integral to one another.

Kiera Phyo, Tearfund Youth and Emerging Generation team

I remember John Stott telling me that he did not believe the gospel included social action, but that our mission did. So it's a case of proclamation and demonstration!

Lyndon Bowring, Head of CARE

There is a huge temptation for Christians to live compartmentalised lives and as a result to be less effective than we could be in our daily witness to the power of the gospel to transform. HOPE offers us the opportunity to be much more intentional about joining up what we think and say with what we do, to truly offer to God the worship of our lives and to offer our neighbours the life-giving Word of God. The Bible is always a book in translation and the most telling translation is the translation of our lives.

Ann Holt OBE, Director of External Relations, Bible Society

In Acts 20:24 Paul says: *'However, I consider my life worth nothing to me; my only aim is to finish the race and complete the task the Lord Jesus has given me – the task of testifying to the good news of God's grace.'* These words came from a man for whom the grace of God resonated so deeply, that he was prepared to risk his life so that others too might come to know the King! Having encountered the love and mercy of God we too know the gospel is the very best news there is. May Paul's words motivate us all to reach out through word and action to those in our neighbourhood who desperately need the love of Jesus!

Manoj Raithatha, South Asian Forum National Co-ordinator

Word and deed are inseparable. How can we preach good news but fail to help those in need actually experience it? How can we help the needy but not tell them that there is a destiny that awaits them and therefore choices to be made? For me it's summed up in Luke 4:18 which says: *'The Spirit of the Lord is on me, because he has anointed me to proclaim good news to the poor. He has sent me to proclaim freedom for the prisoners and recovery of sight for the blind, to set the oppressed free.'*

Carl Beech, Christian Vision For Men

Sharing something of your own faith journey and the love of God can be transformative.

Rural churches are very good at identifying and serving the needs of their communities, through deep involvement in the life of the village. But whilst the activities that we do make a difference, talking about our faith is also key. Jesus calls us to make new disciples. Sharing something of your own faith journey and the love of God can feel risky but it can be transformative, bringing new life to others.

Jill Hopkinson, National Rural Officer for the Church of England

This wonderful manual is a saturation of great ideas to help us bring God's love to everyone. But here's a health warning: don't try to do all these good things at the same time! We need the Holy Spirit's guidance to know how each of us can contribute. We will also need to be 'filled with the Spirit' (continuous tense – Ephesians 5:18) if we are to bring God's presence to those we are serving.

Secondly, don't forget to love and serve your church fellowship too. As Paul said in Galatians 6:10, 'Do good to all people, especially to those of the household of faith'. It is a lack of love and kindness in the Church which turns many away from Jesus, yet the Church should be a revelation of heaven on earth. Thirdly, if some of the projects seem 'too big' for smaller churches, this is an opportunity to work with other churches, expressing God's desire for unity, and for us to become 'of one heart and soul' (Acts 4:32).

As we continue lovingly to do good works in our communities, explaining the message of Jesus, we may together see God's purpose for the planet and the human race completed.

Roger T Forster, Icthus Christian Fellowship

How to Use This Resource

Welcome to the HOPE resource guide. In these next few pages we want to help you maximise the usefulness of this guide and make it as easy to use as possible.

Over the years of HOPE-filled mission we have learnt a number of lessons that we hope will be helpful to you as you plan your future activities.

Firstly, this all begins in the heart. There have been many initiatives over the years where church leaders and denominations have strongly encouraged people to be missional and, for a period of time, this external pressure creates a positive result. But once the initiative is over there is a huge drop in transformational and missional activity, so HOPE is seeking to do something different. We believe that mission begins in our hearts, and as churches and church members we embrace the underlying truth of John 3:16 that God so loved the world that he sent his son. We need to begin this HOPE initiative by asking God for big hearts so that we can see the true value of people. We need to understand that Christian love is unconditional. God loves us regardless of whether we respond or not and therefore we are to love all those around us in the same way.

Secondly, we understand the significance of prayer and in the resource we have many prayer ideas for churches to think about. A preacher once likened prayer to the power of a magnifying glass that can focus the rays of the sun to burn in one place. The magnifying glass can't of course make the sun hotter but it can provide a way to focus its energies. When we pray it doesn't make God love people more, but it does focus the love of God and the power of God into the lives of those we pray for so that people can begin to get a glimpse of the goodness of God.

Thirdly, in this resource we have gathered together what we hope is a comprehensive list of missional ideas that can be used in as many contexts as possible. They can be used by individuals, small groups/cell groups, individual churches or groups of churches. They can be used in cities, villages, and towns, and in our workplaces. They can be used by anyone who is taking their first step into a new missional adventure and those who have been doing mission for many years.

Building a rhythm of mission

We have once again emphasised the importance of the Church calendar in having key points in the year that make up the framework of our activity. They also provide us with a helpful picture of the three steps of our missional activity. Step one is reflected in Christmas as the time we focus on the incarnation and God coming into the world through the birth of Jesus. The ideas in this resource that are labelled 'ONE' are therefore all about helping us connect with our communities. These ideas provide us with lots of practical ways to demonstrate the love of God and preach the gospel through our actions. We have included a selection of radical, new examples of Christians running incredible programmes to love and care for the needs of people in their communities. Each of these organisations is willing to provide resources, help and support to enable you to replicate their work in your area. There are ideas for helping those who are in debt, ways you can be a positive presence on the streets, resources to help you create foodbanks and many more. There are also plenty of other ways to connect with your community whether that's through music, putting on free Fun Days, giving away Hot Cross Buns or holding a Harvest Supper. All the ideas that are about connecting with your community are labelled '**ONE**'.

The second point in the Church calendar is Easter when we think about what the death and resurrection of Jesus really mean. This is the heart of the Christian message and so the ideas in here that are labelled 'TWO' highlight opportunities to share the gospel message through our words. As we've been on this journey of HOPE, we've had many people ask us how we can effectively communicate the gospel in our postmodern culture. What language, metaphor and connection points really work? Likewise we've found that, whilst churches have been amazing at putting on all sorts of events and running different outreach programmes, this doesn't always create a spiritual hunger. We have taken this question and this challenge seriously and know that as the Body of Christ we need to find ways to explain clearly the wonders of the love of God as well as the cost and implications of following Jesus. Within this resource we have a whole section about the Word, unpacking this a little bit more, and we have labelled ideas that relate to giving a clear gospel presentation as '**TWO**'. These ideas include things like showing *The Nativity* or *The Passion* films, the use of literature, biographies of Christians and fiction like *The Shack* that raise questions of faith.

The third point in the calendar is Harvest – a time of reaping. If we sow the Word in a way that is understandable to people, it will have an impact on some and we will reap a harvest as they follow Christ. Ideas that are labelled 'THREE' will give those who have already come into contact with an incarnational idea, and those who perhaps have had an opportunity to hear and understand, an opportunity to respond to the gospel for themselves. Over the last few years we have seen the Church grow in a number of ways through initiatives such as Alpha and Christianity Explored and you will find these ideas and more labelled as '**THREE**'.

ONE

CONNECTING WITH YOUR COMMUNITY

TWO

SHARING THE GOSPEL WITH WORDS

GIVING OPPORTNITIES TO RESPOND

We hope that these categories will help you build a plan for mission that incorporates reaching out in practical ways to your community, building relationships and sharing the gospel in your words, and giving people opportunities to respond to the gospel and begin to follow Jesus. The next step will of course be to provide discipleship for those who are new to the church family.

Our prayer is that we would all allow God to give us such a love for those around us that we would be motivated to preach the gospel through our words and actions through 2014 and far beyond. We hope this rhythm of mission will serve you in 2014 but will also become a pattern that you can use for many years to come as we seek to transform our nation in the name of Jesus.

ONE ***ideas for reaching out to your community in practical ways***

ideas for relevant ways to share the gospel through your words

THREE ***opportunities for people to respond to the gospel message***

Building a strategy

To help you understand how this works here is an example of a strategy that a local church might follow using the three levels described (one, two and three). There is a choice to be made between each level and so naturally there will be fewer people who will enter into each stage.

Stage one

This incorporates two important things – demonstrating God's love through meeting needs within our communities and finding ways to build local relationships and friendships. So for example a church might run a pancake party and a Harvest Supper, whilst also setting up a foodbank and a debt advice service for the community. These help us connect with our communities, and help people to see that God is good and that Christians are OK!

Stage two

Once relationships have been built, we have an opportunity to invite people to go further in their spiritual journey. Not all will choose to do so and that is fine. As we've said, it's important that we continue to love and serve people regardless of what they choose to believe. This stage is about developing spiritual hunger and sharing some content of the Christian message. So for example a church might choose to have guest services at Christmas and Easter and have events that show DVDs such as *The Nativity* and *The Passion* to share some of the gospel.

Stage three

The next stage of the journey is giving people a chance to respond to the gospel – so, for example, a church might run an Alpha or Christianity Explored course where the gospel is clearly explained. Implicit in giving people an opportunity to respond, we need to think of ways we can connect people who do make a commitment into the life of churches over the long-term.

You will find many ideas throughout the resource on each of these stages so you can find a strategy that works best for your church and your community.

Missional Support Structures

It is the dream of the HOPE initiative not just to help churches to one great year of mission in 2014, but that 2014 will be the launch pad of a new missional journey that will empower churches on a year by year basis.

The question is how to support such a long-term, missional approach. Here are a few suggestions taken from the good practice of churches that have retained missional energy over a number of years.

IT IS THE DREAM OF THE HOPE INITIATIVE NOT JUST TO HELP CHURCHES TO ONE GREAT YEAR OF MISSION IN 2014, BUT THAT 2014 WILL BE THE LAUNCH PAD OF A NEW MISSIONAL JOURNEY.

Intentionality/enthusiasm

The petrol of church energy is enthusiasm about the communities church members live in and about what people do Monday to Friday. So missional churches intentionally focus on services, small groups, individuals' testimonies, and anything that keeps the missional agenda at the forefront of people's thinking. Reaching out is always sacrificial and through prayer, reliance on God and our encouragement, this agenda is kept alive.

Preaching and teaching

Churches that maintain missional energy have at least three or four messages a year in their preaching and teaching that relate to the challenge of reaching out, how we need to be big hearted and how the responsibility to be missional belongs to every member of the congregation. These themes are picked up year after year within the context of the preaching and teaching schedule.

Holistic small groups with a missional heartbeat

Many churches around the country have realised that it is people power that makes the difference, with small groups being a fantastic place to work on the two ingredients of mission. One: the authenticity and discipleship of every church member (people are encouraged in their own personal spiritual growth) and Two: individuals are encouraged in what they do Monday to Friday and are prayed for and supported in that. They are also encouraged in what they do in their neighbourhood, in their hospitality, in the church-based projects they may be involved in, and in their community projects and social activities (whether that be sports clubs, book clubs or political groups).

Missional communities

Some churches have found that creating groups of around 30 to 40 people around a specific interest that meet once a month is another way to keep mission on the agenda. These groups might focus on the workplace, what people do at work and how everyone can be more effective in the salt-and-light mandate. There might be a missional cluster that focuses on youth or young adults or on the practical social needs of the community. These missional groups not only encourage but help develop strategies and put into place programmes and initiatives related to their focus which help and empower the church to reach out.

Resources

There is no doubt that to stay missional takes a steady stream of resources, and throughout this HOPE book we have given a number of resources in terms of books, websites, and connections to organisations that will give you training and support for different initiatives.

Word and Action Theology

Paula Gooder

Many years ago, I went to a conference where there were optional workshops after the main talk. A big sign on the wall pointed left to a session on evangelism and right to a session on social action. I remember pausing and wondering how you were meant to choose. That sign implied a belief that evangelism and social action are two entirely different things; in reality the two cannot be so easily split apart. Proclaiming the gospel means little if we tell people God loves them but do not show them love. Caring for people is all very well, but what if they never realise we do it because God loves them?

We need to recognise, deep down, that words and deeds are deeply and profoundly linked and always have been. Right at the dawn of time itself in Genesis 1, creation only happened because God spoke. He spoke and the world came into being. What God formed in creation flowed directly out of the words he spoke. This dynamic, which links word and deed, lies at the heart of who God is and therefore must also lie at the heart of who we are. Indeed it also lies at the heart of who Jesus is.

One of the really important things to recognise about the Gospels is that they are an equal mix of what Jesus said and what Jesus did. We can sometimes focus too much on one or the other when the whole point is that Jesus' words had substance because he lived them out, and his deeds had meaning because of the words he spoke.

We need to recognise, deep down, that words and deeds are deeply and profoundly linked and always have been.

Think, for example, about the sermon in the synagogue recorded in Luke 4. There Jesus used Isaiah's moving prophecy in which he says that:

> *The Spirit of the Lord is upon me, because he has anointed me to bring good news to the poor. He has sent me to proclaim release to the captives and recovery of sight to the blind, to let the oppressed go free, to proclaim the year of the Lord's favour.*
>
> Luke 4:18-19

This sermon of Jesus is so powerful largely because Jesus then went out and spent his ministry with the poor, the captives, the blind and the oppressed. His deeds lived out the words he proclaimed, or in more modern parlance 'he put his money where his mouth was'. The whole power of Jesus' life was that he lived to the utmost every message that he spoke. We know he loves us, not just because he said so but because he opened wide his arms and died for us. We in our turn are called to love extravagantly in what we do just like Jesus did – and we do it because he first loved us.

Words without deeds are ephemeral and unconvincing. But even more than that, we act because it is a sign of who we are as Christians. Time and time again the New Testament writers remind us that our life in Christ has to bear fruit. There is no point claiming a life in the Spirit if our lives show no sign of the Spirit's fruit (love, joy, peace, patience, kindness, generosity, faithfulness and self-control, Galatians 5:22-23). In a similar way, the epistle of James points out that there is simply no point to our fine words, brilliant thoughts and clever concepts if we do not live them out in our lives. We have to be doers of the Word and not just hearers or speakers of it (James 1:22-24). What we say must be lived out or our words are quite simply pointless.

Jesus saved some of his most stinging criticisms for those who said that they believed one thing and did another. Take for example Mark 7:8-12, where he attacked those who said they honoured their father and mother and then avoid supporting them by declaring their money 'corban' (which is the ancient equivalent of a tax loop hole).

It is clear that our deeds must match our words or what we say will have little value for anyone. But what of the other way around, do we need to put words with our deeds? There is a lovely saying, attributed to St Francis, that goes 'Preach the gospel at all times, use words if necessary'. The idea behind it is that so often we assume that preaching involves standing around spouting, whereas the most powerful sermons (again as we so often see in Jesus' own life) can be preached with few, if any, words, as we stretch out our hands to lift up those who have fallen, to care for the sick or to comfort the grieving.

The problem, however, is that we can take this too far. The point about St Francis' saying is that the gospel is preached. It is all too easy for Christians to care for people but never actually tell them why. We can immerse ourselves in the most loving of deeds but if, at the end, those whom we have loved know nothing more of Jesus than they did at the beginning, have we not, in some way, failed them?

WE PLANT, WE WATER, WE WEED, WE WATER AGAIN, WE WEED AGAIN, AND SLOWLY WE SEE GROWTH.

1 Peter talks extensively around this kind of idea. Peter talks about living in such a way that it causes people to comment (1 Peter 2:12). He also recommends that women live with unbelieving husbands in such a transformative way that their husbands are 'won over without a word' (1 Peter 3:1). In 1 Peter 3:15 he talks about always being ready to give a defence or explanation of the hope that is in you. In other words, we act out of love but we never miss an opportunity to say why we do what we do, what our hope is, where it comes from and why it makes us act as we do.

Loving people, however, is no short-term project. It's very clear right from the start of the New Testament that loving people and seeing change is a very long process. Paul says, 'I planted the seed and Apollos watered it' (1 Corinthians 3:6). Plants don't grow overnight and they need a lot of care and attention over a long time to grow. So it is with our HOPE actions: we plant, we water, we weed, we water again, we weed again, and slowly we see growth. We may not see all the fruit ourselves but we have to trust people to God and know he is working in their lives.

Our HOPE actions are an essential part of who we are as Christians. Jesus loves us all so much and lived a life that simply oozed that love to everyone he met. He calls each one of us to do the same, and as we love with every fibre of our being, he calls us to proclaim in word AND in deed that we have the very best news of all, the gospel, the good news of Jesus Christ.

Dr Paula Gooder is a writer and lecturer in biblical studies

The Mission Process

Marty Woods

The ultimate goal of mission is for people to respond to God's love for them, demonstrated by Jesus' life, death and resurrection and expressed through the Church – in words and actions. Each individual can become more of who they were created to be as they respond to Jesus – the rescuer in God's epic story.

Over many years Fusion Youth and Community has developed a 'Process of Mission,' as mission is most effective when all of the stages of the process are being serviced, either by local churches, the community or by mission agencies (and ideally by a combination of these groups). Here is an outline of how it works.

1. Prayer: the starting point is a heart for God and his will for the community. For the world to be changed as God intends, there always needs to be a sustained commitment to prayer.

2. Research: we have our eyes and ears open to the needs and the available resources of the community through various forms of research.

3. Broad and legitimate contact: contact is made with a significant number within the community in a way that builds legitimacy and trust.

4. Role modelling: this is quite literally rubbing shoulders with the community, allowing them to see the difference faith and hope make in our daily lives.

The ultimate goal of mission is for people to respond to God's love for them.

5. Education: at this point in the process of mission, trust has built and people are seeking to understand the difference they have been experiencing. Education now enables them to engage with God's truth in a way that they can hear and understand.

6. Opportunity for commitment: while deeply respecting the individual's need to choose for themselves, this is where a clear opportunity to respond to God's call is given.

7. Integration into a local worshipping community: intentionally helping people find a community within the Body of Christ that they can belong to, building on the relationships between the church and community that have formed.

8. Helping people find their role in God's global purpose: the final goal of mission is to help people discover God's unique plan for their lives and to follow it wholeheartedly.

Marty Woods is European Director of Fusion Youth and Community

Community Franchising

Matt Bird

The Cinnamon Network, which has created the concept of Community Franchising, is able to help your church financially. A grant of £2,000 is available for your local church (or your group of local churches working together) to help start any of the projects with The Cinnamon Network mark in this resource!
For more information please see www.cinnamonnetwork.co.uk

Community Franchising is the new name for replicating the best of what the local church does to help those people most at need in their communities.

If you walk down the high street you will pass business franchises such as Costa Coffee, McDonalds, Thorntons, Boots, and Thrifty Car Rentals. Community Franchising projects are different in that they exist for community benefit rather than commercial gain.

One of the big benefits of Community Franchise projects is that the average local church can own and deliver them. The core service along with other elements such as the brand, best practice and funding model have been put in a 'box' so they can be replicated by hundreds of local churches. They have a number of key advantages:

- An 'off the peg' community transformation project which can adapted to fit the local context without having to reinvent the wheel.
- A community transformation project that has an established track record of delivering results across multiple other communities.
- A cost effective community transformation project because research, identification of success factors and training are already developed.
- A way of working which honours and serves local churches without having to raise significant costs for a central charity.

Each Community Franchise project addresses one of ten specific issues of poverty. The first five issues have been adopted from the Centre for Social Justice research into the pathways of poverty: family breakdown, educational failure, worklessness, addiction and debt. The other five areas of poverty have been identified by The Cinnamon Network action research: antisocial behaviour and offending, vulnerable elderly, homelessness, community health and wellbeing, and food poverty.

DURING THIS TIME OF GREAT SOCIAL NEED IN OUR SOCIETY THERE IS AN OPPORTUNITY FOR THE CHURCH TO STEP UP AND STEP OUT.

Even though each project has a specific poverty focus, every project is ultimately about one person coming alongside another person to walk with them through a very difficult time in their lives, to encourage, to help, to advise, to pray and to show them the love of God.

During this time of great social need in our society there is an opportunity for the Church to step up and step out. Currently there are over 2,000 local churches (5% of the UK Church) involved in serving their neighbourhoods through a Community Franchising project. It is anticipated that 10,000 local churches (25% of the UK Church) will become involved over the next five years.

It is time for the Church to do for community transformation what Alpha has done for evangelism, McDonalds has done for fast food and Costa Coffee has done for coffee. Let's put Jesus-filled community service on every high street and in every neighbourhood!

Matt Bird chairs The Cinnamon Network

A Step Further with Fresh Expressions

Graham Cray

In England, 34% of adults have never had any significant connection to any church. They are not waiting to be invited back; they have never been, and Church is an alien culture to them. Another 26% used to go, many as children, and show no interest in returning. They see no connection between the major concerns of their life and the Church. Those who know Jesus owe the gospel to those who don't (Romans 1:14-15) but if we are to reach people outside of the Church we will need to plant congregations which are not like the ones we have already. It is vital that we show Christian love in action, but we must recognise that many people will still not be drawn into existing churches through these demonstrations. The cultural gap is often too wide and we need to find ways to bridge this gap.

We call these new congregations 'fresh expressions' of church and they are being established all over the country. There is no single model to copy but a wide variety of approaches for a wide variety of contexts and constituencies, by a whole variety of denominations and church traditions.

The Church exists, not for its own sake, but for the place where it is located in the light of God's purposes in Christ. The purpose of a fresh expression is to be a community for networks, or parts of a neighbourhood, where the Church is not already engaged, in order to fulfil this calling. The emphasis is on planting something which is appropriate to its context, rather than cloning something which works elsewhere. The Fresh Expressions team has been encouraging and resourcing these developments for the past seven years and, reflecting on their experience, they coined a working definition of a fresh expression of church:

AS NEW PEOPLE GATHER ROUND THE FOUNDING GROUP, SO THEY SEE A MODEL OF CHRISTIAN DISCIPLESHIP WHICH EXPRESSES ITSELF IN SUCH SERVICE.

'A fresh expression is a form of church for our changing culture established primarily for the benefit of people who are not yet members of any church. It will come into being through principles of listening, service, incarnational mission and making disciples. It will have the potential to become a mature expression of church shaped by the gospel and the enduring marks of the church and for its cultural context.'

Another way of describing them is that they are to be:

- ***Missional*** - seeking to benefit non churchgoers
- ***Contextual*** - seeking to fit the context
- ***Formational*** - aiming to form disciples
- ***Ecclesial*** - intending to become church

Fresh expressions of church are birthed in listening to God. They are based on the assumption that the missionary Spirit is at work ahead of the Church in any place to which he calls his people. Developing out of this listening process, fresh expressions begin with service; service that is neither patronising nor manipulative. It is an end in itself; a little anticipation of the new creation, whatever else may or may not follow. These servant ministries being 'for' the place where God has sent or located them, in the light of the work of Christ, can lead to the establishment of communities which continue and develop that ministry.

As new people gather round the founding group, so they see a model of Christian discipleship which expresses itself in such service. Church and Kingdom are seen as inseparable. Fresh expressions, which are birthed out of service to their locality, model a life of discipleship, as do the founders who have sacrificed their personal, spiritual preferences to plant a community for those with different needs. Evangelism and disciple-making are inseparable.

Evangelism calls people to life-long discipleship by setting before them a way of life, as a follower of Christ the King. This relational approach to mission and discipleship can prove to be a further converting process for founding members of the fresh expression, who find themselves beginning to be changed through it.

It is often a mistake to start a fresh expression with a regular public act of worship to which new people are invited. It is not necessarily wrong, but there are two dangers:

- The fresh expression is seen as an event to attend rather than a community of disciples to join. It invites a consumer approach to the church.
- The event may be being designed for people with whom there is, as yet, no relationship. It has not been formed with them, for them.

A worshipping community can emerge through service, a focus on the Kingdom of God and the hospitality of Jesus. Good practice in establishing a fresh expression should lead organically to establishing Christian communities with a Kingdom orientation.

Resources

Fresh Expressions produces a wide range of materials to help you on your missional journey in your community and to take the next step in reaching those who would not otherwise be reached.

Those resources include a free six-session course (each session is between 90 and 120 minutes), called *msi (mission shaped intro)* which explores mission-shaped thinking in more detail. Find out more and download from www.freshexpressions.org.uk/missionshapedintro

There are also audio and video clips, guides and hand-outs as well as *Share* booklets which aim to encourage good conversations about starting new fresh expressions of church without telling you what to do! Details of all the resources available, and further information about Fresh Expressions, can be found at www.freshexpressions.org.uk.

Bishop Graham Cray is Archbishops' Missioner and leader of the Fresh Expressions team.

A WORSHIPPING COMMUNITY CAN EMERGE THROUGH SERVICE, A FOCUS ON THE KINGDOM OF GOD AND THE HOSPITALITY OF JESUS.

GraceSpace

GraceSpace in Bradford is 'a church for people who don't go to church'. Pioneer minister Colin Blake explains how GraceSpace started life in 2007 when Vicars Café was set up in Saltaire as part of the vision to create a community in the Aire Valley.

The Café provides a safe 'third space' where people can enjoy its hospitality and atmosphere while building relationships and hearing more about God's love. When the original founders moved away, the Café became a social enterprise with a board of management and a project manager running it day by day.

When we arrived on the scene we had no idea what the project was for or how to take it forward. Many people associated with the community travelled from all over the place in those early years but they weren't actually relating to each other very strongly.

So we began to move a lot of events away from Vicars Café and host them in our own home. We meet together as a group around meals and the people now coming range from families with teenage or adult children through to people in their 50s and 60s.

As we move forward, we have taken a long, hard look at our purpose in all of this. How do we look outside and make a difference? We have started to explore how we might do that by volunteering elsewhere. Perhaps we could give our support to a community or local Christian project rather than start one ourselves? All we can do is be honest that we are working out our faith in fear and trembling and trust God for the rest.

The Escalator

Philip Jinadu

If only churches were more like department stores, our evangelism would be a whole lot more effective. I don't mean this in a consumerist way, but in a structural way. Department stores are built from the ground up for those on the outside, to help them journey *through* the store to get what they're looking for. They are literally structured for seekers.

The central point of any major department store is the escalator. Usually the first thing you see when entering, the escalators are easily accessible, always on and automatic. Take but one step on to the escalator and it will carry you up to the next level. You can browse that level, stay on it as long as you like, but the moment that you're ready to go to the next level there's another escalator waiting for you. You don't have to hunt for it, you don't have to wait for it, you just have to take another step. It is utterly intuitive and wholly seeker-focused. So in that way, at your own pace, you can get through the whole store, right to the Holy Grail of electrical goods on the top floor.

When a person is on a journey of faith there are different levels they go through. Felt spiritual need, curiosity/intrigue about church, willingness to explore faith, questions to work through, opportunities to respond, integration into community, on-going discipleship and so on. The point is, people need to take these steps in their own time. For some, coming to faith is a dramatic crisis encounter. For others, it is months of gingerly finding their way.

The problem with most churches is that there are no escalators to help people move through these different levels. We expect seekers to do all the work themselves. We don't have easily identifiable entry points - there's no ground floor. We can put on great guest events from time to time, but there's no easy next step. It's almost like we've got a flight of stairs on one floor, a rope-ladder on another, a lift on the next, and they're all hard to find and erratic in operation. If you run an Alpha course - or something like it - every September, then it's useless to seekers who turn up in January. It's a lift that only works once a year, when you need escalators that turn over continuously.

Churches with an escalator mentality make sure that there are regular social guest events, appropriate for anybody and everybody. Flowing from them are process events like Christianity Explored and Alpha. There are regular seeker-appropriate services, like Baptisms, Dedications, Carol Services and Easter specials. There are events at small group level, events for those into sport or art or food. There are regular newcomers' presentations and new discipleship groups to join. Doors are always open, opportunities are always being created for seekers.

At Woodlands, when people come to our Bonfire Parties we make sure they're invited to the Christmas specials. At those Christmas events, there are flyers and publicity for our January Comedy Cabaret. During that, a presentation is made about the term's Alpha course, which is about to start. We use publicity, volunteers, the internet and social media to make things as simple and seeker-driven as possible.

Not everyone processes through in a nice, neat way. Sometimes people will spend a year just coming to the fun guest events, before finally making their way to a Sunday service.

But we work hard to make sure that the escalators are always running, always there, always accessible. When people are ready to take their next step, they know where to go.

Philip Jinadu is an Associate Minister at Woodlands Church, Bristol

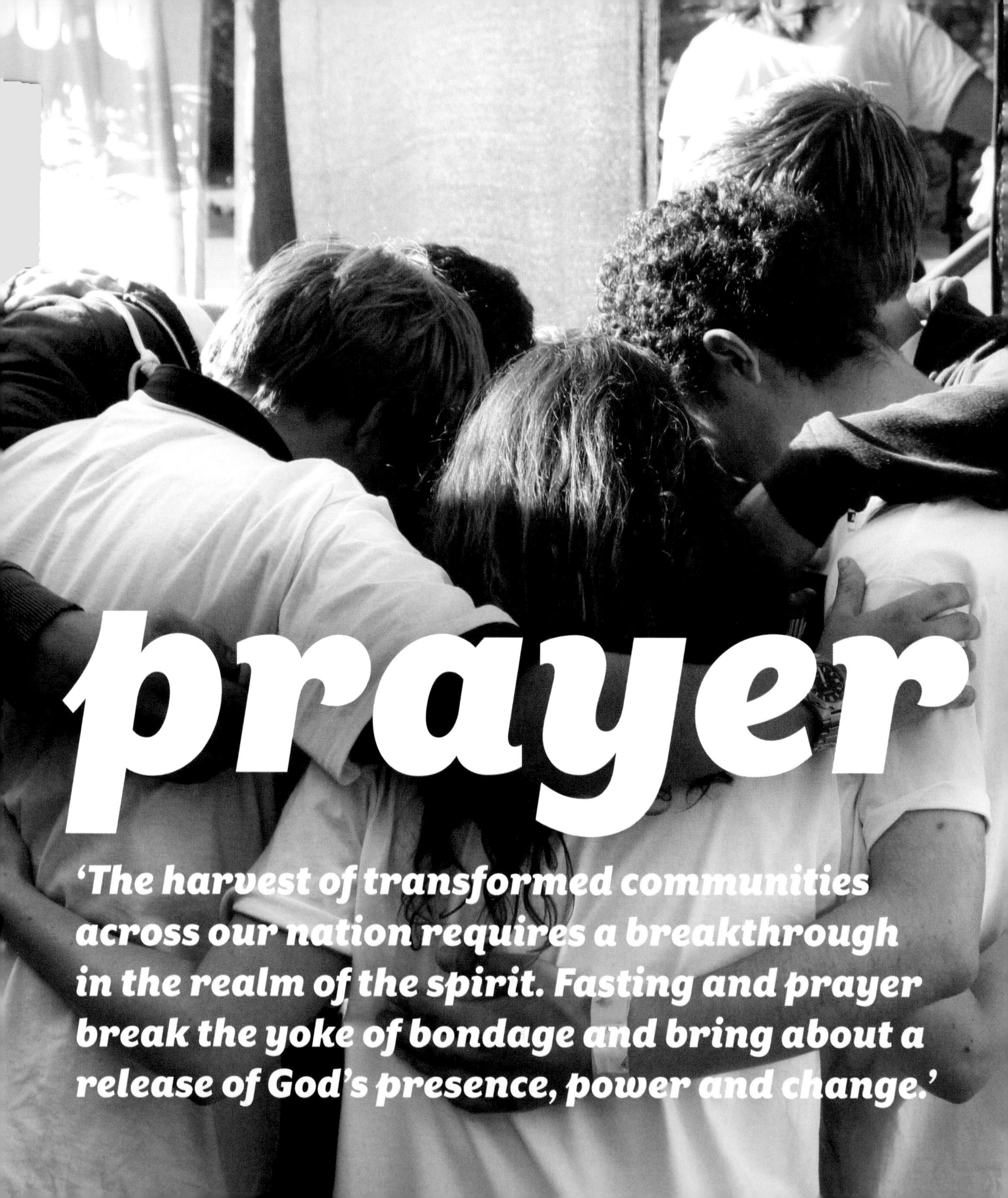
prayer
'The harvest of transformed communities across our nation requires a breakthrough in the realm of the spirit. Fasting and prayer break the yoke of bondage and bring about a release of God's presence, power and change.'

Harvesting a Community of Transformed People Through Prayer and Fasting

Agu Irukwu

In nature we see that the Harvest season for crops produced by the land is the result of a period of sowing and growing. Likewise, the harvest of transformed communities of new believers also requires an intentional period of sowing through prayer and fasting. Someone once said to me, 'Didn't fasting and prayer go out of style decades ago?' It was a genuine and honest question that may be in the minds of many more good Christians. The truth is that fasting and prayer are needed today more than ever if we are serious about seeing our communities transformed by God. The combination of fasting and praying is not a fad or a novelty but a spiritual discipline for all believers of all ages throughout the centuries and across the world.

The Bible taught about both fasting and praying, and gave us commands to do both. The Bible also gives examples of people who fasted and prayed, using different types of fasts for different reasons, and all of which had very positive results. Jesus fasted and prayed. Jesus' disciples fasted and prayed after the resurrection. Many of the Old Testament heroes and heroines of the faith fasted and prayed. The followers of John the Baptist fasted and prayed. Many people in the early Church fasted and prayed. What the Scriptures have taught us, both directly and by the examples of the saints, is that this is something we are to do.

The harvest of transformed communities across our nation requires a breakthrough in the realm of the spirit. Fasting and prayer break the yoke of bondage and bring about a release of God's presence, power and change. Our mission becomes God's mission when it begins in the crucible of prayer and fasting. I have seen this borne out in the course of my ministry and in the growth of our church. I have learned that fasting strengthens prayer as iron whets the sword. This is why 30,000 parishes of the denomination that I belong to, dedicate every February to prayer and fasting for their communities. At my church (Jesus House London) we also add the month of June. These are, of course, in addition to other days regularly taken out to pray and fast during the week.

Our mission becomes God's mission when it begins in the crucible of prayer and fasting.

The more seriously we approach prayer and fasting, the more serious the results we will experience in our missional journey. A spiritual fast involves our hearts and the way in which we relate to and trust God. It relates to discerning and receiving strength to follow through what God might reveal to us about circumstances in our lives or a direction we are to take in making a difference in our communities.

When we fast, we are suddenly aware of what is good and evil. We have a heightened awareness not only of God's goodness and of God's commandments, but of the evil that abounds in the world around us. We experience a greater discernment of good and God seems to give us an opportunity to take a look again at our lives and the world around us, and to discern his will and purposes as we partake in his mission. Let us pray and fast, taking control in the spiritual realm, that we might see a continuous transformation of souls in our communities and our nation for Jesus.

Pastor Agu Irukwu is Chair of the Executive Council of RCCG UK and Senior Pastor of Jesus House, London

How Did I Get This Busy?

Christopher Jamison

Life is busy but many of us speak as though 'being busy' is a force beyond our control. I have taken to asking people who come to the monastery where they find sanctuary in their life, meaning a sacred space or a place of refuge, and many say they find none. To reach out to our communities effectively, to be able to offer them the hope that is so often lacking today, we need first to be finding that hope for ourselves from God. That doesn't mean you have to spend hours every week on a retreat but finding time for stillness and silence in our everyday lives is vital to our connection with our creator. Simple meditation techniques that can be practised when alone or going about your day, are just one way to make space for sanctuary in your life and to open yourself up to hearing the voice of God.

The monastic tradition offers two ways to help us in the silent times: the use of a repeated phrase, and the slow reading of sacred texts. Here we will look at the use of the repeated phrase. Such use was commended strongly by the desert fathers; it was their portable, internal sanctuary. When being still and silent it kept their distracting thoughts at bay; when they were working, it helped to turn the work into prayer. One favourite phrase of the first monks was 'O God, come to my assistance; O Lord make haste to help me.' This phrase which is taken from the Psalms, can be spoken individually, repeated internally or said communally when Christians gather to pray.

In solitude, the phrase, or a similar one, can be spoken in time with breathing rhythmically: 'O God, come to my assistance' as you breathe in, and 'O Lord make haste to help me' as you breathe out. The rhythm of this helps to lift you out of yourself and away from the noises in your head. If those distractions become insistent, one way to handle them is to pause from the phrase, consider the distraction (if it's important, write it down for attention later) and then consciously say to yourself you are putting it aside. If you combine this repeated use of a phrase with the advice on fixing times of silence in your day, then gradually the phrase enters your soul, starts to overflow into your day and begins to transform your perception of life.

> We must know that God regards our purity of heart and tears of compunction, not our many words.

Within the Christian tradition there is also the Jesus Prayer that is so popular in the Orthodox Churches of south-eastern Europe and Russia. This prayer involves the constant repetition of the phrase 'Lord Jesus Christ, have mercy on me, a sinner', to be said inwardly at all times of the day and night.

Other techniques can also help you prepare the body: sit four square (in the lotus position or on a chair with your limbs uncrossed), keep your neck and back straight, breathe deeply a few times. All these can prepare the body for what is not an art of relaxation but an art of concentration. Imagine you are preparing to hear something very important from somebody important: you would automatically uncross your legs, sit up and concentrate.

In meditation, preparing your mind and body is done not as a mental and physical exercise but primarily to allow you to speak to God and finally to let God speak to you. Once I am speaking to the divine 'you' then anything can happen, and usually does, so let the conversation flow freely. The aim is purity of heart. St Benedict said, 'We must know that God regards our purity of heart and tears of compunction, not our many words. Prayer, therefore, should be short and pure' (Rule of St Benedict, 20:3–4). Benedict does not see a single prayer or mantra as the whole of prayer. He insists rather on the need for community life and community prayer as the essential framework for promoting prayer in its various forms, the many ways by which the diverse individuals come to address God as 'you'. This freedom of spirit within a framework is something that anybody can replicate in their life: you need a framework for your meditation, but let prayer flow freely within it.

I hope that you will find these simple techniques helpful as you seek God's inspiration for your HOPE activities and for the life of your community. I pray that you will find sanctuary for yourself from the busyness of everyday life so that as God's Spirit flows, the hope he places in you will overflow to all you meet.

A fuller account of this approach can be found in the author's best-selling book *Finding Sanctuary – Monastic Steps for Everyday Life* (Orion, 2010).

Christopher Jamison OSB is a Benedictine monk and former Abbot of Worth Abbey

Daily thankful prayer

Christopher Jamison has encouraged us through a spiritual meditation to listen and to connect to God on a regular basis. Let us consider putting this into practice, focusing on the words of Luke 10:2 which say: *'The harvest is plentiful, but the workers are few. Ask the Lord of the harvest, therefore, to send out workers into his harvest field.'*

- ***Find a place*** to be still for a few minutes.
- ***Use a prayer*** as you breathe in and out, e.g. 'O God, come to my assistance' as you breathe in, and 'O Lord make haste to help me' as you breathe out.
- ***Listen:*** read through Luke 10:2 slowly and stop to reflect on any word or phrase which stands out. What is the Holy Spirit saying to you?

'THE HARVEST IS PLENTIFUL, BUT THE WORKERS ARE FEW. ASK THE LORD OF THE HARVEST, THEREFORE, TO SEND OUT WORKERS INTO HIS HARVEST FIELD.'

- ***Meditate:*** repeat, reading this verse once or twice, allowing time to reflect on what is being highlighted. What is God saying to you in this?
- ***Pray:*** then turn to prayer, offer back to God what you are discovering and talk to God about all that he is showing you in this verse and how this impacts others.
- ***Contemplate:*** from prayer move to stillness and rest in God's presence remaining open to his love.
- ***Finish by saying*** 'O Lord fill me with your love' as you breathe in and 'O God guide me today' as you breathe out.

The challenge of Luke 10:2 is recognising that we are living in a time when the Harvest is plentiful but that there are not enough workers. So let us pray for ourselves and for our churches that as we go out into our workplaces and communities we might be:

- Full of God's compassion and love so we might seek the salvation of many.
- Generous with our hearts and lives.
- People who overflow with thankfulness for all that God has done for us, and we would be motivated by that to reach others with his love.
- A Church that sees all the opportunities in our work and community to share the love of God through our words and actions.
- People who know God's hope and share it with those around us.

Ideas for Prayer

Jane Holloway

The Church is not just a social work agency, or just a bunch of people who do good. It is a bunch of people who should be dependent on God and therefore, more than anything else, what the Church should do is pray.

Paul Bayes, Bishop of Hertford

Prayer has always been an important value in HOPE and it is exciting to see how prayer is being integrated more and more into mission. Jesus' teaching from John 15 makes it very clear that his invitation is for his people to remain (or make their home) in him. As we learn to do that day by day and surrender to his love (v9) we are then invited to soak in his friendship (v15), the aim being that 'we might go and bear fruit, fruit that will last' (v16). Then we are promised that, '...whatever you ask in my name the Father will give you'. Our prayer is that more and more individual churches and groups of churches will ensure that ongoing prayer takes place in every season of the year, to ensure that all mission activity is underpinned by prayer. Let's pray more, pray with others, and pray as part of our mission.

A growing number of churches have been exploring creative ways not only to mobilise prayer for their communities, but also to involve different churches and expressions of spirituality in the process. Rhythms of prayer are becoming an essential part of a church's programme.

Weeks of continuous prayer (using different models) as well as days of prayer are proving vitally important in all mission activity. Whole nights of prayer (for example the Festival of Life run by the Redeemed Church of God in London) draw thousands of believers to pray from 7pm to 7am the following day. (See www.festivaloflife.org.uk for more details.) Churches are using Lent (40 days before Easter) and the 10 days from Ascension Day to Pentecost Sunday, as well as Advent as times to have continuous prayer to pray deeper into the issues of community and nation.

PRAYER HAS ALWAYS BEEN AN IMPORTANT VALUE IN HOPE AND IT IS EXCITING TO SEE HOW PRAYER IS BEING INTEGRATED MORE AND MORE INTO MISSION.

Ideas for prayer

A week of prayer. You might want to base this on the 24-7 prayer model of having one dedicated prayer space or you could involve more churches by rotating the prayer meetings and rooms for prayer around your community, circulating prayer information so that every sector of the community can be prayed for with relevant information. You might even be able to cover the whole year in prayer 24-7 if you involve enough people! There are free resources and plenty of ideas to get you started at www.24-7prayer.com.

HOPE Community Prayer Treasure Hunt. Take your small group, church or group of churches on a treasure hunt around your community! You'll find all the info you need for a 60 minute prayer treasure hunt at www.hopetogether.org.uk .

Praying in the workplace. The Prayerworks initiative of the London Institute of Contemporary Christianity equips Christians to pray creatively for colleagues, workplaces and organisations with 40 day prompts for prayer. www.licc.org.uk/prayerworks

Pray at 12 noon. A number of churches and organisations are encouraging people to set their alarms and stop wherever they are to pray the Lord's Prayer at noon. Why not join in, as an opportunity to pause in the busyness of the day and commit yourself to God?

Adopt a Street. This is based on Luke 10 where Jesus tells his disciples to speak peace over the city. As the name suggests, individuals adopt a street where they live or work and pray a blessing on it, for at least a year. Adopt a Street is working in partnership with Neighbourhood Prayer Network, together with several other similar initiatives. Together they are aiming to see every street in the UK covered in Christian prayer. Sign up your street at www.neighbourhoodprayer.net

'We started Adopt a Street in Southend on Sea in mid-April and we have around 200 streets adopted now. Crime figures showed that from April to October antisocial behaviour fell by an average of 40% and by December had fallen by 64%'.

Prayer Spaces in Schools. An initiative of 24-7 prayer, this enables children and young people to explore faith and spirituality from a broadly Christian perspective in a safe, creative and interactive way. Flexible resources are available which can be adapted to work for participants aged five to 18 bringing an experiential dimension to a variety of subject areas and to pastoral aspects of school life. Find out how to get started at www.prayerspacesinschools.com.

'This was my first experience of a Prayer Space, so I really did not know what to expect. But the next four days were some of the most incredible in my 20 years of ministry. I feel incredibly privileged that the children allowed me to stand with them on such holy ground.' (Church leader)

Friday Focus. Each Friday send out a themed email highlighting local, regional and national issues for prayer around your area.

Prayer walking

You can prayer walk around your home community, your area of work, and around schools and college campuses.

The following extract is taken from *Neighbours, Transform Your Street* by Rebekah Brettle and Lyndall Bywater. You can find a couple of prayer walking guides that pray blessing over our streets at www.neighbourhoodprayer.net

Prayer walking simply involves walking around your community praying for the places and people you see around you.

1. What is a prayer walk and why is it a good thing to do?

'How beautiful on the mountains are the feet of the messenger bringing good news, breaking the news that all's well, proclaiming good times, announcing salvation, telling Zion, "Your God reigns!"' (Isaiah 52:7 The Message)

A prayer walk is exactly as it sounds: a walk filled with prayer. Prayer walking has been woven through the history of the British Church for centuries. People would walk from cathedral city to cathedral city on pilgrimage, and these pilgrimages were all about prayer. Today, many Anglican churches still mark Rogation Sunday with a prayer walk around their parish boundaries. This tradition, called 'beating the bounds', is an act of claiming the ground for God in prayer.

Prayer walking simply involves walking around your community (either alone or in a group), praying for the places and people you see around you. You may stop at specific locations, or you might just walk and see where the Spirit leads – either way, it's an exciting and engaging way to pray.

God told Joshua: *'I will give you every place where you set your foot'* (Joshua 1:3), and there is something powerful and significant about making our prayers physical: expressing our longings for places by going and standing there to pray.

Blessed to be a blessing

'Because those who are led by the Spirit of God are sons of God. For you did not receive a spirit that makes you a slave again to fear, but you received the Spirit of sonship. And by him we cry, "Abba, Father." The Spirit himself testifies with our spirit that we are God's children. Now if we are children, then we are heirs–heirs of God and co-heirs with Christ, if indeed we share in his sufferings in order that we may also share in his glory.' (Romans 8:14-17; see also Ephesians 1:3-14)

We are truly blessed. It is this amazing privilege of blessing which we want to invite you to use as you walk your community. This walk isn't about praying complicated prayers, tackling spiritual forces or solving social problems, it's about blessing your community with God's life, love and power. It's standing in your identity as a child of God, and speaking the good things of your Father's Kingdom into being in your local neighbourhood.

From the very earliest stories of God's interaction with humankind, we see a particular pattern of blessing emerging. God blessed Abram in order that he might give that blessing away to others:

'The Lord had said to Abram: "Leave your country, your people and your father's household and go to a land I will show you. I will make you a great nation and I will bless you; I will make your name great and you will be a blessing."' (Genesis 12:1-2)

Having blessed his people Israel, God expected them to extend his blessings to the foreigners in their midst:

'When an alien lives with you in your land, do not mistreat him. The alien living with you must be treated as one of your native-born. Love him as yourself, for you were aliens in Egypt: I am the Lord your God.' (Leviticus 19:33-34)

Jesus continued that same mandate of blessing: no sooner had he won salvation and freedom for his disciples on the cross, than he sent them out to carry this ultimate blessing to the very ends of the earth.

'But you shall receive power when the Holy Spirit comes on you; and you will be my witnesses in Jerusalem, and in all Judea and Samaria, and to the ends of the earth' (Acts 1:8; see also Matthew 28:18-20)

The moment we open our hands to receive blessing from God, we are nudged by the Holy Spirit to go out and give it away.

This business of blessing is not just some well-intentioned positive thinking. God's blessings are powerful and life-changing. They can unlock the strangle-hold of death in desert places, and cause life to spring up:

The moment we open our hands to receive blessing from God, we are nudged by the Holy Spirit to go out and give it away.

'Instead of the thornbush will grow the pine tree, and instead of briers the myrtle will grow. This will be for the Lord's renown, for an everlasting sign, which will not be destroyed.' (Isaiah 55:13)

God's words can reverse the effects of sickness:

'The centurion replied, "Lord, I do not deserve to have you come under my roof. But just say the word, and my servant will be healed."' (Matthew 8:8)

God's words can bring impossible peace in the midst of impossible pain:

'Peace I leave with you; my peace I give you. I do not give to you as the world gives. Do not let your hearts be troubled and do not be afraid.' (John 14:27)

'And the peace of God, which transcends all understanding, will guard your hearts and your minds in Christ Jesus.' (Philippians 4:7)

When God speaks in blessing, the world is changed. And we, his children, are given the privilege of accessing those same blessings. We get to experience them in our own lives, but we're also given the privilege of speaking them into being for the people and places around us. Jesus gave his disciples authority to reverse the works of the enemy, and to cause life to spring up:

'I have given you authority to trample on snakes and scorpions and to overcome all the power of the enemy; nothing will harm you.' (Luke 10:19; see also Mark 16:17-18)

He intended us not only to be present where there is pain and sin, but also to speak out the blessings which will turn those situations around.

As we walk the streets of our communities, whether on our own or on a church prayer walk, let's resolve to be good news... to be those who carry the blessings of God in our thoughts, words and actions.

Jane Holloway is National Prayer Director at the World Prayer Centre in Birmingham and a member of the HOPE leadership team

Resources

Websites

Community and church prayer resources

www.24-7prayer.com – how to run weeks of prayer, podcasts, stories of answered prayer and all the 24-7 books and manuals

www.prayerspacesinschools.com – helping children and young people explore faith as part of their education

www.schoolsprayernetwork.org.uk – mobilising prayer for every school

www.healingroomsengland.com – **www.healingrooms-scotland.com** – offering prayer for healing

www.healingonthestreets.com – resources from Healing on the Streets

Individual/family prayer resources

www.when2pray.net – helping couples pray together

www.pray-as-you-go.org – free downloads

www.waymakers.org – an email guide helping to focus prayer for those not following Jesus Christ

National/global prayer

www.worldprayer.org.uk – runs monthly prayer days, links with houses of prayer and all prayer organisations and networks across the British Isles, and globally through the International Prayer Council

Prayer resources for seekers

www.rejesus.co.uk/spirituality - post or download prayers, explore praying

www.trypraying.org - resources written to be used by those who have never prayed before

Books

Heal the Land - *reflections on a corporate prayer journey for the transformation of Stoke on Trent* by Robert Mountford
An inspiring reflection on the impact of united prayer in community engagement.
(Tentmaker Press)

Neighbours, Transform your Street!
by Rebekah Brettle and Lyndall Bywater
Profiles of UK initiatives that are currently involved in praying, caring and sharing the good news.
(Sovereign World)

God is Still Speaking: *Sparking a strategic prayer revival throughout the Church* by Brian Mills.
An overview of how churches integrate prayer and mission. (Sovereign World)

Prayer – a beginner's guide by Jane Holloway (BRF)

Supernatural Communication
by Rachel Hickson (New Wine Ministries)

Redeeming our Communities by Debra Green (New Wine Ministries)

The Dynamics of Effective Prayer by Alistair Cole (Life Publications)

The Grace Outpouring – blessing others through prayer by Roy Godwin and Dave Roberts
(DC Cook)

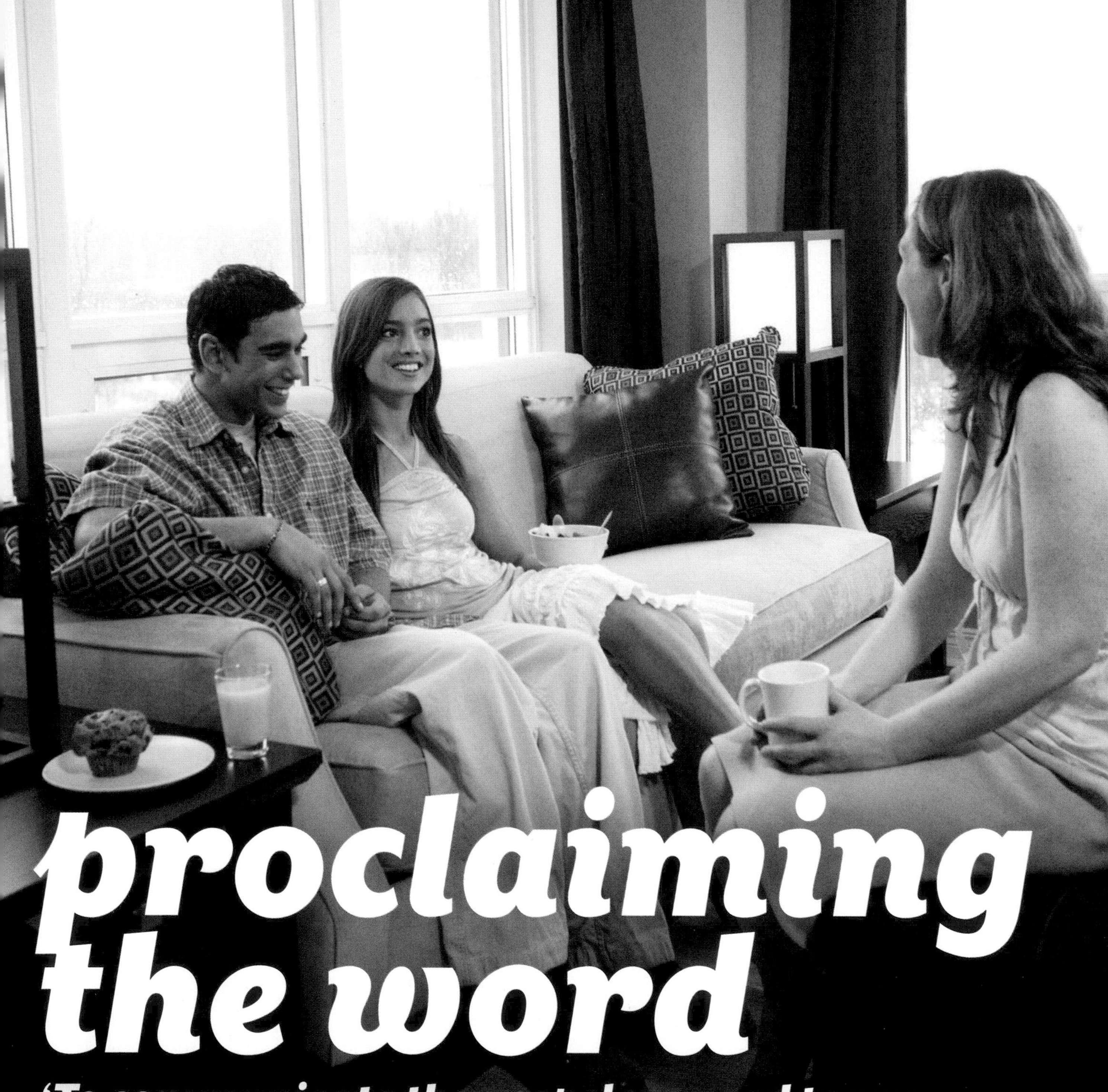

proclaiming the word

'To communicate the gospel we need to use both our words and our actions.'

Communicating the Gospel with Words

Roy Crowne

To communicate the gospel we need to use both our words and our actions. Many of the ideas within this resource relate to the actions, so here we want to focus on the importance of the word element. If we want people to know about God, at some point we need to communicate what we believe, telling them about Jesus and what he has done. It often seems that this is the place where we have the most difficulty. Here are some keys you may find helpful as we journey together to communicate the message of the gospel effectively.

The first is: know your audience. In other words think about the context of the event and the people who will be there. This was something that Jesus was brilliant at doing. Whether it was talking about the leaven in the bread, farming or money, his stories and parables were about things that people knew and understood. He then moved from there to the truths that he wanted to present. Let's present the gospel with the language, signs and symbols that people can understand.

The second principle to be effective in communicating the gospel is to tell people what they know to be true. The parable of the sower talks about various different soils where the seed of the word of God is planted in each soil but has a different impact. Telling people what they know to be true opens them up to an 'A-ha!' moment when they realise that what is being said is true in their lives.

LET'S PRESENT THE GOSPEL WITH THE LANGUAGE, SIGNS AND SYMBOLS THAT PEOPLE CAN UNDERSTAND.

The final piece of advice is that Jesus would then put the message into a Kingdom context. He didn't seem to feel that he had to tell the whole gospel, but could leave that one seed that the Holy Spirit could use to bring people along on their journey of faith. We don't have to cram everything in to each event, but we can reflect on one aspect of the gospel that seems to fit the context, then pray that Jesus would be seen through our words and actions and that he would draw people to himself.

Roy Crowne is Executive Director of HOPE

Preaching the Word in Today's Culture

Laurence Singlehurst

At the end of Hope08 the HOPE leadership team did an extensive evaluation of what had and hadn't worked, asking churches that had been involved for their input. It seemed that, on the whole, churches felt they had connected with the need for putting their faith and their love into action in the community and had seen a positive response. However a key piece of feedback was that people wanted help with how to communicate the gospel in words. Church leaders recognised that there is a crisis of confidence about the words of the gospel. They wanted advice on how to communicate the Christian message using connection points, language and metaphors that people understand in today's culture.

As a result of this feedback the HOPE leadership team and many others have been have been thinking through this issue and we'd like to present some ideas as part of a process of creativity, of re-imagining, and of contextualising the words of the gospel. We hope these thoughts will be a springboard to your creativity.

We want to look at these ideas and thoughts firstly in the spirit of contextualisation. This is the process by which missionaries seek to present the Christian message in a way that is relevant and dynamic in a new culture, so that it can be understood by the hearers because it is spoken through connection points, metaphors and language that are familiar to them. We understand this process for missionaries going to unreached people groups, but every now and again our own culture changes to the extent that our approach also needs to change.

We need a new season of being prepared to experiment; and, if and when we fail, we learn from it and try again.

This process has perhaps four dynamics to it:

1. **Confusion** - where you realise you have a problem
2. ***Creativity*** - where you begin to think about how you deal with the problem
3. ***Early models*** - prototypes, where experimentations are being made
4. ***Working models***

The third stage is perhaps the most important part of these. Engineers tell us that prototypes have two dynamics: they can work or they can fail, but they do not see failure as their enemy, but as a friend that teaches them something so they can try again. It is this attitude that the Church needs to take on board. We need a new season of being prepared to experiment; and, if and when we fail, we learn from it and try again. Is it a strange thing to say that for a period of time the Church needs to fail so that it can learn and grow?

A lesson from history

We see the early contextualisation of the gospel in the book of Acts where the apostle Paul wrestled with the Jewish culture that had become intertwined with the Christian message. He sought to find a more dynamic and worldwide contextualisation that would set the message free. But another interesting lesson from history might be St Patrick. In his book, *How the Irish Saved Civilisation*, Thomas Cahill gives a hypothesis that St Patrick realised he could not take on the Roman approach to mission in its entirety. He did take some ideas from this tradition but it would appear that, having been a slave and having lived within

Irish culture, he also understood their ways and contextualised the message in this way.

Firstly, he understood they were a martyr culture. Celtic men had an aspiration to die in battle; to lay down their lives. He gave them a new aspiration: to take up the sword of the Spirit and to lay down their lives to be martyrs for the Christian message.

Secondly, he dealt with fear. They were afraid of the trees and he preached in woodland clearings to demonstrate that he had spiritual authority. They were afraid of the forests, and he told them that God had made the trees and the forests so they did not have to be afraid.

Thirdly, he spoke some good news. In their culture there was child and adult sacrifice and he told them that Jesus had died for all, therefore no one else had to die.

Fourthly, he dealt with a social issue, campaigning against slavery more than 1,400 years before Wilberforce.

Now this gives us a way to think about contextualisation. What is an aspiration of our culture that we could relate to? What are some of the fears in our society that grip people that we could relate the Christian message to? What is good news for us? How could we describe the life and death and resurrection of Jesus in a way that sets people free? As St Patrick did, we must connect the Christian message to the real needs of society, which is what HOPE has been doing through our actions already.

AS ST PATRICK DID, WE MUST CONNECT THE CHRISTIAN MESSAGE TO THE REAL NEEDS OF SOCIETY, WHICH IS WHAT HOPE HAS BEEN DOING THROUGH OUR ACTIONS ALREADY.

Another way for us to think about this is to look at what the Scriptures say. In Matthew 13:18 Jesus begins to explain the parable of the sower which is recognised by theologians as one of the main passages where Jesus deals with the process of conversion and understanding the message of the Kingdom. What is interesting about this parable is that it is not about whether people hear the Word or not, it is about whether they understand the Word. We see that the hard soil, the path, is like people who hear the Word but understand nothing and it is taken away. The rocky and thorny soil is like people who understand something because they receive the message with great joy so they understand some of the benefits but not the cost and sacrifice. But the good soil is people who hear and understand and they become fruitful followers of Christ, which is our dream.

So what does this parable tell us? That understanding – not hearing – is the goal. We can use words like sin, repent, born again, saved, washed in the blood of the lamb – all words that were once used in Sunday schools when Christianity was a major part of our culture and so these words were understood. Now, for many people, these words are a mystery. They have never heard them before and they really don't know what they mean.

The warning for us is that the gospel must be explained both in its benefits and in its implications otherwise, as the parable teaches, people will respond with joy but then fall away. Perhaps the weakness of preaching in the last 20 years is that we have overemphasised the benefits and not really described the implications and cost.

So we have a language issue. The words that are meaningful to us may not work for others. In my book *Sowing Reaping Keeping* I provide a list of words that we commonly use when preaching the gospel which are not perhaps as understandable as they once where and offer some alternatives:

Sin = principle of self rule = selfishness

Repent = change your values

Love = sacrificial love

Sanctification = clean, walking free

Saved = surrendered

Conversion = new start

Disciple = follower, friend

Lordship = surrender, give up rights

Worship = honour

Born again = new start

Baptism in the Holy Spirit = power to love

Hell = separation from God

Kingdom = God's rule

Evangelism = unconditional love

Give your heart to God = commitment

Give your life to Christ = put Jesus at the centre

Crucified with Christ = dead to self

Redemption = rescue

Church = God's people

Election = chosen

You may not agree with all these suggestions but I hope it helps you to rethink the language you use and its relevance to today's culture.

Connection points

There are four component parts of the Christian message:

Good news

There is some good news, something fantastic, something useful. In the parable of the treasure and the parable of the pearl, what Jesus alludes to is that if people can find the treasure and see the pearl (Matthew 13:44-45) in all its wonder, then actually selling everything and obtaining the pearl or the treasure is not a problem. Billy Graham in 1954 emphasised the need of forgiveness as a connection point for the good news, and in a society with a strong moral plumb-line, this was indeed good news. But in today's culture many people don't feel they have done anything wrong and therefore don't see the need for forgiveness. So what is good news now? Jesus talked about the Kingdom mandate that he had come to set the oppressed free. Maybe we should emphasise that the Christian message brings justice, freedom and love. Historically we have explained the good news in very personal terms and we could perhaps consider, not forgiveness as the emphasis, but 'you matter'. Others might include 'friendship with God', 'your life has purpose', 'love is the answer' and 'generosity makes a difference'.

In today's culture many people don't feel they have done anything wrong and therefore don't see the need for forgiveness.

Addressing a problem

Another aspect of the gospel message is it deals with an overwhelming problem, something that destroyed relationship with God and relationships with people. Historically this is described as sin – again, a word which is meaningful to Christians but has lost meaning in our society today. So we need to find a new way to describe this. In 2 Corinthians 5 we see the apostle Paul dealing with the same issue in a pavement culture that was in some ways similar to ours. In his letters to the Corinthians Paul describes the gospel in this way – 'He died for all, that those who live should no longer live for themselves but for him who died for them and was raised again' (2 Corinthians 5:15). So for the apostle Paul the universal problem here is living for ourselves. It has been said by some that our postmodern culture is one of the most 'live for ourselves' cultures the world has ever seen. We place ourselves and our own happiness at the centre of everything. The *Daily Mail* had a headline saying 'Is greed the new religion' as they recognised that our culture has taken a huge step away from the values of selflessness and altruism, which were part of our Christian heritage, and has turned to greed and selfishness. These are issues that affect everybody and perhaps in this way sin can be explained using language and connection points that make sense.

Finding answers

Thirdly, we must have some good news. Again Paul's message in the 2 Corinthians passage says that we can be set free by no longer living for ourselves, but by surrendering to Christ we can be changed and transformed. So in a sense the good news of Jesus' life, his incarnation, his identification, his demonstration of the wonder of the love of God and who God is, and ultimately his death and resurrection, is perhaps the one area of the good news that is still dynamic today. We need to describe the wonder of this love that God has shown us: so that we can be set free; so we can live differently, and so that we can not only experience this for ourselves but also be a part of God's great purpose.

A life lived out

Fourthly, a life lived out. Historically we have often talked about repentance and Lordship as the key issues of the Christian life lived out, and maybe we need to find new ways to describe this. Lordship is certainly an idea that has very little meaning in today's culture, so perhaps for us the concept of surrender is more dynamic. We understand that we are in control of our own lives; we decide what is right and wrong; we decide what we should or should not do and how we should live. Yet the Christian challenge is to surrender our understanding and embrace Christ and his understanding. Repentance is definitely a word that we struggle with today, especially as so often we think it means to change direction when in fact it means to change your mind; perhaps this is a better concept for us. Again the apostle Paul, who was also struggling in a pagan culture, wrote to the Romans in chapter 12:2: 'be transformed by the renewing of your mind. Then you will be able to test and approve what God's will is – his good, pleasing and perfect will'. Alan Krieder, in his helpful book about the early church[1] speaks of why catechism was so important to them. This was the process by which people understood that their Roman values, the pagan values derived from false gods, were not the way forward. Instead they were taught to embrace Christian values of love and sacrifice, integrity and honesty. This challenge to our culture, to change our value systems, is something we increasingly hear secular commentators and politicians talking about. So let's not let the secular world steal our thunder. Let's proclaim that the life lived out is about a relationship with God through Christ; it is about changing our value systems and living in a different way. Thinking about the gospel broken down in these four ways may appear a little mechanical, but can be helpful.

Repentance is definitely a word that we struggle with today, especially as so often we think it means to change direction when in fact it means to change your mind.

There is a growing movement around the world which suggests that in preaching the gospel today, we should talk more about Jesus. It may sound simplistic, but we need to recognise that our secular society today knows very little about Jesus. They don't know what he said or what he did, so how can we ask people to follow him? We need to put Jesus back at the centre, telling people who he was, and what his incarnation, life, death and resurrection mean.

[1] *The Change of Conversion and the Origin of Christendom* (Continuum International Publishing Group)

The use of stories

It may help to suggest that we each think about four stories about Jesus in the New Testament that are most meaningful to us, so that when we are asked about our faith we can tell a Jesus story. This would help us tell the story without a religious angle, but with authenticity and emotional strength as it is personal.

Another issue for us might be that as individuals and church leaders, when the gospel in any form is described, it tends to be described in a 'I have the truth and you don't' tone. This is hard to stomach for many listeners, and can appear unfriendly and accusatory. Perhaps what we need is a softer tone of voice in our culture today. Explanation and story are much more easily understood by people, and perhaps our preaching of the gospel needs to explain we are not ashamed of these truths and ideas. Then we let people think for themselves whether it is true or not and what they want to do with it. In a sense we see this worked out with both Alpha and Christianity Explored courses in that they give space for people to share their thoughts and ideas whether they are right or wrong. There is a growing explanation through the course and, in the end, people decide for themselves whether they want to believe or not.

We have made the above comments and have included the other contents of this section as part of the creative process. The truth is that none of us is absolutely certain what works and what doesn't work in today's culture, but in the spirit of contextualisation we need to experiment, be creative and learn together.

Resources

The Gospel Message Today
by Laurence Singlehurst (Grove)

Sowing, Reaping, Keeping by Laurence Singlehurst (IVP)

The Evangelical Alliance have conducted research into how Christians have come to faith, how they share their faith, what they believe the barriers are to sharing the gospel and where they are most likely to interact with non-believers. To find the report entitled ***Confidently Sharing the Gospel?*** please visit their website www.eauk.org.

Inductive Preaching by Ralph and Gregg Lewis (Crossway Books)

Biblical Perspectives on Evangelism
by Walter Brueggemann (Abingdon Press)

The Practice of the Prophetic Imagination
by Walter Brueggemann (Fortress Press)

Laurence Singlehurst is Director of Cell UK and a member of the HOPE leadership team

Invitation

Roy Crowne

Invitation is right at the heart of Christianity. Throughout the Old Testament we see God inviting his people to follow, to serve, and to love him. Likewise in the New Testament, God extended that invitation through Jesus so that it was available to all. In view of this, and of Paul's words that God makes his appeal through us (2 Corinthians 5:20), we should live a lifestyle of invitation. We need to ask God for the courage we need to step out and invite others into relationship with him.

So often we can feel frustrated when people say no to our invitations to events like carol services, Alpha courses, or other church activities. We feel that if they don't come, we've failed, but actually we don't have any control over their decision – it is simply our job to ask. We may feel rejected if they say no, but we have to remember there could be any number of reasons they can't attend. With these things in mind, we may create a culture where we're prepared to just ask people, having confidence in the fact that we're inviting people to take a step on the best journey they'll ever take. Let's aim to increase the number of invitations we make, remembering invitation is at the heart of our faith.

Extending an invitation

Michael Harvey

Many of us cannot remember the last time we invited someone to church, because we have simply stopped inviting people. One reason might be that we fear someone saying 'no' to our invitation, or perhaps we've asked people before and been disappointed by their response. Why do we give up so easily? I have heard countless stories from Christians who had to be asked several times before they ever accepted an invitation. We need to learn from the persistence shown in the story of the lost coin (Luke 15:8-10) or the lost sheep (Luke 15:1-7), where a true persistence and determination was shown because the thing that was lost was worth searching for. It would also help us to remember that 'success' is doing our bit and inviting someone; we cannot control or claim responsibility for the answer they give. It's OK for someone to say no, the important thing is that they were invited.

'SUCCESS' IS DOING OUR BIT AND INVITING SOMEONE; WE CANNOT CONTROL OR CLAIM RESPONSIBILITY FOR THE ANSWER THEY GIVE.

Some of us fear that we might spoil a good friendship. We don't ask because we are afraid it will cause irreparable damage, but frankly it is very unlikely that we are going to spoil a true relationship over a simple invitation. And of course there's every chance it might change the relationship for the better! But fear of being rejected can just stop the whole process. I have been rejected hundreds of times and yet I can still take it personally. I have to remind myself that it's not a rejection of me; that person is just not yet ready to come to church. We need to be people who live by faith rather than fear. Fear stands for **f**alse, **e**vidence, **a**ppearing, **r**eal. Fear is a thief that steals and destroys but it will only become big if we allow it to grow. We can stop it growing by recognising it; then we can resist and reject it. Our doubts and fears will usually step aside when we make an unyielding commitment to action.

For church members to feel confident in extending invitations, it's also important for church leaders to be clear about seeker-friendly services. Harvest is a great time to have a guest service and for church leaders to tell their members in advance how that service will be delivered so they can feel confident in asking friends.

So let's all take courage and be generous in inviting others to come along to our church activities and services, for by doing so we will reap a rich harvest.

Michael Harvey is Principal Consultant for Back to Church Sunday.

Back to Church Sunday

Back to Church Sunday is an opportunity to extend an invitation to friends or family and ensure they receive a warm welcome when they come to church. To make the most of Back to Church Sunday, hold it in September, perhaps the week before your Harvest celebrations and make sure you invite people who attend, to
join you for your Harvest service the following week. You can find out more about Back to Church Sunday and order resources at www.backtochurch.co.uk.

Resources

Table Talk is a series of games designed to help friends and family engage in meaningful conversation. There are games that are themed (for example around Easter and Christmas) and ones that are aimed at different age ranges (from 10 years and up). Each game has six big questions which can be explored over six weeks. To find out more and to purchase games please visit www.table-talk.org.

Unlocking the Growth by Michael Harvey (Monarch)
A book about the power of invitation; looking at how churches can grow through members of the congregation inviting their friends.

The Big Welcome

The Big Welcome is a simple church-facing campaign to encourage Christians to invite someone they know to something they love. With its roots in Back to Church Sunday, this Free Church initiative, a partnership between Elim and the Baptist Union, is about making people feel really welcome in any church activity.

The word 'church' is purposefully not in the title so you can be really creative about what you would invite people to, whether that's a meal, a concert, a quiz night, a coffee bar or even a church service.

With the theme around God's big embrace and the story of the prodigal, the Big Welcome is an initiative by which churches can encourage people to take an invitation, trust in the power of prayer and take big steps in reaching out to their friends and family. The Big Welcome is supported by resources including posters, invitation cards, prayer cards and a bookmark give away, alongside service resources, teaching, and resources for churches in their planning to get ready to truly make church, or an event, a really welcoming occasion, without the cringe-factor. (The invitations and posters are available in both English and Welsh.) For more information and resources visit www.thebigwelcome.org.

For church members to feel confident in extending invitations, it's also important for church leaders to be clear about seeker-friendly services.

Young people

Soul Survivor

Soul Survivor is a great place to take young people to give them an opportunity to hear the gospel in a clear and relevant way. Every summer Soul Survivor gathers around 25,000 young people together over three events in Stafford and Somerset, and each year they have seen thousands give their lives to Jesus. Main meetings are focused on worshipping God in song, hearing from God's Word, and praying for one another in the power of the Holy Spirit. Young Christians feel comfortable inviting their friends along as everything is explained for those who have never been to a church event before, and there are lots of activities each day and evening including cafes, sports, films and music venues.

For more information go to www.soulsurvivor.com

Releasing the Workers for Evangelism

Mark Greene

As a church leader, you naturally want your congregation to be engaged in mission and evangelism all the time. The reality, however, is that they can't be engaged in mission and evangelism *in the same way* all the time. Every context is different – work, neighbourhood, door-to-door, mums and toddlers, Alpha – so your people all need to be supported in prayer but they need to be equipped in different ways.

As it relates to workplace evangelism, the three dominant emotions that a huge number of Christians feel are guilt, fear and inadequacy. They feel guilty because they think that evangelistic conversations are the only thing that really counts to their church – and they just don't get that many opportunities. They feel fearful because they rightly recognise that the people they share the gospel with today are going to be the people they share the office or the building site with tomorrow and it might go horribly wrong. They feel inadequate because maybe they haven't seen much fruit and don't seem very good at taking the opportunities that do come their way.

Well, with that in mind, there's a great opportunity for church leaders who want to help. Sometimes, however, church leaders feel ill-equipped to know precisely how. The most important thing, however, is not that you have the perfect evangelism model for every possible context but rather that you are a leader who wants to encourage your people for a life of workplace evangelism that is purposeful but not driven; Spirit-sensitive not impatient; bold but not impetuous; loving not mechanistic. And that you, like them, are ready to learn and use your own wisdom and skills and resources to help them work out the way forward.

As his people we do what we can in loving, cheerful obedience to his call and in the power of the Holy Spirit. And then we leave the results to him.

There for lots of practical ideas for your people in my book *Thank God it's Monday* but here are five things you, as a leader, can do:

1. You can reassure and envision

You can remind your people that God loves their co-workers. And because he loves them he is quite likely to be actively working in their lives to draw them to himself. The Christian may be the only Christian in the workplace, and very significant for that reason, but they may not be the only person or means of communication that God is using in the non-Christian's life: there's the witness of the Word, the witness of creation, the witness of other Christians, the witness of the Spirit and the witness of miraculous divine intervention.

Secondly, you can remind Christians that they spend quite a lot of time with the people they work with. So there's time to build credibility and trust and relationship. That said, you can also reassure them that you understand that, though there may be lots of opportunities to show the gospel in a day, there are usually rather few opportunities to share it.

Thirdly, you can remind workers that God is the evangelist. He draws people to himself. As his people we do what we can in loving, cheerful obedience to his call and in the power of the Holy Spirit. And then we leave the results to him. Sometimes people see fruit instantly, sometimes it takes years, sometimes we find out in heaven.

www.URBANSAINTS.org

ince 1906 we have been helping young people live lives of Faith, Hope and Love through Jesus Christ.

Through...

- Weekly resources
- Holidays
- Special events
- Community projects
- Training programmes

Together we can make a difference

Find Out How...
01582 589850
email@urbansaints.org - www.URBANSAINTS.org
facebook.com/urbansaints - twitter.com/urbansaints

2. You can demonstrate that you want to understand

Every workplace is like a foreign country. And they can be as different from one another as Norway is from the Sudan. It's one thing, for example, to be a young waiter in a suburban restaurant where the other waiters and waitresses are all young, the atmosphere open and there are plenty of opportunities to chat about life, the universe and Jesus. However, it is quite another thing to be a young lawyer in a city law firm working 70 hours a week, where every minute has to be accounted for, everyone around you is a rival and people don't tend to go much deeper in personal conversation than the latest episode of *EastEnders* or the football results. The point is that usually the opportunity to share a testimony or the gospel arises out of a relationship where the person trusts the Christian enough to let them in. And that will take a whole lot longer in that city law firm than in the restaurant.

So, you can ask your people questions, find out what their particular work is like, what the people are like, what someone's boss is like. You could simply decide to use five minutes after every service to ask one person a week: 'How do you see God working in your daily occupation?' After a while that will change your congregation. One of the most transformative things pastors can do, according to those who have done it, is to visit someone in their workplace. You might aim for one person every six weeks. You may never visit everyone but the word will get round that you are interested and that will send a powerful message to your people that God is too. Beyond that it will almost certainly further enrich your preaching, teaching and prayer.

3. You can pray and you can enlist pray-ers

Prayer is the most powerful tool we have. So you could begin to pray systematically for your workers – annotating a church list with information on where they work and what they do. You could look at the church's prayer diary and make sure that work is included with other missional areas.

Just imagine what God might do through your church's ministry among the people they spend so much time with at work. The Lord be with you. And them.

You could encourage small groups to pray for each other's non-Christian co-workers by name. It only has to be one person and people who don't work outside the home can bring the name of someone they are concerned about.

4. You can harvest stories of fruitfulness and blessing in the workplace

Testimony inspires. And as people begin to hear stories of fruitfulness they too will recognise how they may already be fruitful themselves and how God might use them. Ideally, these need to be shared publicly – either in a service or through a newsletter.

5. You can ask workers: what would help you be more fruitful?

Some people will need training to be ready for and alert to opportunities, others might need help in identifying a next step. Pathways abound: from a Christmas card, to a Christian book on an issue, to a novel with an interesting theme that triggers a conversation, to a verse for a particular occasion, to a one-on-one Bible study in the local coffee shop before or after work, to an invitation to a talk in a curry house/course in a home/service in a church . . . to a barbecue, to a Cup Final party, to a bake-in for the homeless in the Christian's home . . .

Just imagine what God might do through your church's ministry among the people they spend so much time with at work. The Lord be with you. And them.

Mark Greene is Executive Director of the London Institute for Contemporary Christianity

Contextualising Evangelism

Adrian Holloway

For the past 16 years I've been employed by churches to advise them on their evangelistic strategy. In this time, I've worked closely with around 80 churches in the UK to try and help them find the most effective way to make an impact for Christ. Of these churches, the ones that are making the most significant advances are the ones who have been the best at 'contextualizing the gospel'.

Let me explain the jargon by referring to the supreme example I have come across in the recent past. Five years ago I first heard Tim Keller preach at Redeemer Presbyterian Church in New York City. I had never ever heard any public speaker do such a great job of tailoring his message for the group of people he was trying to reach. It seemed Keller had sat down and thought to himself: 'If I were a 25 year old trainee lawyer living in Manhattan, if I had a privileged background, but a very stressful job, which bits of the gospel message would most connect with me?'

I have listened to about 50 of his talks. No matter what the text, no matter which book of the Bible he was expositing, he would find a way of drilling down into the most pressing heart issues facing the non-Christians who he was trying to reach on the fringes of his Sunday congregation. For example, Keller majors on the 'tendency to perfectionism'. Sermons are peppered with 'Why are you working so hard?' 'You've passed your exams, you've got the job you've always wanted, and the boyfriend you've dreamed of, so why aren't you happier?' 'Why are you so bothered about your personal appearance?' 'Why do you care so much about what others think about you?' He even did sermons targeted at obsessive types who have to be the first to arrive at the office in the morning and the last to leave.

THE VAST MAJORITY OF CHURCHES IN THE UK ARE RELATIVELY SMALL. HOWEVER THE GREAT COMMISSION IS VERY BIG AND THE NUMBER OF DIFFERENT CULTURES AND PEOPLE GROUPS IN OUR TOWN AND CITIES IS HUGE.

Of course it's taken Keller years to get to this level of precision. He's studied the hopes, fears and neurosis of a certain type of New Yorker, and they flock to hear him. The result is not in question; he has seen hundreds of converts. However (and here's the point) if I preached about the 'tendency to perfectionism' in some churches I visit, they wouldn't have a clue what I was on about. And here's the slightly controversial and uncomfortable conclusion I've reached . . .

Yes, the vast majority of churches in the UK are relatively small. However the Great Commission is very big and the number of different cultures and people groups in our town and cities is huge. Churches of 50 to 100 members will often have 10 to 15 different ministries, reaching out to every spectrum of society. Of course all of these outreach ministries (to the disadvantaged, to the elderly, to those raising autistic children, to the affluent members of a local golf club, and many more) are all exactly what we as Christians are called to do, but it leaves the pastor with a tremendous challenge. If all these outreach ministries were to bring non-Christians onto the fringes of the church, how does the pastor find the right 'voice' to reach them all? How do you contextualize the gospel?

The churches that I know that have done best at winning large numbers to Christ and sustaining growth over a long period of years, typically began by seeking to reach just one type of person. They contextualized the gospel to reach a certain people of a certain class or background. They spoke their language. They got inside their idiom. They studied their culture and inhabited their world. They incarnated the gospel. Once they had success in fishing that pond, they moved on to seek to win other types of people to Christ. This is 100 times easier once you already have momentum, once you already have 10 or 15% growth in numbers attending and income year on year.

The churches I've worked with who are most frustrated and disillusioned are those who have faithfully sought to reach their whole community, even with 50 members. They run kids clubs, soup kitchens, cross-cultural missions and 10 other things. They are exhausted and perplexed that when they do bring people along on Sundays those people don't stick and join the core community.

If I could say anything to the UK evangelical church it would be that making disciples of our nation is best thought of as a marathon rather than a sprint, and that we must learn to contextualize the gospel. Jesus was a carpenter, who made a point of using farming illustrations much more than carpentry ones. Why? He was contextualizing the gospel to his culture where most people were not carpenters, but many worked the land, or worked off the land.

Jesus was a carpenter, who made a point of using farming illustrations much more than carpentry ones.

Once any church has found a way of reaching and keeping people from any particular target background, then Christians who have written themselves off as ever making any kind of evangelistic contribution, suddenly see that the church can grow, and that 21st Century people living in the UK can very easily be saved and added, provided they hear the gospel in the right context and provided they don't have to cross too many cultural barriers. Five years on, and once the church is made up of 20% new Christians, everyone begins to see that 'this works!' Then it's much easier to diversify and gradually launch various ministries, so that in the end, once we are 600 or 700 strong we can resource outreach to many of the cultural niche communities that make up our towns and cities.

Adrian Holloway is an evangelist based at ChristChurch, London

Connection Points

Laurence Singlehurst

How do we make our preaching relevant for guest services and at other meetings where we may have guests or people from un-churched backgrounds? How do we show the dynamic nature and the relevance of the gospel in today's culture in order to create spiritual interest and hunger? We need to find connection points – ways in which we can speak the truth of the gospel in response to a need of those around us.

Family

For example, in a recent survey, it was shown that amongst young people less than 4% had any interest in God *per se*. However, they were very interested in family and making family work. This is a good example of a connection point as we know that God invites us to be a part of his family. This also gives us an opportunity to talk about how the selfishness in our culture is destroying family but that the gospel looks to restore that brokenness.

Joy

Joy is also another good connection point in a society where personal happiness is so highly prized. We might want to think of discussion points around where real joy comes from, how we lose joy, and how joy can be found in being who we were created to be. Many young people in particular today are desperate to find out who they are and what they have to offer the world. The gospel of course deals with this and gives us opportunity to talk about God's purpose for each of us to use our gifts. Jesus talked of us being one body, where everyone has a role. Again we can see how selfishness in our society, in our background, can stop this taking place and why the Christian message is redemptive and empowers us to be who we are really called to be.

IN SEEKING TO MAKE THE CHRISTIAN MESSAGE RELEVANT, WE ARE IN NO WAY SUGGESTING A WATERING DOWN OF THE TRUTH. FAR FROM IT.

Fear

What are the fears that people have? Many people are held captive to all sorts of fear. How can we address that, how can we connect to that fear and show how the Christian message can liberate us?

In seeking to make the Christian message relevant, we are in no way suggesting a watering down of the truth. Far from it. We should at all times be willing to explain both the benefits and the cost of the Christian message, this is simply about finding ways in to that discussion in places where people aren't asking questions about God.

The gospel is as relevant today as it was 2,000 years ago, so let's use our imaginations and think of ways to connect our teaching and preaching to our community and to the people around us.

Responsive Evangelism

Andy Paterson

'Why does the Bible have so little to say about evangelism? For such an important subject you'd think there'd be more!' That's a question faced by Christians who recognise that the wonderful good news about Jesus must be shared, but look in vain for a detailed biblical blueprint. They've seen and heard evangelists at work, boldly and courageously speaking to people they've never met. But somehow, for reasons not to do with cowardice, this feels so alien and unnatural to them. And so they live their Christian lives under the continual shadow of guilt, happier to retreat into their safe Christian ghetto than engage with the people they know don't yet know Jesus.

If you were to ask the early believers about their strategy for evangelism, they'd look at you with incredulity. For them, talking about Jesus Christ was as natural and instinctive as breathing! You don't need a plan; you just live that deliciously different life and give an answer to those who ask what makes you tick. That's why the two key Bible verses about sharing your faith are all about responding to those who ask.

Paul tells us in Colossians 4:5-6 '... *make the most of every opportunity. Let your conversation be always full of grace, seasoned with salt, so that you may know how to answer everyone.*'

And Peter tells us (just so we don't think it was all Paul's idea) in 1 Peter 3:15 *'But in your hearts revere Christ as Lord. Always be prepared to give an answer to everyone who asks you to give the reason for the hope that you have. But do this with gentleness and respect.'*

'MAKE THE MOST OF EVERY OPPORTUNITY. LET YOUR CONVERSATION BE ALWAYS FULL OF GRACE, SEASONED WITH SALT, SO THAT YOU MAY KNOW HOW TO ANSWER EVERYONE.'

In other words, the New Testament pattern for everyday evangelism is that of responding to opportunities provoked by a redeemed life and provided by a sovereign God.

Understanding this can be both liberating and fruitful. It removes the false guilt that has disabled many: it's not down to me to force openings. But rather, it frees me up to achieve excellence in my tasks and integrity in my friendships. We love people for who they are and trust that within that genuine relationship, God will open up ways for us to speak about the person and work of Jesus.

It also means that when I respond to others, I'm not intruding into 'their space'. They've chosen the time, the place and the subject. They're relaxed and enquiring, and I know that I'll be sharing a subject that's touching upon what concerns them. What's more, this approach embraces all personality types. So often evangelism is associated with thrusting, extrovert personalities, but when my responsibility is to respond to the opportunities that God provides, then I can be myself and share honestly and openly how Jesus Christ impacts my life. This involves every believer and it excludes none.

It sounds simple, doesn't it? Well, yes it is but there's a lot that's assumed by such a straight forward approach. Firstly, it assumes that Christians will live 'deliciously different' lives, and not conform to the norms of a sin-saturated society. This was the regular thrust of the New Testament letters. Be different. March to a different beat. Be as much like Jesus as a rescued sinner can be. So we won't worship the false idols of materialism. We'll delight in God's plan for sex. We'll find our satisfaction in Christ and not all the cheap and trivial alternatives that the world has on offer.

Then secondly, it assumes that we will genuinely love other people. And that will naturally overflow in caring actions and practical service. Not because we have to but because we want to. It means that we'll share in their lives, and listen to their stories, and share in their sorrows, and be there with them and for them.

Thirdly, it means that when we do get a chance to respond to the questions of our friends, we'll have the wisdom and passion to grasp those opportunities. We'll start from where they are, using language and illustrations that connect, and identifying points of contact. We'll be able to articulate what Christ did to rescue sinners and how he saved us.

If you're a Christian you have a unique grace story to tell and you should be able to tell it in under five minutes. Are you ready? Are you living the sort of life that provokes questions? Are you praying for the opportunity?

Andy Paterson is Mission Director for the Fellowship of Independent Evangelical Churches (FIEC)

If you're a Christian you have a unique grace story to tell and you should be able to tell it in under five minutes. Are you ready?

Resources

Who? by Paul Langham

If someone is interested in Jesus and finding out more about our faith, we of course point them towards the Bible. The Bible is where the story unfolds and we read about God's purposes for man from creation to eternity. But sometimes it's hard to get to grips with – especially for people who've never read it before.

The Bible Society have a brilliant resource called *'Who?'* – an easily accessible book for people who don't read the Bible but would like to find out about its message. Whilst it is faithful to the original text, the language is modern and written as though the authors were alive today. It's a great stepping stone for people who have never made it past the cover of a New Testament, and a refresher for those who have got stuck. At its heart *'Who?'* helps us get to grips with who Jesus really is.

Might There Be More? is a booklet produced by Bible Society, designed to help you and your church get conversations started and keep them going as you share your faith. *Might There Be More?* is easy to follow and the first section looks at questions like 'Is God bad for your brain?', and 'Should God come with a health warning?' They explore whether there was a historic figure named Jesus of Nazareth, and whether they can trust what the New Testament says about his death and resurrection. The booklet also touches on biblical wisdom for present-day issues and the question of ultimate purpose and meaning. The second section is the Gospel of Mark, which comes in the easily accessible, Contemporary English Version. So readers can start out by thinking about Jesus in general terms, and then go deeper, letting the written Word and the living Word speak for itself.

Sold in packs of ten copies from shop.biblesociety.org.uk

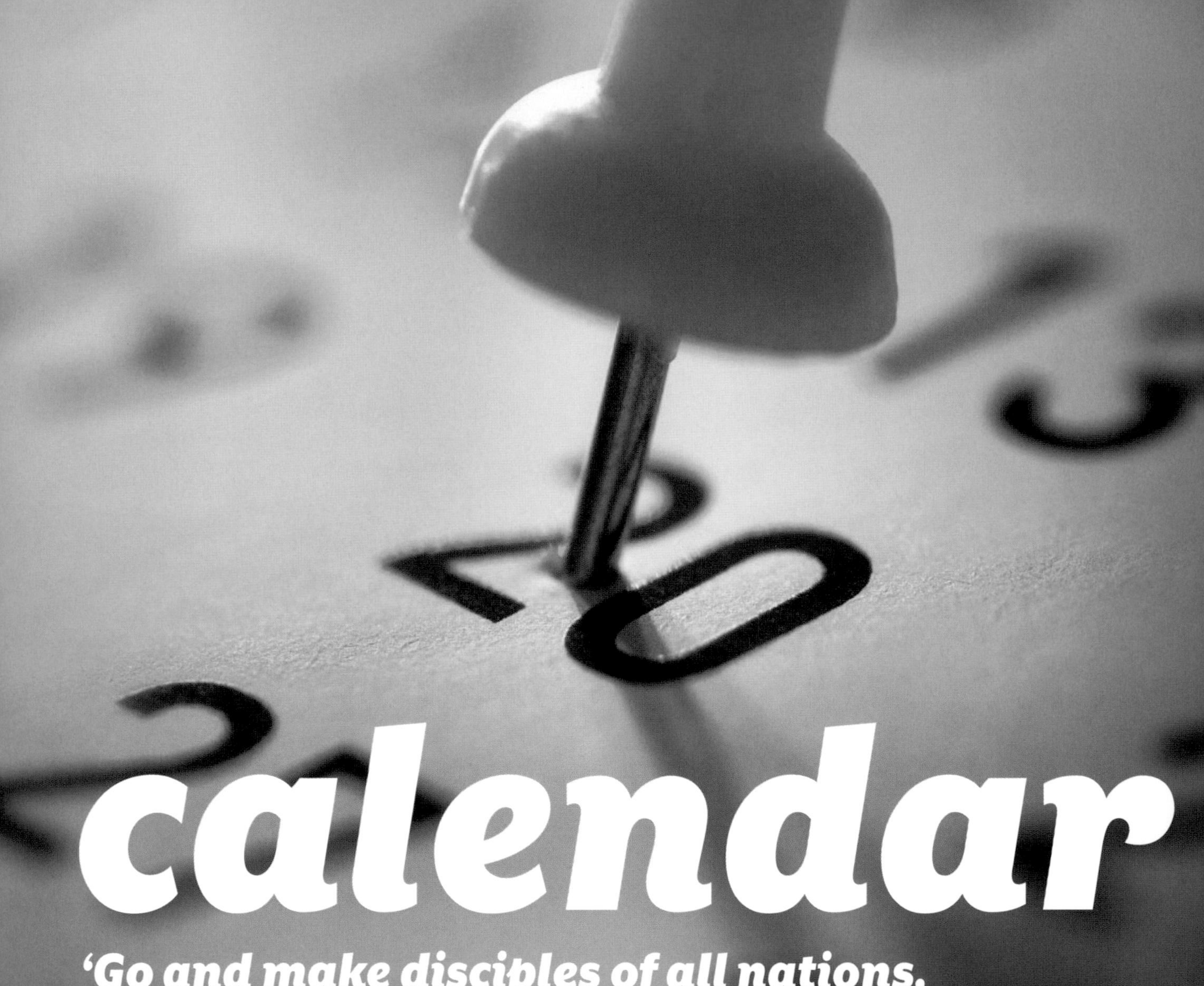

calendar

'Go and make disciples of all nations, baptising them in the name of the Father and of the Son and of the Holy Spirit, and teaching them to obey everything I have commanded you.'

A Rhythm of Mission

Steven Croft

'All authority in heaven and on earth has been given to me. Therefore go and make disciples of all nations, baptising them in the name of the Father and of the Son and of the Holy Spirit, and teaching them to obey everything I have commanded you. And surely I am with you always to the very end of the age.'

Matthew 28:19-20

We are all used to the cycle of the Christian year (Advent and Christmas; Lent and Easter; Pentecost and Harvest) and this pattern began as a way of helping the Church make disciples annually with Lent being a time of preparation for baptism on Easter Day. We can continue to use this model as a pattern for teaching the faith, for telling the story of the gospel and for making sure our church diet is balanced.

We live now in a society where people are in many different places in relation to faith:

- Many people have never been part of a local church and know almost nothing of the Christian story
- Some know and understand the story but don't understand what it means for their own lives
- Some are very new Christians and need support and nurture
- Some are established as disciples and need ongoing teaching and care

If we want the Church to grow we need to give priority to making disciples through the life of every local church and this will mean giving due priority once again to three core habits of growing new Christians within the life of church and congregation.

The first is sowing the seed: offering the gospel to those who are outside the life of the church. There are a thousand ways to do this in our workplaces, our schools, through friendships, in pubs and on the streets. The most fruitful places to sow the seed of the gospel are often the communities where the Church is already engaged in loving service.

> The most fruitful places to sow the seed of the gospel are often the communities where the Church is already engaged in loving service.

The second is nurture: offering ways for people to explore the Christian gospel for the first time that may lead to baptism and confirmation. This is critical. There are many different courses and resources you can use but what matters is offering something regularly and prayerfully which suits those in your community who are ready to explore faith.

The third is growth: a regular diet to help new Christians so they are able to grow to maturity as disciples within the life of the church. This can be done in many different ways through small groups, Bible study, training and teaching courses, to help the whole body to grow.

Each of these three core disciplines will be worked out in different ways for children, for young people and for adults.

So how do local churches with few resources make sure that they are doing each of these things regularly? The best way is to follow a simple, annual cycle to give a pattern and rhythm to the task of making disciples structured around three seasons.

Sowing the seed of the gospel

From the late summer through the autumn, focus on proclaiming the gospel to those who haven't heard it before. Make sure you get outside the church, onto the streets and into the market place, the schools and the meeting places. The great festivals of Harvest, Remembrance and Christmas give us lots of opportunity to share the gospel.

Offering nurture groups

Then from the late autumn through to Easter every church should focus on seeking to nurture the

The Yearly Cycle

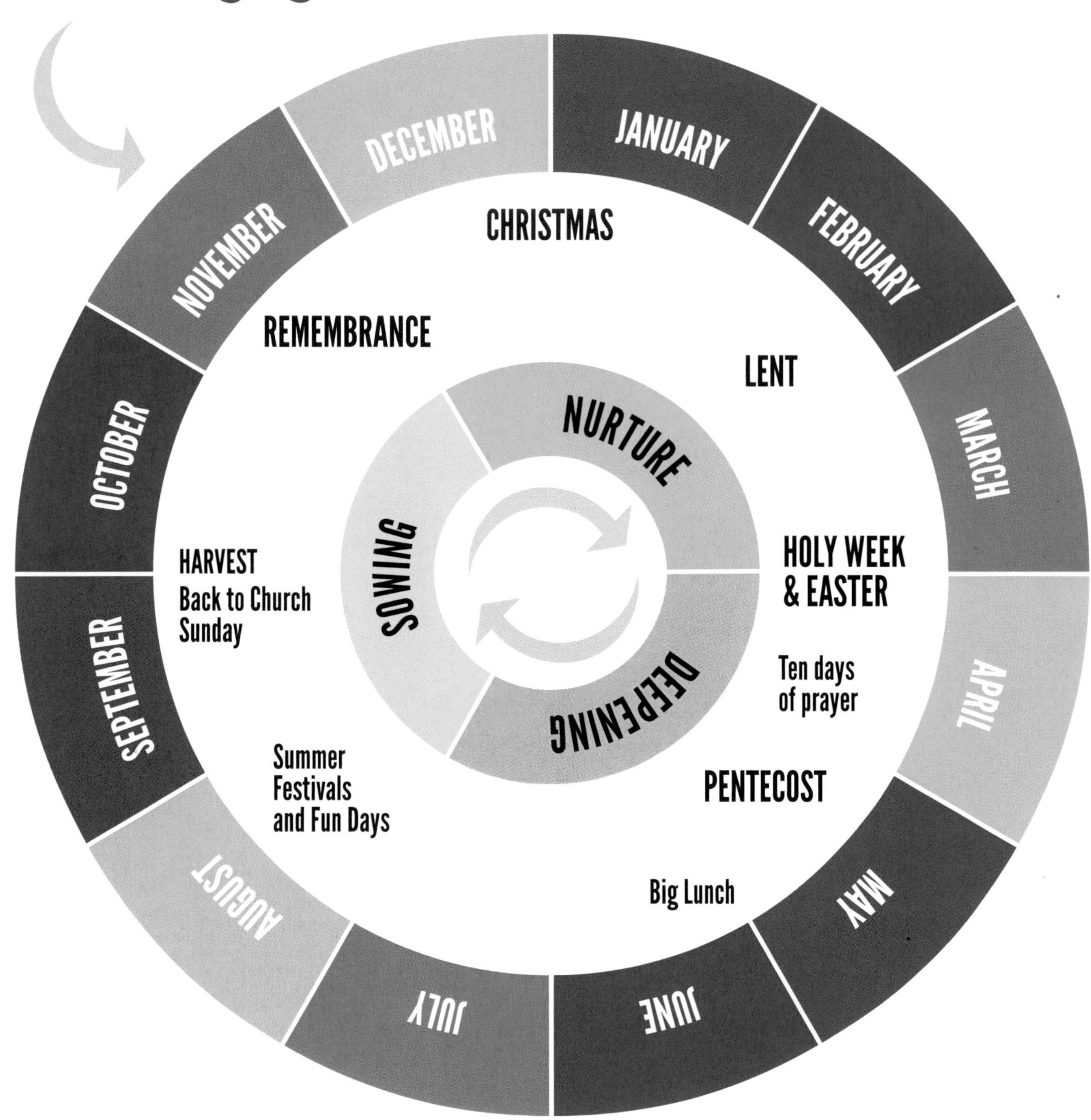

faith of enquirers and new believers. Some churches might be working with just one or two people each year; praise God for them and care for them. Others might be working with half a dozen people exploring faith or more. Groups might begin in November, January or later and run up to Easter.

Deepening disciples

From Easter to the summer, focus on deepening the faith of the disciples, both the new Christians and the existing church. Let that be a time of encountering Christ in deeper ways, of spiritual refreshment, pilgrimage, renewal and learning. Keep the ancient tradition, which goes back to the apostles, of Ten Days of Prayer between Ascension and Pentecost as year by year we seek God's grace for this cycle of proclaiming the faith; working with the enquirers who come and deepening the discipleship of the whole people of God.

If we keep it well, this annual cycle will be more of a three dimensional spiral which will deepen our life year by year. Through its dependence on prayer, it reflects the truth that growth is a gift of God. Evangelism and making disciples will not become a separate activity but a stronger and more normal part of the life of every congregation.

The lines between the seasons are not exact. Some of each season will be present in every other season. There are no rules to follow, nor is it meant to be a continuous cycle of activity. There will need to be times for resting and fallow years in every community.

Evangelism and the making of disciples is not something we bolt on to the life of the church but something which flows from and into our worship and community. They are not activities for a few enthusiasts but part of the normal and organic life of the people of God.

The task of making disciples should be as ordinary and normal in the life of the local church as digging the garden and putting in seed potatoes in the spring or mowing the lawn in the summer. Let's take the next five years to learn and reset that rhythm in the life of every church in the land.

Steven Croft is Bishop of Sheffield

EVANGELISM AND THE MAKING OF DISCIPLES IS NOT SOMETHING WE BOLT ON TO THE LIFE OF THE CHURCH BUT SOMETHING WHICH FLOWS FROM AND INTO OUR WORSHIP AND COMMUNITY.

Beyond 2014

It is the expectation of the HOPE leadership team and those behind the HOPE initiative that this does not finish at the end of 2014 but that every church will create their own missional and transformational rhythm for the future. The end of each year is a timely moment to give thanks for the lives that have been impacted and changed in the preceding 12 months and to dedicate ourselves to God's service through incarnational mission in the coming year.

A rhythm of mission and justice for young people

Tearfund Rhythms takes 'word and deed' and makes it part of our everyday lives. It's a website and phone app that help young people offer their ordinary lives in extraordinary ways to God, with the heart that a generation who invest in small, regular actions can transform our world.

Rhythms helps its users to weave these actions into their daily life. You pick one of the four lifestyle rhythms and live it out for 30 days – to let these actions become habits and to let those habits form your character. It's a great resource that can be used alone, with friends, with a youth group, cell group or a Christian Union.

The four rhythms are Connection, Advocacy, Contentment and Generosity. Each rhythm gives 25 ideas of small actions that you could start doing, for example: holding the door open for others, buying The Big Issue, *praying for your local community, or writing a thank you letter to a neighbour.*

Rhythms is word and deed in action in a way that will have a deep and profound impact on our communities and the world, as we act on our calling to love God and love the world.

You can join the community at rhythms.org

christmas

'As we focus on how God came and got involved in our world... we can find many ways to demonstrate to our communities that God loves them.'

Christmas

Christmas is a fantastic opportunity for us to demonstrate the gospel message. As we focus on how God came and got involved in our world by coming to earth as a baby, we can find many ways to demonstrate to our communities that God loves them. Whilst Christmas is a time of rejoicing, there are many for whom it brings stress and loneliness so there are many opportunities to bless our communities and bring God's light and life.

Christmas is also, of course, the busiest time for the church in terms of welcoming visitors so it is a brilliant time of year to get to know new people and invite them along to church. Here we've included lots of different ideas for prayer, building relationships, sharing the gospel and ways to make our Christmas services as friendly as possible.

LOCAL CHRISTIANS WERE EXCITED TO HEAR GOOD STORIES OF PEOPLE SURPRISED BY GOD AS A RESULT OF THE PROJECT AND THEY ARE KEEN REPEAT THE EVENT TO SEE WHAT ELSE GOD WANTS TO DO.

A light in every street

Over 3,750 candles and prayer cards were distributed around the city of Hull over Advent, with an estimated 10,000 people joining in praying for the city and region on Christmas Eve.

People went to a stall in St Stephen's Shopping Centre each Thursday evening during Advent, marked their street on a map, and collected a professionally designed and printed prayer card and candle. Then, as the first star appeared on Christmas Eve, each lit the candle and as they placed it in a window, they said the short prayer – 'Jesus, Light of the World, please shine your light on me, on my family, on my home, on my street, on my city. Amen.'

The candle light on Christmas Eve, a reflection of the star over the manger, added a new tradition to local life and brought a focus on God back to a consumer-hijacked season. Local Christians were excited to hear good stories of people surprised by God as a result of the project and they are keen repeat the event to see what else God wants to do.

The project was run by Hope - The Next Chapter, with One Voice (Hull), Kings Breakfast and Try Praying.

Mission ideas

Free Christmas present wrapping in your local

ONE

shopping centre. Ask your church members to donate paper, bows and gift tags and to volunteer to wrap presents during shopping centre opening hours.

This is a great way to bless people when they're stressed – and an opportunity to invite shoppers along to your Christmas carol services.

Providing Christmas presents

ONE

Work with local agencies and charities to find young or elderly people in your area who will not be receiving many presents this Christmas. Get your church to donate (unwrapped) presents in November to be passed on.

Schools work

TWO

Offer to take assemblies or classes in local schools on the meaning of Christmas.

Village fete

ONE

Liaise with the police to close off your high street for a few hours one evening to have a fun open-air Christmas event. Work with local traders and see whether they would like to stay open, provide mulled wine and mince pies, place Nativity displays in shop windows, have a band and/or carol singers – you could even run your own stall with homemade cards and gifts from your church members.

Christmas dinner

ONE

Many find Christmas a painfully lonely time so it can be a huge blessing for churches to host a Christmas lunch for those who would otherwise be alone.

The Nativity

TWO

The BBC four-part drama *The Nativity* is a compelling retelling of the Christmas story in a fresh and contemporary way. The Bible Society has a DVD with a special licence to show the drama in schools and churches, and have provided downloadable resources to aid discussion and engagement with the story. Visit shop.biblesociety.org.uk for more information, to order your copy and to download resources.

> THANK YOU TO ALL INVOLVED WITH THE HAMPERS. IT WAS A LOVELY SURPRISE AND JUST MADE MY CHRISTMAS TO KNOW THAT PEOPLE ACTUALLY DO CARE ABOUT OTHERS.

Operation Rudolph

ONE

'To say I was speechless would be an understatement! Thank all of you at Operation Rudolph from the bottom of our hearts.' Family who received a hamper

Vision

Operation Rudolph gives quality hampers to those who face a difficult or lonely Christmas in Nottingham. These 'hampers of hope' have items that are carefully chosen, lovingly packed and faithfully delivered to contacts of the church and those recommended by local agencies.

In the first 10 years the team packed and delivered more than 8,800 hampers with a combined value in the region of £525,000.

'The joy that your wonderful hampers have given to the families that we have supported cannot be put into words–your gift has made their Christmas.' Nominating Agency

Benefits

Receiving an Operation Rudolph hamper has multiple impacts upon individuals and families across the city. The most tangible benefit for so many is the gift of food including seasonal treats such as mince pies, chocolates and Christmas crackers that they may not otherwise have enjoyed. For one family the delivery of an Operation Rudolph hamper on a Saturday morning a few days before Christmas was incredibly timely as until that point there was no food in the house for the children to have breakfast. In additional to practically providing food, the hampers make people feel loved and valued. Over the years the gift of a hamper has triggered the establishment of new friendships and transformation in people's lives as they have come along to services at the Christian Centre and encountered the love of Jesus.

For the people who serve

Through helping to make Operation Rudolph happen volunteers and sponsors contribute to bringing hope and joy to people in their city at Christmas. Delivering the hampers repeatedly has a significant impact upon volunteers, expanding their awareness of the poverty, vulnerability and isolation many people experience within our own city. 'It was a fantastic and warming experience, delivering to worthy causes,' said one volunteer driver.

Operation Rudolph also provides an ideal opportunity for people within the congregation to buy an alternative gift for friends and family at Christmas, raise sponsorship amongst colleagues instead of buying each other Christmas cards, bring the whole family or a group of pupils/colleagues/friends to pack and/or deliver hampers together. In recent years, groups of people living in specific neighbourhoods have worked together to deliver hampers within their locality, providing opportunities to get to know their neighbours.

'The contents of that box are magnificent, thank you so very much for making an old man very happy.'
90 year old, housebound, man who received a hamper

'It was a fantastic and warming experience, delivering to worthy causes,' said one volunteer driver.

Challenges

- Deciding how to allocate hampers if nominations exceed capacity to produce hampers.
- Timing of hamper allocation and stock procurement compared to receiving sponsorship (often continues coming in after the event).
- Liaising with external agencies regarding hamper nominations, allocations and delivery details.

How easy is it to replicate this idea?

The concept is simple and could be easily replicated, even on a much smaller scale. It does however require months of planning and organisation by a few committed people prior to all the volunteers helping assemble and deliver the hampers over a three day period. Sufficient space is required to set up a production line with all stock (and possibly storage in the weeks leading up to this) as well as stacking packed hampers awaiting collection/delivery. A computer, transportation, financial resources, and commitment from the congregation are all vital.

How much does it cost?

It is approximately £20,000 for 1,000 hampers (contents and packing) and all other costs associated with running the project. This is in addition to any stock received through corporate donations.

Materials/training

Contact the Christian Centre in Nottingham if you would like to view copies of promotional literature, forms (nomination, sponsorship, volunteer), or a corporate information pack.

Tips

- Make a plan at the beginning and be clear on who you want to give hampers to (elderly, vulnerable, isolated, families...) and what you do/not want to include in the hampers (food, toiletries, games, Christian literature/advertising for events etc).
- As soon as you can, ask companies for corporate donations of stock. Contact external nominating agencies in early September to start the nomination process, allowing sufficient time to review all nominations, make allocations of hampers and receive recipients' name and address details.
- Promote the project from early October within the congregation, and repeatedly up to the time you will assemble and deliver the hampers (the weekend before Christmas works well).

'Thank you to all involved with the hampers. It was a lovely surprise and just made my Christmas to know that people actually do care about others.'
Hamper recipient

There are four ways the congregation can get involved:

1. Nominate someone to receive a hamper - Ask 'Do you know someone on your street, at work or school who is isolated, vulnerable or feeling hopeless? Would they benefit from receiving a surprise hamper packed full of Christmas treats?'

2. Sponsor a hamper. Sponsoring a hamper costs £20, yet the contents are worth so much more due to special offers and stock donations. Encourage people to Gift Aid their donation. Gift cards could be available to allow people to sponsor a hamper as an alternative to buying a gift for friends/relatives.

'Do you know someone on your street, at work or school who is isolated, vulnerable or feeling hopeless?

3. Be a Rudolph Champion. Encourage family, friends, classmates and colleagues to sponsor hampers too or ask your boss for a corporate donation (financial or in kind). Provide promotional resources for this.

4. Volunteer. Help unload stock, pack and/or deliver hampers. Ask people to sign up for specific volunteer slots in advance.

Make a sample hamper in advance so you know what order to place things on the production line when stock arrives. If making more than one type of hamper (e.g. different contents for families) use different coloured tape to seal boxes so it is easy to identify which type of hamper is which.

Contact details

www.operationrudolph.org
E: luke@christiancentre.org
T: 0115 947 4038

Stories

Rachel's story

'This time last year I was the one receiving a hamper and realised it was because of the mums and toddlers group run by the Christian Centre. After talking to the team leader about re connecting with God I came to the Christian Centre. A few weeks later my sister came too, and we are now both regular attendees. We have also made some amazing life-long friends along the way, and we all share the same passion for our Lord. Before the Christian Centre I didn't have many friends, but now I have lots! So this year my sister and I decided to help out with packing and delivering the hampers. And you know what? It felt just as good delivering the hampers as receiving one! Now we have a strong Christian bond in the local community, and it feels great! And all because of an act of true kindness this time last year; all because of a Christmas hamper!'

The Operation Rudolph team said, 'We delivered a hamper to Kate and her three small children who had fled to the UK to seek asylum after her husband was abducted by the military in the Congo. Kate had been kidnapped and raped, her husband had been killed, and her fourth child was missing in the Congo. The gift of an Operation Rudolph hamper was a blessing to Kate as she received minimal support from the National Asylum Support Service and was not eligible for benefits.'

Gospel message

TWO Brislington Christian Fellowship in Bristol has been producing tract leaflets for a number of years. They drop them through local doors each quarter to share the good news in a non-threatening way, and produce a special edition each Christmas. The tracts use local interest stories as a way to open up the gospel message.

Small group idea: why not invite the neighbours round for mince pies and mulled wine?

INVITE LOCAL SCHOOLS TO TAKE PART IN A NATIVITY EXHIBITION WHERE THEY CAN DISPLAY PICTURES OR PERFORM DRAMA AND SONGS.

Ideas for busy towns

Get in the picture

ONE Set up a Nativity scene in an area where there is good footfall and have costumes and props that allow passers-by to come and be a part of the picture. Take their photograph and upload it to a website that they can access to download and use as they wish. Hand out refreshments to busy shoppers as they go and include details of church services on the website.

Find out more at www.getinthepicture.org.uk

Community advent calendar

TWO Christ Church in Staffordshire arranged a giant community advent calendar in local shops. With all the windows revealed by Christmas Eve, they held a guided walk through the town to see the displays, singing carols as they went. Many of the displays were made by school children so it could be a great opportunity to work with your local schools to do something similar.

Get crafty

ONE Hold a craft session for children so they can make symbols and decorations for a Christmas tree. You could then hold a special service for the decorations to be placed on the tree.

Nativity exhibition

TWO Invite local schools to take part in a Nativity exhibition where they can display pictures or perform drama and songs. Invite parents and the local community to come and watch.

Billboards

TWO One man in Oldham was so encouraged by a mission visit to Ghana and how people there openly shared their faith in their towns, he and his mates decided to create billboard adverts in their home town, encouraging people to visit a website to ask questions about Jesus.

Ideas for young people

Christmas showcase

ONE Run drama, dance or music workshops for young people during the autumn and then give them an opportunity to show off their new talents at a Christmas showcase for parents and friends.

Blessed to be a blessing

ONE Genetik (the Message Trust's year out training ground for missional leadership) send out students to randomly bless people in Jesus' name. Students are given an area, a people group or a specific task and they would have to try to bless as many people as they can. This blessing could include: buying bunches of flowers and delivering them to elderly neighbours; handing out money for nothing to people in the high street; going door to door offering to do any odd jobs free of charge; or baking cakes and taking them to homeless people on the streets.

- For some events it's useful to warn people in advance, for example if you are offering odd jobs door to door, post a flyer advertising this a few days in advance to get a better response.
- Have a base, like a gazebo, where people can check in or get more information, and wearing branded clothing – such as HOPE t-shirts - helps make it look more professional and trustworthy.
- Be aware of CRB requirements or food hygiene issues for the various tasks.

The key to the event is to have a clear understanding as to *why* you are doing what you are doing. Creating a tag line response that everyone can use is helpful like 'We just wanted to show you God's love in a practical way,' or 'We are part of X church and we wanted to bless the local community.'

Hot chocolate for skaters

ONE During their 'Beyond Belief' mission week, churches in Cambridge found that some of the most fruitful projects on which young people served, were those that required them to be creative and to take opportunities as they arose. One church had planned an afternoon programme for children and families, but no-one came. As a result, the young volunteers decided to take trays of hot chocolate out to the skate park which is on the church doorstep. They were amazed at how many good conversations were possible as they hung out with young people they met. The church suddenly discovered a mission opportunity that they had been previously missing, and set up a new weekly outreach to skaters.

'I turned my front room into a cinema. It's a really brilliant way to get your friends together. Have a go!'

Raising money

ONE Get your young people to raise money for charity by holding a 'Front Room Fundraiser'. Watch a film or sporting event, play some games or have some food – anything you like that gathers a group and provides a good social atmosphere. Take a few minutes to talk about the chosen charity and why their work is important, and then ask for donations as people leave. It's an easy and fun way to raise money for and awareness of great charities.

'I turned my front room into a cinema. It's a really brilliant way to get your friends together. Have a go! All you need are people, a front room, a DVD player and a money box.' Liz, Twickenham

See http://village.rhythms.org/howto for more info.

No slumber challenge

ONE Use the Tearfund 'No Slumber' challenge with your young people to help them connect with the reality of life for children who have lost parents to AIDS around the world. Each participant is given a character (a bit like in a Murder Mystery game) and during the evening they make choices as that character. It's a great way to involve young people on the edge of your youth group and have a fun but challenging evening. For full resources please see www.tearfund.org/noslumber.

Why not try an Advent Labyrinth? We've designed a short journey to help you connect with the Christmas story in a creative and reflective way. Visit www.hopetogether.org.uk for more details.

You are loved

Giveaways are a great way to engage with people, and offer a free gift as an act of love and kindness. Even better when they can signify something of the gospel truth.

- Have two or three young people dress up as angels or shepherds.
- Buy some simple, glass tea light candle holders and 200 candles, and write on the holder 'You are loved'. Leave a space on some for a name and just write 'is loved', giving you the opportunity to personalise one for people you speak to.
- Place the holders in a rustic basket and give them out to passers-by in a busy location. You will be amazed at who wants a candle; people will even queue up to receive one!
- As you give them out take the opportunity to discuss God's gift of Jesus who said that *'God so loved the world that he gave his one and only son, that whoever believes in him, shall not perish but have eternal life.'* John 3:16

'GOD SO LOVED THE WORLD THAT HE GAVE HIS ONE AND ONLY SON, THAT WHOEVER BELIEVES IN HIM, SHALL NOT PERISH BUT HAVE ETERNAL LIFE.'

Consider

- You could display or give away a card with a scripture such as John 8:12 *'I am the light of the world. Whoever follows me will never walk in darkness, but will have the light of life.'*
- For adults you could use this give-away idea by taking the gifts into pubs as an alternative pub-crawl!

Christmas prayers

TWO

Most people enjoy seeing, and decorating, a Christmas tree. This provides a great opportunity to see people engaging with prayer and enjoying the Christmas festivities.

- Purchase a Christmas tree and set it up securely in your town centre, decorating it creatively.
- Have an area where passers-by are invited to write the name of someone or a circumstance that they would like to pray for this Christmas onto a Christmas tree bauble. Give them the opportunity to place it onto the prayer Christmas tree.

This is a great way to engage people in meaningful conversation about some of life's hurts and concerns and an opportunity to bring the love of Jesus into their situation.

Consider

- Make sure you buy baubles that can be written on easily with a marker. The cheapest plastic ones are often the best.
- After the day, consider giving out the baubles to your congregation so they can pray for the people and situations each day leading up to Christmas.
- You could also offer to pray for these people and circumstances there and then.
- Perhaps give away a free glow stick to all who participate explaining that Jesus is the light of the world.

Alternative carol singing

ONE Organise a group of people to practise singing some carols and then go door to door singing Christmas carols for all. But instead of asking for money, why not surprise your neighbours by giving a gift instead? You could give some chocolate coins, or something with a spiritual significance such as a candle, a prayer, or an invitation to a Christmas carol service.

Consider

- Make sure your singers are wearing big smiles - it seems obvious, but it's surprising how many people fail to smile when singing!
- Involve people of all ages. It's always extra special when you can involve both the old and the young.
- Dress up for extra effect. At least put on a tinsel scarf!
- Wrap up warmly. We don't want you catching a cold!
- Surprise your local pub and sing carols for the customers.

Christmas Cot

TWO If you want to draw a crowd, why not set up a cot in a busy place and mark out a small area around it with cones or tape? Have two people standing around it wearing high-vis jackets. This will draw people to ask what you are doing and you can get creative with your answers, explaining the story of Christmas and how eagerly the birth of Jesus was awaited.

Consider

- Set up a table where craft activities could be offered for smaller children. Perhaps they could make a crown to hang on their Christmas tree. This gives an extended opportunity to build relationship and discuss the Christmas story further.
- Have booklets ready to hand out that detail the Christmas story, or give a copy of Matthew or Luke's Gospel which detail the birth of Jesus.

For more creative mission ideas check out the adventures of Chris Duffett, an evangelist, Baptist minister, artist and poet at Duffett.wordpress.com

We had a superb evening at the Queen's Head pub. We got to know people in the community and the landlady wants to get involved with the church.

Children's musicals

TWO Why not use one of Sheila Wilson's great musicals themed around the Nativity to engage with children? There are different musicals for various age groups – find out more at www.redheadmusic.co.uk

Sing Christmas

'We had a superb evening at the Queen's Head pub. We got to know people in the community and the landlady wants to get involved with the church.'

Here's a really simple way you could get people in pubs, clubs, community centres, care homes or anywhere people come together, listening to and celebrating the real meaning of Christmas. How? Follow the example of churches in Leicestershire by working with a local radio station to broadcast a live carol service for the community to tune in and sing along.

Venues throughout the county are invited to Sing Christmas by joining in with the service broadcast on BBC Radio Leicester. The churches have created the website singchristmas.org.uk where venues can register and be listed free, and invitations, posters and song sheets can be downloaded for printing.

Thousands of people in over 100 venues in the city and in towns and villages across the region join in with the interactive carol service. Everyone is invited to sing along with the carols and text the radio station during the broadcast to try to get a mention on air - over 250 text messages are received which is a huge response for a local radio station. Local and national

well-known personalities read the Christmas story from the Bible and there are prayers and a Christmas thought.

Churches play a vital part in Sing Christmas by inviting a local venue such as a pub, club or care home to join in. They help with preparations and are there on the night to encourage the singing. It's a great way for churches to be involved in their community, meet people who don't come to church and be part of an interactive project that takes the real meaning of Christmas to people where they are.

Sing Christmas is organised by Leicestershire Churches Media (part of Churches Together), the Diocese of Leicester and BBC Radio Leicester. The brewers Everards encourage their pubs to be involved and provide ideas and resources. Local authorities and East Midlands CARE let care providers know about Sing Christmas. This great idea could be easily replicated in your area by working with your local radio station. To find out more about Sing Christmas go to www.singchristmas.org.uk

'We all sang carols at Hood Court Flats. There were people who wouldn't normally come to any church events. We had a lot of fun and there was a lovely atmosphere. People didn't want to go home.'

- **If you're looking for a more simple idea, why not take a group of you to sing Christmas carols in your local supermarket, shopping centre, hospital or old people's home? Hand out Christmas goodies like mince pies, and offer invitations to your Christmas carol services.**

WE ALL SANG CAROLS AT HOOD COURT FLATS. THERE WERE PEOPLE WHO WOULDN'T NORMALLY COME TO ANY CHURCH EVENTS. WE HAD A LOT OF FUN AND THERE WAS A LOVELY ATMOSPHERE. PEOPLE DIDN'T WANT TO GO HOME.

Sports crowds gather to sing for the Boy Jesus!

TWO The last place you may imagine for a Christian act of worship is a sports stadium. But across the land, from Portsmouth to Leeds, from Shrewsbury to Sheffield, more and more clubs are now open to using Christmas as a great opportunity to gather supporters together with their local community for community carol services. These may offer a lively mixture of carols, readings and creative ideas reminding people who'd never step inside a church of the Prince of Peace who came to save the world.

At AFC Bournemouth they've been running their Community Carol Service since 2003. The Club Chaplain, Andy Rimmer, has organised a number of the services and says, 'Christmas is a time when it's OK to talk about Jesus in an open way and we see this service as a great way to bring people together to sing their favourite carols as well as hear a low-key message about Jesus. It's enabled us to build bridges into the life of the club and the community. Numbers have varied between 300 and 1,000 but it's always been a positive family occasion.' The hour-long service usually involves the whole first team squad plus staff who do the readings, a Salvation Army band and school choirs. It has mainly been outdoors apart from a couple of years when it was held in the main bar. 'It takes quite a bit of work to pull off well,' says Andy, 'and we're looking to draw in more local churches over the next few years but it really is worth it – we even raise money for local homeless charities!'

Elsewhere in the country Bolton Wanderers hold a service for about 600 which is recorded by local radio and aired on Christmas Day. Portsmouth had over 3,000 in 2009 for a joint churches' carol event at Fratton Park, and Leeds United uses puppets, local choirs and music groups to prepare for the Christmas period. In the next few years the hope is that sports club chaplains and local churches will be able to host more such events in local stadiums up and down the land.

'It's a win-win situation,' says Andy from AFC Bournemouth. 'The club get to put on a community event. It's run by local churches and Christians working together. It's a natural opportunity for the good news of Jesus to ring out, and it even helps to make a difference through the offerings and food brought along, to help some of the more disadvantaged in the local community!'

Why not get together with your local sports club and churches to hold a Christmas carol service?

If you'd like more information about sports chaplaincy you can contact Sports Chaplaincy through their website at www.sportschaplaincy.org.uk.

Why not get together with your local sports club and churches to hold a Christmas carol service?

The Nativity with a difference

ONE

Hundreds of people came through the doors of Hadleigh, Suffolk United Reformed Church over the Advent season to witness something of the truth of the Nativity portrayed in one of today's disaster relief tents. ShelterBox is a charity that provides emergency shelter and lifesaving supplies for families around the world who are affected by disasters and need basic shelter and equipment. People caught up in the Haiti earthquake, the Indonesian tsunami and the Thailand floods have all benefitted. Each tent along with key items such as blankets, water treatment equipment, a stove and pans, tools and gifts for the children are sent out in the ShelterBox. This durable plastic box is the size of a couple of large suit cases and itself can be used for storage and even as a cot, which at Hadleigh made it central to the Christmas story! More than 800 people visited the Nativity and donated enough for four ShelterBoxes (at £590 each).
www.shelterbox.org

Advent pageants

TWO

Imagine a community celebration where young people are the stars and they have an opportunity to re-enact the Christmas story in their local community. An Advent Pageant is just that, by offering a simple parade through the main street of your community, finishing with a celebration concert or festival.

What does it look like?

An Advent Pageant re-enacts the Christmas story with songs and drama. It starts with a parade, led by a Master of Ceremonies which stops at planned places along the way asking if there is room for Mary to spend the night (to which the answer is always 'no'!). The parade finishes at a high profile civic location where a celebration is held with a telling of the Christmas story, singing and drama performances.

Who is involved?

Schools are invited to participate and classes are encouraged to put together items from an extensive range of resources for the event or to create their own. The programme may be over-seen by a group of teachers alongside people from local churches.

A pageant can be as big as your resources will allow. Some schools and church groups have very simple costumes with a few songs while others make banners and all the students in the school perform.

Find out more at www.adventpageants.com

Seeker-friendly services - Christmas at KingsGate

Christmas is the season when people in the UK are most likely to say yes to an invitation to come to church so, it is vital that we make the most of this annual opportunity.

For nearly 20 years, KingsGate in Peterborough have placed a major emphasis on Christmas and Easter as highpoints in the church calendar, and have reaped a considerable harvest as a result. We asked them for some top tips:

Develop an invitational culture

In the weeks before Christmas remind people about the importance of fulfilling our missional responsibility. If possible share testimonies of people who took their first steps to faith at a previous guest event, and include an emphasis on invitational evangelism in the Sunday sermons. Vital to increasing an invitational culture is the church's confidence that they are bringing people to something good. Hence, the second step is to:

Produce good quality services...

- ***That are guest-friendly but are 'presence-filled'***

Be committed to providing an environment where both seekers and the Holy Spirit feel welcome. Remove unnecessary cringe elements and provide an authentic worship service in which people can really meet God.

- ***That are creative but have a clear message***

Connect the whole service under a unified message, so that the worship, creative elements and sermon have a common theme. In an increasingly un-biblical culture it is important that we help people understand the Big Story of the gospel.

- ***That are excellent and authentic***

With obvious constraints of budget and personnel it is important to do the best you can! It is probably best not to attempt something very creative if the singers can't sing solos, the dancers can't dance, and the actors can't act! However, whilst excellence is important, authenticity is even more important. People may be impressed with a great performance, but they will only be spiritually moved by the reality of Christ amongst his people.

PRAY THAT GOD WILL VISIT YOU, AND YOUR UN-CHURCHED FRIENDS WITH A FRESH MOVE OF HIS SPIRIT. MAY YOU SOW, REAP, KEEP AND ENJOY THE FRUITS OF YOUR DIVINE PARTNERSHIP!

Think about 'next steps'

It is one thing to get people to come; it is another to encourage them to stay. On the day give people a clear opportunity to respond to the gospel, to receive prayer and follow-up literature, as well as varied opportunities of informal connection around coffees and cakes. Contact people beyond the service and make sure that you have a key new sermon series, Alpha course or social activities ready for them to come to.

Pray!

That God will visit you, and your un-churched friends with a fresh move of his Spirit. May you sow, reap, keep and enjoy the fruits of your divine partnership!

Other ideas

Make your service as friendly as possible:

- Invite local schools to bring their choirs to sing at the service offering proud parents the chance to come and hear them sing.
- Have mince pies and mulled wine after the service so your church members can chat to visitors.
- Provide a welcome pack for visitors that includes information about your church and your services/events the rest of the year. Consider adding a small gift such as a Christmas decoration or chocolate, or add a booklet that shares the gospel message.
- Make sure visitors have space to park – have welcomers guiding people to parking spaces.
- Have a team of welcoming people on the door who can help everyone find a seat and can talk to anyone who comes alone.

- Be aware of visitors' needs, especially if they have hearing difficulties, are visually impaired or are wheel-chair users.
- During your service advertise any upcoming Alpha-style courses (see the Autumn: Hope Explored section) and future social activities so visitors know how they can continue to connect with the church.

Run a HOPE New Year Prayer Party!

'Couldn't you keep watch for one hour?' Jesus asked his disciples in the Garden of Gethsemane (Mark 14:37). Why not hold a 60 minute HOPE prayer party over New Year?

Youth cafés

ONE The cold winter months are a great time to launch a youth café to give young people something to do. Café in a Box offers all the information you need to set up a café that will welcome young people into a safe environment, giving them a chance to make friends, play games, have fun and experience true community. www.cafeinabox.info

Grants available

If you would like to start this community franchise project The Cinnamon Network can provide a micro-grant of £2,000 to help you get started. For more information about how to apply visit www.cinnamonnetwork.co.uk

Christmas Lunch on Jesus

ONE This is a great opportunity to work with other churches in your area!

'Receiving the hamper makes you feel good, like someone cares about you.' Francisco

Vision

Christmas Lunch on Jesus (CLOJ) is an outreach project initiated by Jesus House in London which distributes free Christmas hampers to residents of the most deprived wards in the London Borough of Barnet. They focus particularly on making sure children and single parents living in deprived conditions can enjoy a Christmas lunch with all the trimmings.

The idea is easy to replicate in other areas where people are in need and it's a great opportunity to work with other churches in your area to show the love of Jesus in a practical way at Christmas.

Benefits

The CLOJ project serves to alleviate the cost of Christmas for those in our community who might not be able to afford it otherwise. They provide everything required to have a Christmas dinner with all the frills including a turkey, potatoes,

I would just like to thank you all for the good work you all do by allowing us to have such beautiful hampers this year again. It is so appreciated not only by me but by my daughter too, Amanda, who has two children with disabilities. You really do not know how much this has helped out. Once again, thank you all so much, and may God bless you always.
Maureen & Amanda

Transform
Travel with Tearfund
THERE ARE MOMENTS IN LIFE THAT CHANGE THE WAY WE SEE THE WORLD
www.tearfund.org/transform
tearfund
Registered Charity No. 265464 (England and Wales)
Registered Charity No. SC037624 (Scotland)

vegetables, gravy, mince pies and Christmas pudding.

Volunteers who help pack and deliver the hampers find it is a great opportunity to meet other church members who are serving, and to meet members of the community who the hampers go to.

Challenges

As the success of the entire project is fully dependent on the charity and time of volunteers, challenges may arise in finances and the availability of manpower. To ensure adequate resources, it's helpful if requests for volunteers and financiers are consistently publicised approximately five months before the resources are required.

How to replicate this idea

The idea is relatively easy to replicate and Jesus House has training material available for groups who may be interested in starting their own CLOJ community project. A training session may also be scheduled to answer any questions that may arise. This will help groups to avoid practical pitfalls which they might otherwise encounter in the course of running a CLOJ project.

Resources needed

Finances: the aim is to raise enough money to cover the costs of the entire project. These costs include advertising, stationery, travel and transportation of hampers, refreshments for volunteers and hamper boxes, as well as the entire contents of the hampers. Requests for donations should be publicised months before the event to ensure adequate finances are secured before the project commences.

Manpower: the project depends on the time and commitment of volunteers who register to participate in the CLOJ project. Jesus House recommend you recruit as many volunteers as possible to ensure the success of the project, ideally across churches.

Just the chance to put a smile on people's faces was fulfilling.

Tips

- Publicity is carried out using a range of media including newspaper adverts, flyers and posters and it's also a good idea to speak to other churches who can publicise the project in their congregations.
- Consider speaking to your local council about what you're doing – they may want to get involved in the publicity, packing and distribution.

Contact details

If there is a need for a CLOJ project in your community, you have a planning team and the ability to acquire funding, you can contact Ayo Adedoyin at Jesus House to find out more:

E: adedoyina@jesushouse.org.UK
T: 020 8438 8285
www.christmaslunchonjesus.com

'I got involved with the CLOJ project because I wanted to help make a difference in someone's life at Christmas. The opportunity to reach out and make Christmas better for people who might otherwise not have a good Christmas resonated with my heart. The distribution day was amazing! I volunteered with one of the participating churches in Colindale who were very warm and friendly. It was nice to meet and work with new people and the planning and organisation was excellent. The recipients of the hampers were also amazing. It was interesting to go into a new area of the borough to share God's love. Just the chance to put a smile on people's faces was fulfilling. An old lady burst into tears when she opened her door to us; it was clear that without this, Christmas wouldn't have happened for her and for others. CLOJ brought it home to me that we all need the love of God and it was a very fulfilling experience. I have now participated in CLOJ for two consecutive years and am looking forward to more!'

Mollie, a Jesus House volunteer on the CLOJ project

Highway Homeless project from Highway of Holiness Church

Our mission is to engage the church in the effort of finding lasting solutions to alleviate social problems regarding homelessness. We provide food, shelter, counselling, training and spiritual guidance for 40 homeless men, seven days a week and 365 days a year in our community.

In 2009, our church was inspired by a homeless project from another church. During one of our evangelistic outreaches, we came across two homeless alcoholics, and shared the gospel with them. They asked for our help and we responded by starting to feed them three days a week at church. Suddenly, the numbers grew as the two men began inviting friends, and in a few weeks we had more than 20 people to care for. The men asked for a shower so they could clean up for job interviews, so we converted one of our toilets into a shower room for them. We then said the men could sleep in the church for three nights each week, which soon became every night during the cold winter.

We have had some challenges at first including anti-social behaviour which caused problems with our neighbours and the Police, and we had to overcome the cultural gaps between our African and Caribbean congregation and the mainly Eastern European men we were working with. But God has blessed us and we have seen Muslims, Buddhist, Sikhs, Atheist, Hindus and Agnostics give their lives to Christ through the practical demonstration of the love of God and the power of the Holy Spirit.

Many alcoholics have recovered from alcohol abuse and found jobs, and moved into their own accommodation. We have a dedicated intercessory team that prays consistently for the project and the people involved which I believe has made a great difference.

'I love living here because of how diverse it is and the fact that you can never feel alone.'

Girts Silins, Latvia

Find out more at www.highwayofholiness.co.uk

WE PROVIDE FOOD, SHELTER, COUNSELLING, TRAINING AND SPIRITUAL GUIDANCE FOR 40 HOMELESS MEN, SEVEN DAYS A WEEK AND 365 DAYS A YEAR IN OUR COMMUNITY.

Grants available

If you would like to start this community franchise project The Cinnamon Network can provide a micro-grant of £2,000 to help you get started. For more information about how to apply visit www.cinnamonnetwork.co.uk

Hope Into Action

Enabling the church to house the vulnerable

Vision

Hope Into Action has a vision for every church in every community to provide accommodation and support for at least two vulnerable homeless adults.

Hope Into Action began when a group of Christians opened a house for an ex-offender and an ex heroin addict. The house was linked to the local church who offered pastoral support, ultimately seeing the first tenant get baptised and the second become a Street Pastor. In less than two years they opened a further eight houses, with a number of others in the pipeline, and a passion to see churches across the country replicate the same model.

Benefits

Hope Into Action don't offer rooms in a house, they offer a home, meeting the essential needs of having a safe place and an opportunity to be in genuine, loving relationships. Each person who before was homeless, becomes surrounded with love, prayer, positive role models and mentoring from members of the church.

Opportunities

This model is a great way to put your faith into action. All you need is a small group from your church to engage with and form relationships with vulnerable people. Hope Into Action also provide a model where you can share your investment capital with the poor by investing in a house for a minimum of five years and getting a return on that money, while at the same time seeing vulnerable people helped.

Challenges

Helping people out of poverty is full of challenges but one of the root causes of poverty is often a deficit of love and relationships in lives. The homes Hope Into Action offer are tools to enable the church to reach people and meet their deeper, relational needs and then transform lives. This is not a short-term commitment: volunteers will need to be willing to give time to build relationships with those who are housed. They must be willing to work through any setbacks and deal with disappointment along the way, but there is great opportunity to see God transform people's lives.

How easy is it to replicate this idea?

If your church is thinking of buying a house for vulnerable people then get in touch with Hope Into Action and they will be able to advise you on housing regulations, assessments of tenants, management of clients, housing benefit, rent collection, tenancy agreements and tenancy law, investor input and returns, and much more. They will also train your church members in mentoring skills and guide them in their relationships with the tenants in the house.

Contact details

www.hopeintoaction.org.uk
E: admin@hopeintoaction.org.uk
T: 01733 558301

A different church acts as host each night, offering a place of safety, a hot meal, a warm, dry place to sleep and breakfast in the morning.

Grants available see www.cinnamonnetwork.co.uk for details

Hope Into Action stories

- John was in a state of despair after eight years of hostel life. Methodone kept him off heroin but his cannabis habit made him paranoid and depressed. Through Hope Into Action John has now given up cannabis and reduced his methodone. He has found employment through a church member and is a fully trained street pastor. 'Helping others helps me,' he says.
- Rachel and her daughter fled from the city where she was a victim of domestic violence. Hope Into Action housed her and the local church is able to give her support with parenting and accessing courses.
- Cameron was living on the streets for many years. His life changed around when he moved into one of the Hope Into Action houses. *'I just needed a stable environment,'* he said. He has now given up a long-term habit of heroin misuse and has asked to be baptised in the church.
- Peter was met inside HMP Peterborough by a member of the Salvation Army and a Hope Into Action project worker. When he left prison he was met at the gate by the church, given food and support. The church supported him through fork-lift truck training, he passed and was able to get an interview with an employer.

Housing Justice Night Shelters

ONE *'Our aim at Housing Justice is to develop a nationwide network of Night Shelters to show a living, caring faith in Christ to the homeless, by meeting their practical and spiritual needs.'*

Vision

Housing Justice supports churches and other groups to set up, run and develop winter night shelters. They are a well-established way of meeting the challenge of helping destitute and homeless people. In collaboration with other churches, a 'Rolling Shelter' system is set up where Christian hospitality is offered nightly to vulnerable rough sleepers during the winter period. A different church acts as host each night, offering a place of safety, a hot meal, a warm, dry place to sleep and breakfast in the morning. Training, help and support can also be given to the homeless guests to assist them in getting their lives back together.

A night shelter ministry doesn't require masses of resources, and if the appropriate approach is adopted, there are few risks and dangers. Importantly, it is also a way of getting virtually everyone in the church involved, because whatever a person's gift, it can be used in this valuable service to the marginalised. What is more, it is a way for churches that might not naturally come together to work together in the service of Christ.

Benefits

When weather conditions are extreme, a night shelter can be the difference between life and death: a matter of physical survival. The physical benefits are great, but so is the emotional and spiritual help that is given. Night shelter guests appreciate the fact that they are accorded respect and dignity and acknowledged as people in their own right. It is a world apart from being kicked in the gutter. For many guests a stay can be the 'helping hand' that they need to get their lives back on track. The support given by the volunteers and the professional case workers, who often work alongside the night shelters, can make all the difference to the guest as they handle what is happening in their lives. For many, the picture of an 'alternative reality' to that of mixing with people who are dependent upon alcohol or other substances, can be the impetus they need to get them back to a place of 'greater normality'. For others, they come to know the inner transformation of Jesus in their lives as they discover him for themselves, often through the love that has been shown to them.

WITH A SMALL GROUP OF KEEN AND MOTIVATED VOLUNTEERS, AND WITH RELATIVELY LIMITED RESOURCES, A NIGHT SHELTER CAN BEGIN.

For the volunteers, there is the principle that however much you think you may give, you get more back from God. There is an obvious sense of satisfaction as people see the difference that their small act of caring can make, and some volunteers go on a journey of personal discovery as they find and develop skills and gifts that they didn't know that they had. The sense of completeness that comes from working alongside people who are quite different to you can be a wonderful discovery. On the broader scale, churches in towns that have little to do with each other find that what binds them together is greater than what separates them. Additionally, there is a dimension of 'social cohesion' as volunteers from outside regular church circles get involved.

Challenges

Getting started can be a challenge: overcoming the perceived difficulties, naming the fears and anxieties, and getting people to own the project at an organisational level are all hurdles that Housing Justice can help churches overcome. Gathering volunteers together is often not a problem, because so many people are keen to be involved in this simple act of caring. There is a fellowship between night shelters that means that a relatively new night shelter is often the first to come forward to help another new Night Shelter in a nearby area get off the ground.

How easy is it to replicate this idea?

With a small group of keen and motivated volunteers, and with relatively limited resources, a night shelter can begin. Local context determines exactly how it will work out, but 'small and manageable' is always the best way to start. One church with half a dozen volunteers can begin just by using the premises that they have, with donations of food and basic equipment. This can then be multiplied, and often is, as others see how straightforward and effective this caring work is. Other localities will have a large team, employed staff and greater financial resources. The principle is that people work with what they have: there is no one size fits all blueprint for a night shelter. The principles that Housing Justice teach (and which are available in the free downloadable resource: Shelter in a Pack: http://bit.ly/lhWU2K) are what is needed, rather than a particular level of resources. The wider night shelter family that Housing Justice brings together means that no one needs to feel isolated as they seek to get their night shelter off the ground.

Getting started

The simplest way to get started is to make contact with the Housing Justice office. An experienced and trained staff member will be available to discuss the vision and to help you crystallise your ideas. Training and grants are also available.

'He left with tears running down his face and I later discovered he started going to church and that he signed up for a course to learn more about Christianity!'

Contact details

www.housingjustice.org.uk
E: info@housingjustice.org.uk
T: 020 3544 8094

One of the Housing Justice team said: *'Hope is found in the midst of a spiral of hopelessness. One of our guests came to me to ask if I would pray for a friend who had a serious illness, despite the guest being a non-believer himself. After I prayed alongside him for his friend I just thanked God that our guest was with us and asked that God would protect him, guide his life and help him to understand that God really cares for him too. He left with tears running down his face and I later discovered he started going to church and that he signed up for a course to learn more about Christianity!'*

Looking for some Christmas sermon inspiration?

Get a copy of *Proclaiming Christmas* with timeless talks by some of the most creative communicators in the church, edited by J John and available from www.philotrust.com.

new year courses

'Reaching for a goal whilst you are supported by a like-minded community can be very effective.'

New Year Courses

As people start each New Year, they are often full of hope about what the coming 12 months will hold. New Year's resolutions are part and parcel of the season with people hoping to give something up or to develop new and better habits. This hunger for change and a new start provides an excellent opportunity for the church to serve. We could have a huge impact if, in villages, towns and cities across the UK, churches worked together to provide a range of New Year resolution lifestyle courses. For example one church could run a course on financial freedom for those who have resolved to sort their money out. Another church could run a health and fitness course to help local people achieve a common New Year goal. Yet another church could run courses focusing on building better relationships, and all the churches could join together to promote their activities across the village, town or city where they are taking place.

Often we fail with our New Year's resolutions because the only tool we use in bringing about personal change is self-discipline. Whilst self-discipline is an important part of change, alone it is a relatively weak tool. If we depend just on self-discipline, we'll often find ourselves disheartened at our failed efforts. Reaching for a goal whilst you are supported by a like-minded community can be a very effective way to achieve real change.

New Year's resolutions are part and parcel of the season with people hoping to give something up or to develop new and better habits.

Relationship Central

Holy Trinity Brompton (HTB) run *Relationship Central*, offering courses which aim to provide practical, relevant help to parents, couples and individuals in different areas of family life and relationships. The four courses are: The Marriage Course, The Marriage Preparation Course, The Parenting Children Course and The Parenting Teenagers Course.

www.relationshipcentral.org

Revd Graham Singh, Vicar of St John's Hampton Wick said: *'We run the Parenting Children and the Parenting Teenagers Course Relationship at St John's. As a church one of the reasons we love it is because of the open invitation to come to something as easy as learning about parenting. We have lots of other activities in the church which maybe challenge your faith. We find that the idea of learning about parenting is so easy to come to that we get loads of people turning up from our invitations.'*

The Parenting Children Course

ONE

The Parenting Children Course aims to equip parents and carers of children aged 0-10 years, as well as parents-to-be, with tools to build a healthy family life. Over five sessions (or 10 shorter ones) parents and carers learn how to invest in their children's future, model the values they want to pass on, set healthy boundaries and keep love at the centre of their family life.

www.relationshipcentral.org/parenting-children-course

The Parenting Teenagers Course

The aim of The Parenting Teenagers Course is to equip parents and carers of children aged 11-18 years old with strategies to build a healthy relationship with their teenagers while guiding them into adulthood. Over five sessions (or 10 shorter ones), parents and carers learn practical tools to help them support their teenagers, communicate effectively, discover how their teenagers feel loved, set appropriate boundaries and let them go gradually so that they take on increasing responsibility for their own behaviour.

Amanda Smart said: *'I am a pastor at Every Nation Church London, but I am also a full time mum of two boys aged eight and ten. This time last year I did my first Parenting Children Course. As it was something I hadn't done before, I wanted to do a trial run before I ran a big course in our church. So I asked the mums outside the school gates to help me trial the course. I started with four mums in my front room; two were single mums and two married with four different nations between them. We met every week and watched the videos and had discussions; it was absolutely amazing. The one thing they were most excited about was the family time – spending time together. One of the greatest things was that I was able to share the gospel. One lady said 'Who is this Jesus you are talking about?' I really want to encourage church leaders: it doesn't take a lot to get this course going – just buy the DVDs, get a group of friends together and just do it – it is a fantastic course.'*
www.relationshipcentral.org/parenting-teenagers-course

WE MET EVERY WEEK AND WATCHED THE VIDEOS AND HAD DISCUSSIONS; IT WAS ABSOLUTELY AMAZING.

The Marriage Preparation Course

The aim of The Marriage Preparation Course is to give engaged couples the practical tools they need to build a strong and lasting marriage. Over five sessions the couples learn how to invest in their relationship, develop shared goals and values, and keep love growing throughout their marriage. The course is for any couple who is engaged or considering marriage.

www.relationshipcentral.org/marriage-preparation-course

The Marriage Course

The Marriage Course allows couples to escape from the hustle and bustle of everyday life and take time to relax, eat, drink and invest in their relationship.

Over seven sessions, set in a fantastic atmosphere with a candlelit meal on a romantic table for two, couples learn practical tools to help them invest time in their marriage. There is never any group work and couples are never asked to share anything about their relationship with anyone other than their partner. The topics covered are: Building Strong Foundations, The Art of Communication, Resolving Conflict, The Power of Forgiveness, The Impact of Family, Good Sex, and Love in Action.

Author and columnist for *The Times*, Tim Lott, and his wife Rachael signed up for the seven-week course and then he wrote about their experience.[2] Though initially reluctant to attend due to its church links, they found the course enjoyable and challenging and were sad when it ended. He said, 'It had put the idea of marriage on the agenda above and beyond what our personal desires were – as something separate, out there, that needed to be nurtured. And Rachael had felt transformed by the experience, saying: "I feel evangelical about it. Understanding that people express their love in different languages, learning to listen and put one another first – these have all been revelations."'

The Marriage Courses, like the Parenting Courses are accessible for people from all walks of life, whether Christian or not.

THE MARRIAGE COURSES, LIKE THE PARENTING COURSES ARE ACCESSIBLE FOR PEOPLE FROM ALL WALKS OF LIFE, WHETHER CHRISTIAN OR NOT.

www.relationshipcentral.org/marriage-course

21st Century Marriage & 21st Century Parent

The 21st Century courses are ideal for small groups. The majority of content is provided by DVD, with eight short talks from Rob Parsons on different aspects of marriage/parenting. Alongside the DVDs you can buy a pack of 'handy hints' booklets which can be used as discussion guides.

Becky from North Wales recently ran 21st Century Marriage in her church. Here's what she said about it:

'Earlier this year some friends and I had the privilege of running 21st Century Marriage. We chose to run the sessions over four weeks, which we thought was a manageable amount of time for people to fit into busy schedules and arrange babysitters. Each DVD topic is quite short so we watched two per evening, to allow plenty of time for the couples to chat through the topics together. We gave everyone a booklet, filled with practical yet simple tips, to take home with them.

[2] *'Can you learn the secret of a happy marriage?',* The Times, *October 2011*

21st Century Marriage was a dream to run – I loved it. It was so fulfilling to encourage couples in their relationships. The feedback forms that were completed afterwards had lots of positive comments and confirmed to us that it was a great success. I highly recommend anyone who fancies running this to go for it! I am sure that you too will be amazed at the great response!'

Positive Parenting courses

There are a wide range of courses for parents available in the Positive Parenting series, including the 'Time Out' courses in Early Years, Primary Years, Teenage Years, Special Needs, ADHD, ASD and a course especially for Dads. The 'How to Drug Proof Your Kids' course concentrates on the important role a parent can play in reducing the risk of their child becoming involved in harmful drug use. 'Quidz In' gives parents the knowledge and skills needed to talk to children about money and budgeting from an early age.

To deliver these programmes you need to be a licensed facilitator, and Care for the Family has developed an accredited training module to equip people with practical skills and understanding to work with parents.

Sian from Gwynedd is using the training and materials at her church to run courses for parents in her community. Here's what she said:

'Our vision is to work alongside families and to support them and create relationships within the local community. One of the main highlights of the course has been to see parents meeting up with each other, being honest with each other, and being supported. Parents from the group have also begun meeting up outside of the group time. One of the families has started to attend the regular Sunday evening family service and through this we are able to give them spiritual support too.'

Parentplay

Parentplay is a fun, seven-week parenting course focusing on parents of children under five years old. It uses informal small-group discussions followed by parents and children sharing an exciting, messy play-time together. To purchase a book and CD-ROM with all the content you need, visit www.parentplay.co.uk.

We had people contact us from all walks of life and at all stages of engagement.

Claire Gooud who ran Parentplay in Leeds said all the mums got on very well with each other, and all entered enthusiastically into discussions. They learned a lot, made many friends and gained confidence. One of the main things they learned was that no matter where you are from, you all go through the same struggles as parents. On the feedback forms the mums listed the things they'd learned, such as 'It's OK to have "me" time'; 'It improved my English'; 'I have become more patient; I praise more; I show love more'.

Marriage by Design

Marriage by Design is a one-day marriage preparation course for engaged couples. Courses are led by trained facilitators who introduce topics using a mixture of DVD content and live presenting. Couples then have the opportunity to discuss topics together using the couples' handbook to generate discussion. Marriage by Design has been developed using research into what makes for the strongest relationships, and it is suitable for couples from any background, with or without a Christian faith.

Maddie from the Isle of Man has delivered Marriage by Design to a number of couples from the community. Here's what she said:

'Running a Marriage by Design course was one of the best volunteering experiences for me and my husband. We chose to advertise it in the local press, Register Offices, shops, community halls, and local churches. We had people contact us from all walks of life and at all stages of engagement. There was a sense of nervous excitement at the beginning of the day and as it progressed each couple relaxed, obviously enjoying the mixture of presentation, DVD inserts and couples' activities. The whole day had a light-hearted feel and the feedback throughout was very positive. One man said that although he had had to leave at 11am, he had learned more about his partner in that first 90 minutes than he had in the rest of their seven years together!'

Parenting in the Teenage Years

In this DVD, Rob Parsons gives the inside track on understanding teenagers and shares some of the lessons he's learned as a parent. The DVD is split into three sessions, and it comes with a free booklet containing helpful tips and discussion starters, which can be easily used within a group setting.

For young people

Romance Academy

This is a 14-weekk intervention project that addresses the underlying causes of risky youth behaviour, such as poor self-esteem, low aspirations and lack of positive family life, by promoting the value of stable relationships. To find out how you can be trained as a facilitator of a Romance Academy visit www.romanceacademy.org.

See page 183 for more information on Romance Academy.

Health and fitness

ONE Why not try a lifestyle course for those who want to lose a bit of weight and live a healthier lifestyle?

- How about a weekly session learning to cook healthy food? You could use something like Rosemary Conley's ***Step By Step Low Fat Cookbook*** or check out more health and fitness ideas at www.rosemary-conley.co.uk.

Grants available see www.cinnamonnetwork.co.uk for details

Walking is a great way to start exercising; it has many health benefits whilst allowing people to go at their own pace and is great for building relationships.

- Walking is a great way to start exercising; it has many health benefits whilst allowing people to go at their own pace and is great for building relationships. If you'd like to start a weekend walking club visit www.whi.org.uk to find out about walks in your area plus lots of useful information including training for walk leaders.
- For youth groups, a sports initiative could be a great way to get active and to bring new people into the group. You could try Youth for Christ's 'Kick Academy' courses; ten-week programmes teaching the gospel and life-skills through football. For more information go to www.yfc.co.uk/kickacademy.
- Start a weight loss programme at your church such as WeightWatchers – see www.weightwatchers.co.uk.

Work and vocation

ONE Lifestyle courses for those who want to do something about their work or the way they work.

- ***The Heart of Success*** is a DVD and workbook by Rob Parsons which will enable individuals to explore the best way to find that elusive balance between life and work. Visit Care for the Family at www.careforthefamily.org.uk.

Feeling Good – Kings Community Church in Southampton

We have been running a toddler group and pre-school from the church for well over a decade, and have run a number of events to help build relationships outside of the sessions as conversations can be hard when children are running around. These have proved to be very effective, however the limitation has always been how to communicate the heart of the gospel at these social times, when

people are signing up to watch a movie, or drink a glass of champagne!

We discovered the Wellsprings Course, developed by Baptist minister Leesa Barton, and published by the Baptist Union, and created our own idea based on this called Feeling Good. It is a four week course looking at key themes facing women today and what the Bible has to say about them, covering areas like worry and anxiety, failure, healing, and forgiveness. Each theme is covered in 5-10 minutes and largely hinges on personal testimony. The rest of the evening then follows on with conversation around the chosen topic. In parallel with that, there is a beauty treatment or pampering session that each guest receives which ties in with the theme. We have done facial treatments, hand massage, foot spas and so on. The evening finishes with a free gift for each guest.

We have found that inviting someone to this evening, being very clear that there will be someone sharing their story about how God has helped them in an area of their life, along with emphasising the beauty treatment, and the food and drink has been very helpful, and much easier than inviting to a heavily evangelistic meeting or course. Once the four weeks are concluded we then try to encourage all those that have come to book in to the launch event of our Alpha course, and to go along as a whole group, reserving their table together.

WE HAVE DONE FACIAL TREATMENTS, HAND MASSAGE, FOOT SPAS AND SO ON. THE EVENING FINISHES WITH A FREE GIFT FOR EACH GUEST.

Grants available see www.cinnamonnetwork.co.uk for details

ONE

CAP – Christians Against Poverty

Debt Centres

'CAP has transformed us as a church. We knew nothing about debt counselling but by partnering with CAP we've helped hundreds of people out of debt and we've seen people come to church and become followers of Christ who would not have come otherwise. God's mandate is for us to care for the poor and this is such an easy way for us to get involved.' Simon Benham, Senior Pastor, Kerith Community Church, Bracknell

'Because of the support from CAP and the amazing family at St John's Church, we are now free from debt, have a wonderful home and, best of all, we have Jesus in our lives.' Gemma, CAP Client

'I would like to thank you from the bottom of my heart for what CAP have done for me. I was suicidal and if it hadn't been for my caseworker and his wife, I don't think I would be here.' Roy, CAP Client

Vision

CAP's mission is to relieve poverty in the UK through top class debt counselling services delivered through local churches. Through this, CAP clients can experience and respond to the love of Jesus.

Before engaging with CAP:

- 76% of clients skipped meals to repay their debts
- 65% struggled to feed or clothe their children
- 37% seriously considered or attempted suicide as a way out of their debt problems

CAP is passionate about empowering you as the local church to tackle the big problems in your community. They invest significantly in every debt centre, providing some or all of the centralised debt counselling services, as well as providing training, management and support to help your centre be as successful as possible.

Benefits

CAP provides an opportunity for churches to share the good news of Jesus with people that they might not normally meet. With a CAP Debt Centre, relationships are sustained at least until a client is debt free giving volunteers and CAP staff countless opportunities to offer prayer, give personal testimonies and share their faith.

Helping people with unmanageable debts get debt free means homes are saved from repossession, children are fed and clothed, and marriages are restored, all alongside the promotion of sustainable financial habits so that clients can stay debt free. On top of this CAP sees hundreds of people discover God and begin a personal relationship with Jesus Christ each year.

Opportunities

There are plenty of volunteer relationship-building opportunities for your congregation. Befrienders provide support for marginalised and vulnerable clients in a variety of ways from a friendly phone call, to meeting for coffee, offering prayer and personal support. This service breaks the cycle of loneliness and isolation, as well as giving the volunteer a chance to grow in their faith and see great results for their efforts.

BEFRIENDERS PROVIDE SUPPORT FOR MARGINALISED AND VULNERABLE CLIENTS IN A VARIETY OF WAYS FROM A FRIENDLY PHONE CALL, TO MEETING FOR COFFEE, OFFERING PRAYER AND PERSONAL SUPPORT.

Challenges

If you're thinking about opening a CAP Debt Centre, consider:

- **Funding** – CAP is a national charity that stands in faith for its finances, as do the churches who partner with them. This is a serious commitment for any church, but 16 years' experience has shown CAP that it is a worthwhile investment.
- **Volunteers** – CAP's service is an amazing opportunity for a church to unite behind a ministry but it can be a logistical challenge to organise and inspire everyone. CAP trains centre staff to create a team of enthusiastic and willing volunteers.
- **Accessibility** – A lot of CAP clients have never been in church before but through their debt counselling they decide to attend. This provides a challenge in ensuring that your church is welcoming and accessible to all members of society, while maintaining core gospel values and teaching. What a brilliant problem to have!
- **PR** – The final challenge is raising the profile of your centre. People with financial problems really need to know that a CAP Debt Centre exists so CAP can offer churches advice on how to let your community know what's on offer.

Tips

If your church is already involved with other community outreach programmes, CAP is an ideal ministry. Debt is often a symptom of other problems and so an active church is the best place for CAP clients to find a complete solution to their unique situation. Churches already running foodbanks, rehabs, parent and tots groups or providing other practical help, often find a great synergy between CAP and these ministries.

How easy is it to replicate this idea?

There are two options for partnering with CAP.

Option 1

Full centralised debt counselling services as well as PR support, literature, evangelism and discipleship aids and access to CAP's Client Aid budget (an emergency fund) and Discovery Breaks (short client holidays). Estimated cost per year: £6,000

Option 2

As a Debt Centre you are responsible for providing part of the debt counselling yourself and the Head Office services (listed above) can be paid for as optional extras, instead of being part of the initial cost. Estimated cost per year: £2,000

(These contributions cover less than half of CAP's costs.)

Getting started

The first step to opening a CAP Debt Centre is for a senior leader from your church to attend a Church Partnership Day. This is an inspiring day that will allow you to experience the culture of CAP first hand. You can ask all the questions you need to get a better understanding of how a partnership between CAP and a church works. Church Partnership Days are free and are held regularly throughout the year.

To book on to a Church Partnership Day, contact CAP using the information below.

Contact details

www.capuk.org/churchpartnershipday
E: openacentre@capuk.org
T: 01274 760 580

Stories from CAP

I had given up. I stayed in my pyjamas all day. Nothing I did would help or change anything. I knew the bailiff was coming to take my stuff, but I just thought, "Come and take what you want. I haven't got anything anyway". I think the nicest bailiff visited me. He sat me down, made me a cup of tea and gave me three numbers to ring for help with my debts. I rang CAP last as the others couldn't help me.

When Irene came, I was ready for a fight. I thought she might try and shove God down my throat and tell me I can't do this and that. But she didn't judge me at all and she offered to pray for me, which was really nice and gentle. Then she came with a Christmas hamper. It had everything for our Christmas dinner from a voucher for the meat, right down to serviettes and little presents for each of us! Little things make a huge difference and I really needed that hamper. To know that someone out there, someone that I have never even met, was thinking of me made me feel loved. I am truly thankful to CAP's supporters.

I went on a CAP Discovery Break as I needed a chance to rest and relax. I have arthritis and fibromyalgia and I was in constant pain. Someone prayed for me and I didn't have any pain the whole time I was there. All of us became Christians on that break. My son now wants to get baptised and we go to Irene's church. Everybody is lovely in that church. God is working in my family.

Now I can answer the door and the phone. I can be confident because CAP's involved. I've got money for food and all my debts are getting paid too. CAP isn't just there to help with your money; Irene calms me down and makes sense of everything. She does the same for all her clients, not just me. You can see Jesus in her. Michelle, CAP Client

CAP Money

'A couple came on an Alpha course with us who were having major problems in their marriage due to struggles with their finances. I took the CAP course to them in their home and in week two it was as if a light switched on for them. Using cash and having a weekly allowance for each of them meant that they didn't argue about what the other was spending their money on. Their marriage was literally saved as a result.'
CAP Coach

Vision

CAP Money is a revolutionary money management course from Christians Against Poverty that teaches people budgeting skills and a simple, cash-based system that really works. This course will help anyone to get more in control of their finances, so they can save, give and prevent debt.

CAP Money teaches delegates three vital principles:

1. **How to build and live on a budget.** This is the cornerstone of managing money well. The course provides delegates with advice on how to increase income and cut costs.
2. **The CAP Money system.** This system helps to simplify the delegate's money and make it understandable. It operates using three accounts: a regular payments account, a cash account and a savings account.

3. How to live from week to week using cash.

Living on cash and getting away from cards means that delegates know exactly where their money is and helps them to spend less.

Through a DVD-based course facilitated by trained CAP Money Coaches, delegates can build a budget and ask any questions they may have. A unique benefit of CAP Money is that, if delegates discover they can't balance their budget and pay off any debts, they will be able to access CAP Money Plus. This is a phone and email debt counselling service provided by Christians Against Poverty.

Benefits

CAP Money is a fantastic outreach tool that any church can use to impact their community. Many people are feeling the pinch and looking at how to reduce their expenses, meaning money management and budgeting are at the top of their agenda. Through CAP Money, your church can reach out to give people the tools to deal with their finances at this crucial time.

CAP Money also reflects Jesus' heart as money was one of the major topics he addressed in his teaching. As his Church, we should do the same. Money affects so much of what we all do and if it is out of control, it has the power to destroy lives. CAP Money empowers people to give and save more as well as preventing the destructive effects of unmanageable debt.

You should look for volunteers who are comfortable and confident when working with a wide variety of people, and happy to lead in an informal teaching environment.

Tips

Volunteers - You should look for volunteers who are comfortable and confident when working with a wide variety of people, and happy to lead in an informal teaching environment. Detailed financial knowledge is not required, although volunteers need to be comfortable handling figures and have a good grasp of basic financial principles. Also, as they are teaching others about money, they must have their own finances in order and be of good character and integrity. They must be people who you are happy to represent your church to the local community.

Inspiring your church - Your congregation are vital to the success of CAP Money. Church members will be needed as CAP Money Coaches, to invite their friends to the course and to pray. To inspire your church, you can book a CAP Speaker (call 01274 760570 or email speakers@capuk.org) or order a free resource pack, which includes a DVD of client stories, sermon notes and more.

Resources

CAP Money is run in thousands of locations throughout the UK by churches that partner with Christians Against Poverty. The course will usually run over three sessions, primarily in the evenings, but some are run during the day. Many courses are run from church buildings and others are run in cafés, people's homes, or community centres. The number of people attending can range from two to 40.

Running CAP Money in your church will have a big impact for church members and those in your community for relatively small effort and cost. All you need to do is recruit volunteers to run the course (called CAP Money Coaches) and allow CAP to present their work at one of your Sunday services. It's recommended to start with a team of at least three CAP Money Coaches and you may find you want to recruit more in the future.

It costs just £45 for each volunteer from your church to become a CAP Money Coach and get CAP Money up and running in your church.

This covers:

- a full day's training, including lunch and all refreshments
- a starter pack of course materials for each new Money Coach (ten Delegate Workbooks, one course DVD, a Money Coach Guide and a selection of posters and flyers)
- ongoing email and telephone support and assistance from the CAP Money Team in Bradford.

There are also additional in-depth training sessions available at regional training days throughout the year for Money Coaches who want to grow their knowledge.

Christians Against Poverty possesses a Group Credit Licence and as part of that there is the option for a CAP Money Coach to train to become a Licensed Money Coach. Being a Licensed Money Coach will enable them to provide more support for delegates who have referred themselves to CAP Money Plus because of unmanageable debt.

'I TRIED TO COMMIT SUICIDE ALL THANKS TO MY STUPIDITY WITH MONEY, BUT WE WERE KEPT GOING BY THE PRAYERS AND LOVE OF FRIENDS.'

Options

Do you have a specific demographic you want to work with? Then the CAP Money Course may be ideal for you. They offer a range of courses including: one aimed at students, one for schools and youth, a specifically tailored course for ministers to work through at home, and one that is suitable for use in prisons.

Getting started

Request an information pack, identify volunteers from your church to be CAP Money Coaches, then book spaces on a regional training day. After attending a training day, you will be ready to run CAP Money in your church and community.

Contact details

www.capmoney.org/en_GB/runacourse
E: info@capmoney.org
T: 01274 760567

'I tried to commit suicide all thanks to my stupidity with money, but we were kept going by the prayers and love of friends. We were put on the CAP Money Course and, for me especially, it changed my life.' Mandy

A CAP volunteer said, *'We worked with a lady who has never understood money management and just spent the money her husband brought home, often barely getting through the month. She is now enthused by the cash system (having been appalled at all she was spending) and is getting her husband on board to run a cash system rather than credit cards.'*

Community Money Advice

'We recently had a couple visit us who were in a complete state. The husband had been borrowing money, without telling his wife, to cover up some financial difficulties. She had found out by accident and dragged him along to us. Their marriage was all but over as she felt she couldn't trust him anymore but admitted that she still loved him. Not only have we been able to negotiate a payment plan with creditors but we also suggested the couple attend the marriage course that was running and starting the following week. Having attended, they have got their marriage very much back on track and are working to sort out their finances.'
CMA centre worker

Vision

The vision of Community Money Advice is to have completely free face-to-face money advice centres in every community across the nation, reaching anyone in need with quality advice from budgeting education, form filling and casework through to personal insolvency. The Community Money Advices ethos is to set people free from debt whilst giving them the tools to remain debt free.

Personal debt has blighted this nation for many years with debt impacting on many different areas of life causing illness, mental health issues, relationship breakdown, isolation, and, in extreme situations, suicide. People need help and practical advice, someone who can listen without judging and then help to find resolution to debt issues as well as providing budgeting education to ensure any solutions offered are sustainable.

Grants available see www.cinnamonnetwork.co.uk for details

Community Money Advice started in 1997 in Sussex and has grown into a network of over 100 money advice centres, with 1,000 trained volunteers impacting thousands of lives a year.

Opportunities

If you would like to open a debt centre, CMA can provide you with all the information and training you need, even if you have no previous experience in this area. They will help you set up your centre, provide a freephone advice-line for questions on starting up a centre and casework concerns, help you with policies and procedures, and provide you with all the guides and resources you need. A Regional Operations Support Manager will also be available to visit your centres and provide guidance and mentoring.

Setting up a debt advice centre takes time and commitment but to see people's lives transformed through spending time listening to them and offering real practical help is enormously rewarding. Taking a professional approach is necessary but the best debt advisers are those who enjoy talking to people and are able to be compassionate and non judgemental.

Resources needed

A centre may have as few as two or three volunteers helping people one evening a week through to a centre staffed with full-time employees open six days a week. A volunteer-led centre will cost in the region of £3,000 to start up and about £1,800 a year to run. Ideally a centre will have space to interview clients, tea and coffee making facilities, access to a photocopier and have a dedicated computer with internet access.

Getting started

Get hold of a copy of a *Setting up a Debt Advice Centre* booklet from www.communitymoneyadvice.com which details how to plan, run and establish your centre.

Contact details

www.communitymoneyadvice.com
E: info@communitymoneyadvice.com
T: 01743 341929

John's story

John was brought to the Debt Advice Centre by his church minister. He had lost his wife two years previously and had subsequently fallen into deep depression. To comfort himself he had gone on a spending spree and run up several credit card debts. Because he felt so ashamed, he kept his debts a secret for nearly two years until they became so unmanageable that he finally confided in his pastor.

At his first visit John was hardly able to speak and was very tearful but he was also relieved that he was finally taking action to get his debts under control.

Over the following weeks we were able to successfully negotiate a reduced payment plan with all his creditors that meant a balance was finally restored to John's finances. He was able to live within his means whilst honouring his debts and the relief and release that this brought to John's life was obvious. His whole demeanour changed and with each visit it became clear that his self-esteem was improving.

Last month he told us that he had a new lady in his life and that right from the start he had been honest with her about his debts, something that he would never have been able to do before. He's off all his anti-depressants and can now look to a much brighter future in every way.

easter

'Over the Easter weekend we come together to reflect and to rejoice again on the story of Jesus' death and resurrection that is central to our faith.'

Easter

Easter is the most significant time in the church calendar. As individuals and churches we spend the 40 days of Lent preparing our hearts to think again about Jesus' sacrifice for us on the cross and to celebrate the amazing victory that he won for us when he rose to life. Over the Easter weekend we come together to reflect and to rejoice again on the story of Jesus' death and resurrection that is central to our faith. Despite all that Easter means to us, to those outside of the church it can be just a long weekend away from work and a chance to eat chocolate eggs. You might like to use some of these ideas to help your celebrations of Easter communicate the gospel to your whole community.

YOU MIGHT LIKE TO USE SOME OF THESE IDEAS TO HELP YOUR CELEBRATIONS OF EASTER COMMUNICATE THE GOSPEL TO YOUR WHOLE COMMUNITY.

Ideas for mission

Pancake party

Shrove Tuesday is a great opportunity to hold a party where you can invite your friends, work colleagues and neighbours round for a pancake.

Pancake racing - a tradition that apparently began when a woman was making pancakes and heard the church bells ringing, calling her to worship. Realising she was late she ran out of the house with the frying pan still in her hand! Modern day racers usually have to toss the pancake a certain number of times before they reach the finish line with their pancake intact.

Pancake tossing – willing participants can challenge each other to see how many pancakes they can toss in two minutes. The official world record stands at well over 400 times!

With Lent starting the following day, Shrove Tuesday is a great time to get people to share what they would like to give up for Lent. You could ask members of your community if they would like to join you in raising money through Lent – read on to find out more!

Sacrificial giving

This idea can be used by used by individuals or churches of any size. The more people who get involved, the bigger the impact!

In the run up to Easter (Lent) we focus on what Jesus sacrificed for us. He gave everything and for us to go without one of our usual comforts for a short amount of time helps us to focus on his great and sacrificial love. But fasting is about more than just stopping doing something, it's about getting our hearts right with God and understanding his heart for the world. We can use Lent as a time to bless our communities and show them God's sacrificial love.

What's the idea?

Think of something you do on a regular basis, that costs you money and that you can give up for Lent. It could be something you give up completely (like chocolate) or something where you pick a cheaper alternative (like inviting a friend round for coffee instead of meeting at a coffee house). Keep a track of the money you save each week and put it in a money box (if you do this as a whole church, make it easy for people to give there too).

Where does the money go?

What needs are there in your community that you could do something about? One church in Watford committed the money collected in Lent to their local hospital that was struggling to buy equipment for its children's ward. The hospital was stunned when the church gave over £5,000 – questioning whether an extra '0' had been added on by mistake! You could talk to local charities and projects about their needs, consider giving the money to a school that would benefit from some new equipment, or speak to the council about whether you could buy play equipment for a park. Alternatively you could use the money to help those in poverty around the world. You could use the money raised to sponsor children through Compassion (www.compassionuk.org) or get involved with a national scheme called 'Lend us your Lent' run by Soul Action, a joint initiative between Soul Survivor and Tearfund. The money raised through Lend us your Lent will go towards Soul Action projects (www.soulaction.org).

Ideas of what you can give up

- Choose a cheaper brand in the supermarket
- Make lunch at home instead of buying it at work
- Rent a DVD instead of going to the cinema
- Have a soft drink when you go to the pub instead of alcohol
- Give up buying chocolate, downloading music or buying magazines for the duration of Lent

If your church members don't spend much money on luxuries, then it might be that they'd like to donate some of their time instead. They could forgo a quiet Saturday morning or Sunday afternoon to clear an overgrown area, or offer a lunch break once a week to help a child in school learn to read. Finding out needs in the community that anyone could meet with a small amount of time gives people a great alternative if they are already living very simply financially.

If your church members don't spend much money on luxuries, then it might be that they'd like to donate some of their time instead

Another option is to 'Count Your Blessings'. Several charities such as Mothers' Union and Christian Aid offer ideas for this scheme, which helps people taking part to thank God for the blessings people in the UK enjoy, when compared with people living in poverty in other parts of the world. Each day during Lent, there's something to count – like the number of taps in your home or the number of books on your shelves. There's a suggested amount to give for each item and a short prayer, giving thanks for running water or education for example. The small amounts set aside daily can mount up to a significant gift.

Make a splash

When all the money has been received make a splash of handing it over to the recipients! Invite local press and members of the clergy to represent all the churches involved and present the money to the charity or organisation receiving it.

If you send round Easter cards to local homes, why not include a way they can send you prayer requests such as a reply slip or an email address?

Giving blood

TWO Flesh and Blood is a campaign by Kore and NHS Blood and Transplant to encourage church members to consider giving blood and donating organs. More than 1,000 people die each year whilst waiting for a transplant, and every day 8,000 units of blood are needed to meet hospital demand. If churches saw this as part of their commitment to giving we could make a huge difference and help save many lives. See www.fleshandblood.org for free resources for your church and community.

John Lampard, a retired Methodist Minister, has been giving blood since he was 25. At 70 his blood is being used for neo-natal transfusions. He says, *'Donating blood is sharing a part of your life with other people so that they can have life. An hour spent donating blood is very little when you consider all the good that comes out of it.'*

An hour spent donating blood is very little when you consider all the good that comes out of it.

The Passion at the heart of your community

Since 2010 around 20,000 people have gathered in Trafalgar Square each Good Friday to watch The Passion of Jesus – a re-enactment of the final hours leading up to Jesus' crucifixion. The large-scale event attracts churchgoers, tourists, passers-by and those who live or work nearby to consider the significance of Jesus' passion for all.

Now, thanks to a partnership between Bible Society and The Wintershall Trust, you can apply to receive the tools, training and tips to put on The Passion of Jesus in your local community on Good Friday 2014.

The Passion of Jesus is a unique opportunity to communicate the compelling message of hope by combining live drama, music and a community festival in a central public space. It offers you the chance to celebrate the skills and talents of individuals across your local community, and the opportunity to engage with local schools, theatrical groups, businesses, artists and churches.

Selected locations will be offered advice from those who have been involved in The Passion of Jesus in Trafalgar Square, as well as the complete script and soundtrack to use at their performances. Training opportunities will take place in advance of Good Friday 2014, including practical tips about logistics and planning, as well as advice about promotion, marketing and working with local and regional media agencies.

To find out more about what's involved and to register your interest in becoming one of the selected locations to stage The Passion of Jesus, visit www.biblesociety.org.uk/passion2014

Stations of the Cross for school children

TWO The Mothers' Union in Bishop's Waltham decided to try to redress the balance between the commercial side of Easter and the true Christian message. Using a programme devised by the Diocese of Gloucester, they invited the Year 6 classes at their local junior school to visit St Peter's Church during school time to experience the true meaning of Easter.

The children were warmly welcomed at the door of the church and then seated at the front of church to hear a brief account of Holy Week. Then in small groups of five or six, they travelled with their teacher or helper to look at the six stations around the church which each represented an event in Holy Week. A member of Mothers' Union was at each station to explain in more detail what happened at that particular event and then gave the children an opportunity to respond reflectively through multisensory activities. There was one station in the main aisle decorated with palms for the entry into Jerusalem on Palm Sunday, another focused on Jesus washing the feet of the disciples and a third, the Last Supper. A corner of the church was decorated with plants and rocks and became the Garden of Gethsemane and in the opposite corner they set up the crucifixion scene. All the groups came together in the chancel for the final station, the Resurrection. They built an empty tomb guarded by an angel under the main altar and used the choir stalls to seat the children.

Each child left with a goody bag that included an Easter egg and colourful invitation to return to St Peter's on Good Friday for a children's workshop and on Easter Sunday for a family service. There was also an Easter card and a leaflet outlining their regular children's activities and groups. The children and the team really enjoyed the experience saying it was, 'Brilliant!'

For more information on Experience Easter and to buy resources email experienceeaster@mail.com or visit gloucester.anglican.org.

THIS IS A GREAT TOWN OR CITY-WIDE IDEA!

Art and photography competition

ONE The arts are a great way to engage with your community and competitions always draw a good response. The more local churches you involve, the bigger and better this idea will become!

What's the idea?

Run a competition to see who can produce the best image around an Easter theme e.g. 'hope' or 'new life'.

- Launch the competition in schools, through community groups, and consider advertising in local media.
- Have three age ranges such as one for Primary School children, one for Secondary School and one for adults. Depending on your budget you could also have runners up in each category.
- Budget some money for a cash prize (say around £250 - £500 for each winner) which, in the adult category, could be donated to the charity of the winner's choice and for the young people could go towards art equipment at their school.
- Create a community celebration by holding an exhibition of all the submitted works and having a prize-giving as part of the event.

THE ARTS ARE A GREAT WAY TO ENGAGE WITH YOUR COMMUNITY AND COMPETITIONS ALWAYS DRAW A GOOD RESPONSE.

Consider

- ***Who your panel of judges will be.*** It's a great idea to include your Mayor, a local art teacher, a local artist, church leaders, a local newspaper editor or a local radio presenter.
- ***Where you will have your exhibition.*** Your church building may be ideal or this could be a great chance to engage with members of the public elsewhere for example at the local shopping centre or library. If you do this, think

about how you will make sure people know this is run by the churches!

- ***Prize alternatives.*** If you'd rather not give a cash prize you could also ask local businesses to provide awards or you could give prizes that will encourage the winner in their creative gift (e.g. art or photography equipment).
- ***Media.*** Invite the local press to take pictures of the prize-giving and to interview one of the organisers. Be clear about why you've run the competition so they have a snappy 'sound-bite' that summarises your aims. (See the chapter on working with the media for more advice.)
- ***Who will be at your exhibition?*** Churches who have held competitions like this have found images around hope have often led to poignant conversations with members of the community so make sure you have some church members on hand during the evening just to talk to people.

Love your street

ONE Wouldn't it be amazing if each street of our community had someone who was committed to praying for it and making it a better place? As individuals, families, small groups, churches and Christians across villages, towns and cities we can make that a reality by adopting a street each! It's a great way to start getting involved in your community and understanding its positive and negative aspects.

Anyone can put this into practice and you don't need any resources to make it happen!

Pick a street to adopt. It could be where you live, where your small group meets, or a road you walk down regularly on your way to work, school, or the shops.

Pray for your street. You could do this every time you walk down it or set aside a specific time each week or month. Thank God for the good things that you see there. Pray about the bad things, asking him to bring change. Ask God what you can be doing to make a difference in that street.

Take action. As God leads you, start to do things to bless that street and make it a better place. It could be as simple as picking up litter as you walk down it, or perhaps you will see a greater need in that area such as meeting someone who is homeless and in need of some food.

Make friends and be hospitable! Purposefully and prayerfully start relationships with people who live or work on your chosen street. Start with one person or family and commit to praying for them and blessing them in any way you can. Open up your home and practise hospitality by inviting people round for dinner or a party.

This idea will be best driven by individuals but could be adopted around villages, towns and cities with someone co-ordinating which streets have been adopted so each one is covered. It would be fantastic to have regular prayer backing up the initiative, praying for situations arising in streets and keeping each Christian covered in prayer as they seek to bring God's Kingdom to their street.

Find out more at www.loveyourstreet.org

Schools are right at the heart of the community and provide a great way to reach young people and their families.

Schools work

All these ideas could be done by one church or you could work with others across your area to make them bigger and better!

Schools are right at the heart of the community and provide a great way to reach young people and their families. Don't be daunted if you've never worked with your local school as Easter offers a multitude of reasons to get involved. Easter is part of the curriculum so teachers are often very grateful for help, plus this could be a great chance to start conversations about other ways your church could be a blessing to them over the whole year.

TWO ***A walk through the Easter story:*** why not invite local school classes to visit your church in the run up to Easter and re-enact the Easter story for them? St Polycarp's in Sheffield did just that with brilliant results! They visited schools first to teach the pupils some songs, choose 12 disciples and make palm leaves. Then they invited all the pupils into their church and walked them through the events using videos, a Passover meal, dramatic story-telling and song. The children and teachers loved it and we think it's an idea that could work brilliantly around the country!

TWO ***Taking lessons or assemblies:*** many schools would welcome a visit from a Christian or a group from a local church to explain what Easter means to them and what happened over 2000 years ago. Why not approach your local school and ask them how you can help? See the resources section for materials to help you get started!

Resources

There are lots of organisations who can help you deliver excellent schools work. Check out www.schoolswork.co.uk, www.yfc.co.uk, and www.scriptureunion.org.uk for more details.

Holiday clubs

TWO

The Easter holidays provide a perfect opportunity to bless families and connect with children in your community. Holiday clubs can be loads of fun, give parents a break and help children engage with church and God through fun activities like song, drama, craft, story-telling and games. There are loads of resources around that will give you plenty of ideas to make your holiday club a success with creative and interesting ideas. Try Scripture Union (www.scriptureunion.org.uk) or visit your local Christian bookshop in store or online to browse a whole range of holiday club materials. Make sure there are easy ways for families you meet through holiday clubs to take further steps into the life of the church and finding faith.

You could consider launching an in-schools lunch time club on the back of this to continue engaging with young people all year round.

Children's musicals

TWO

A creative way to engage children is to put on a children's musical around Easter either through local schools or churches. You could work with other churches in your area to put on a simple performance of the Passion Play – a perfect excuse for a visitor service! Composer Sheila Wilson has written three Easter musicals to suits different age groups (4-8, 5-11 and teenagers) that are around 15-25 minutes long. Each musical captures the hopes, the fears, and finally the joy of the resurrection, bringing Scripture alive powerfully through children's voices. All the resources you need (including backing music if you're short on musicians) can be found at www.redheadmusic.co.uk.

You could consider launching an in-schools lunch time club on the back of this to continue engaging with young people all year round.

Children of Hope – free resources!

TWO

'Children of Hope' is a song for 4-12 year olds, written especially for HOPE by children's composer Sheila Wilson. With optional two-part harmonies, kazoos, and hand-jives, its positive message makes a fun contribution to any event and is a great way to involve children and parents from the community! Download a live recording, a wordsheet, a vocal manuscript and a chord-sheet for free at www.hopetogether.org.uk.

Resources

Pam Pott offers workshops to those who would like help and advice on how to memorise Scripture for dramatised readings. Contact pam.pott@gmail.com

Make your Easter parade a walk of blessing

ONE TWO

For hundreds of years Christians in different villages, towns and cities, have joined together to take part in a walk on Good Friday to remember Jesus' journey from his trial to the place of his crucifixion. Others have been involved in a parade on Easter Sunday to witness to Jesus' resurrection.

If these are key traditions in your church calendar why not use them as another opportunity to show God's love to your community? Consider how your walk could be a blessing to others and how you could invite them to join in the celebration of Easter.

Tips

- Hand out goodies as you walk along with invitations to your Easter Sunday service such as helium balloons, chocolates or Hot Cross Buns. Take time to stop and chat to those around.
- End the walk with an open air service of praise and thanksgiving.
- Or you could finish the walk by stopping somewhere central and offering to pray for local people who would like to be healed. 'Healing on the Streets' started at a church in Northern Ireland and is being replicated around the UK,

seeing many healed and come to faith after they have been prayed for. See page 198 for more details of this initiative.

Creativity at Easter

Easter provides lots of opportunities to use the creative arts and this is a great way to work with other churches across your village, town or city to put on the best show you can! Using drama and music is a great way to engage a wide-audience and to make sure the message of Easter is heard in your community.

Passion Plays

Passion Plays have been part of Church tradition for centuries, telling the story of Jesus' trial, death and resurrection. Often churches perform their play in the open air, attracting passing crowds, and sometimes moving to different locations for changing scenes. Don't forget to pool resources with other churches to make sure you have a big enough team to take care of the scripting, acting, publicity, costumes and sets! If you're going to be doing the play outside, speak to your local council first.

Think about how to make the play relevant to your area. You might want to keep very strictly to the words and actions shown in the Bible, or you could give the play a more contemporary feel using popular music and modern-day language.

Find out more in *The Mystery and The Passion* by Richard Hasnip (Authentic) from www.saltminetrust.org.uk.

Easter choirs – great idea for all ages!

ONE Choirs are becoming increasingly popular with many using modern and popular music and attracting all ages. This is a great opportunity to engage with your local community. Gather a group of enthusiastic singers from both the church and the surrounding community and begin rehearsals. It could just be for the fun of singing together or you could put on a performance over the Easter weekend, perhaps charging a small entrance fee with all proceeds going to a local charity. Encourage the choir to invite all their friends and family to support them!

BRING THE STORY OF EASTER TO LIFE BY HAVING DIFFERENT MEMBERS OF THE CONGREGATION LEARN SECTIONS OF SCRIPTURE AND THEN DELIVER THEM DRAMATICALLY AS PART OF THE SERVICE.

Making the most of your Easter Sunday service

TWO Lots of people come to church at Easter who wouldn't normally be there and hopefully with all the outreach you've been doing over Lent that number will increase this year! This means your Easter Sunday service is a fantastic opportunity to help people understand the significance of Jesus' death and resurrection.

Dramatic storytelling

- Bring the story of Easter to life by having different members of the congregation learn sections of Scripture and then deliver them dramatically as part of the service.
- You could use video clips for some sections (Mark's Gospel reads a little like headline news so you could record someone reporting the events as news).
- You could think about sharing breakfast when you get to the reading in John 21 where Jesus gives his disciples fish for breakfast.
- Think about symbolic gestures like flinging open the church doors when you proclaim the words of the Great Commission.
- Children could perform a short Passion musical.
- You could take your service out on to the streets by doing an Emmaus Walk, going from one place to another and as you go, retelling the story of Jesus meeting the disciples on the road.

Don't forget!

Make sure you have plenty of welcome packs to give to visitors explaining what your church is about and what else you do outside of a Sunday service. You might like to give them a gift too such as a small Easter egg as well as a Gospel to take home to read.

After the service invite people to stay and share Hot Cross Buns with you as part of the celebrations.

Invite visitors to an upcoming social event that will take place a week or two after the service to help cement connections with newcomers.

Fun Day

A free Fun Day is a great way to get the community together and bless people! See the chapter on festivals and fun days for lots more info and think about Easter-themed activities such as:

- Free Hot Cross Buns or Easter eggs
- Egg rolling race
- Easter egg hunt for children
- A Passion play
- Having a large screen showing an Easter film
- Free shoe cleaning (linking to Jesus washing the disciples' feet)
- Kids craft tables making Easter cards and hats
- Kids Easter bonnet competition

Serving the servants

On the Thursday before Easter, also known as Maundy or Holy Thursday, we remember how Jesus washed the feet of disciples, demonstrating the kind of service and love we're to display to the world. This provides us with a great opportunity to go out into our communities and show people the servant-hearted love of Jesus.

There are so many people who work day in, day out to serve our communities. We couldn't function without postal workers, refuse collectors, lollipop men/ladies, nurses, youth workers, bus drivers, doctors, teachers, police officers, local council workers, and many more! Often these servants work long hours, and don't always receive much appreciation. Wouldn't it be amazing if we could show these public servants that their work is noticed and that we're grateful for all they do?

Wouldn't it be amazing if we could show these public servants that their work is noticed and that we're grateful for all they do?

The idea is simple: find a modern day equivalent of washing someone's feet and head out as an individual, family, small group or church to say thank you! You could give out small gifts like flowers or chocolates and accompany them with a card that says the receiver is really appreciated for all they do in your area. You could also say that you're praying for them and give them a way to contact you with any prayer requests (such as an email address). The idea isn't to do a hard-sell, but to find simple ways to say thank you, to bless people and to demonstrate that we serve a loving and generous God.

- Churches Together for Eastbourne say thank you to the town's street cleaners by holding a Street Cleaners Awards Evening, where the Mayor awards trophies after everyone has enjoyed a fish and chip supper.

Why not organise a prayer breakfast for leaders in your community such as MPs, MEPs, local government officials and Police? Ask them how you can best pray for them for their role in the community.

Passover meal. Meals are an effective way to create an informal atmosphere and encourage community and a Passover feast gives an opportunity for everyone to see what Jesus' Last Supper would have been like. For ideas and recipes see the Scripture Union resource ***Easter Cracked***. Or how about a different take on the Last Supper by putting on a Murder Mystery evening for young people?!

Hot Cross Buns. Find significant places in your community where there will be good passing traffic and hand out Hot Cross Buns as a small celebration of Easter. This works well at places like train stations and shopping centres.

Easter eggs are always popular. How about getting your church members to donate eggs then give them to social services or the local hospital to give to children who wouldn't normally receive gifts at Easter?

Films. Use films like *The Passion* to share the Easter story. You could put on a film night at your church, in your home or buy copies of the DVDs to give away.

Narnia. St Mary's Church in Luton used the popular CS Lewis story *The Lion, The Witch and the Wardrobe* to attract attention to their church. They put a wardrobe in their doorway so that people literally entered through it, and hung coats there to make it authentic. It attracted lots of people who were walking past to come and see what was going on! You could then theme your talk around elements of the story and/or show the clips where Aslan is slain/resurrected representing what happened to Jesus.

You've probably got lots of other ideas too! Why not share them with others on the HOPE website? www.hopetogether.org.uk

YOU'VE PROBABLY GOT LOTS OF OTHER IDEAS TOO! WHY NOT SHARE THEM WITH OTHERS ON THE HOPE WEBSITE?

Get the community outside of your church praying!

'Try Praying' is an initiative to invite people who don't currently pray, to start talking to God. There are leaflets you can hand out containing stories of answered prayer and ideas of how to start praying. You could also develop activities around this such as a clinic set up for an hour or afternoon a week where people can drop in with prayer requests. Find out more at www.thereishope.co.uk and www.trypraying.co.uk

Resources

J John Easter *Sonrise* booklets
A short booklet explaining the truth and significance of Easter. Available from www.philotrust.com/shop (bulk order discounts apply).

Bible Society is running a project called 'You've Got the Time' to help people engage with the Bible more deeply by listening to the New Testament over 40 days. To find out more call 01793 418222 or visit www.biblesociety.org.uk.

CPO offers lots of great resources you could use. Find out more at www.cpo-online.org.uk.

For loads more Easter ideas and resources see the HOPE For Easter resource available from the HOPE website www.hopetogether.org.uk.

Easter mission ideas for young people

The gospel according to YouTube

Gateway Church in Leeds looked at the four most popular YouTube videos and held a service talking through how these clips spoke of the gospel. They also included an Easter egg colouring competition, an Easter egg hunt, and provided Hot Cross Buns for everyone.

Collect for charity

A practical way to help a charity while also getting your young people thinking about physical and spiritual 'junk' in their lives.

What's the idea?

At the start of Lent ask your young people to go through their wardrobes and put anything they haven't worn or used for six months in a bag. At Easter ask them to bring in anything in this bag which they still haven't worn or used. Together, take all the contents of these bags to a local charity shop.

Encourage the young people to be really honest about how much they can afford to give away. Challenge them not to go too easy on themselves. On the other hand, try to make sure they're not being over-zealous and giving away a great deal, or expensive items, unnecessarily. It might be wise to let parents know what you're doing so they can help with this.

Egg giveaway

ONE Using chocolate to share the true message of Easter!

TWO

What's the idea?

Challenge your young people to give out a small Easter egg to each of their friends / classmates and use it to explain the importance of new life. Some youth groups lead assemblies in their schools explaining this, with the local church covering the cost of giving a chocolate egg to every student. This is a creative way of sharing the Easter story and challenging the young people to share their faith.

GREAT IDEA FOR THE LAST DAY OF THE SCHOOL TERM.

Consider

How will you get enough eggs? Perhaps contacting a confectionary company to discuss what you're doing could yield a cheap bulk order. It would definitely be worth getting your church's backing for this project and asking for their financial support.

Who will do the talking? Make sure your young people are confident explaining the message of new life behind Easter. If the project involves any public speaking, make sure those doing the talking are comfortable with this role.

24-7 prayer

This can really help to inspire your young people in their prayer lives, and to develop their heart for their community. It can also be surprisingly effective at drawing in your young people's friends or those on the fringes of the group.

A FEW TIMES OF GROUP PRAYER IN THE ROOM CAN ADD RENEWED ENERGY. TRY TO START AND FINISH THE SEASON OF PRAYER WITH CORPORATE PRAYER AND WORSHIP.

What's the idea?

Set aside a particular room for prayer in your church, community centre, or even school. Fill the room with materials to inspire people to pray and to enable them to pray creatively. It helps to cover the walls with paper (to draw on) and to use cushions and throws to make the room more comfortable. You could even put up curtains to form a 'Holy of Holies'.

Encourage your young people to sign up for hour-long slots, and in this way try to cover every hour of a week or weekend with prayer. Involve adults in the church too, and encourage the young people to bring their friends to pray.

Consider

Who will be involved? Your young people are likely to provide the impetus for this kind of season of prayer, but the more people you can get behind the idea, the better. So who else from your church, and from other churches in your area, can you get on board? And how can you encourage young people from your church to get their friends involved?

Logistics. There is work to be done in setting up the room, but also in arranging how people will sign up, how people will access the room, separate rooms to sleep in and the all-important tea and coffee facilities.

Corporate prayer. A few times of group prayer in the room can add renewed energy. Try to start and finish the season of prayer with corporate prayer and worship.

Child protection. Ensure that nobody under 18 is ever left in the building alone or with just one adult. Also provide two separate rooms which boys and girls can sleep in, if they need to.

Resources

For more inspiration, creative ideas and logistical tips, see www.24-7prayer.com.

For resources on running 24-7 prayer rooms in schools go to www.prayerspacesinschools.com/home/

One Voice

Join 24-7 Prayer, Tearfund and hundreds of churches and youth groups around the world for a week of prayer. For more information go to: www.tearfund.org/youth

Spring clean

What's the idea?

Get your young people together for a day cleaning up their town. Provide them with all the equipment they're likely to need, divide them into teams, and set about clearing up rubbish, cleaning graffiti, digging gardens, painting garages and whatever else your community needs.

This project will be much more effective if you spend some time beforehand working out what the real needs of your community are. For example, talk to your local council or residents' association. Then target two or three particular areas and give them a deep clean. Or you could pick a particular street, speak to residents and ask them what they would like your team to do.

If managed well, this project will make a lasting difference to your area and be a brilliant example of how the Church can serve communities. It can also inspire your young people to put their faith into action, and develop group dynamics.

Consider

Equipment. Make sure your group has all the tools they need for the tasks in hand. You may need to enlist the help of the wider church in providing tools or the funds to buy equipment.

Health and safety. Make sure anything you plan is properly risk-assessed. And again, child protection must be a consideration, so make sure you have enough adults helping to lead the project.

Although the young people won't be getting paid for their work, it is important to make sure that they do the best job possible, so leader monitoring on the day is essential.

Local Media. This is a great chance to show others that not all young people fit the media stereotype, so invite the local media along to see the amazing work that the young people are doing.

Arrange a premier for the film, invite the young people and their families plus local dignitaries and possibly a celebrity to give out prizes.

Why I Love... Film Project

Using film to capture moments and thoughts has become a common part of most young people's lives, so why not harness that to produce a piece of history about what your young people think about the place in which they live?

What's the idea?

Challenge young people to film a 2-3 minute video showing or explaining the things that they love about their area and community.

When the videos are collected, the best ones will be compiled together to make a film entitled '*Why I Love (insert town name)*'

Launch the project in schools and youth clubs from around the town, offering a prize and certificate for all the films included in the final film.

Create a website or YouTube channel where the videos can be uploaded and viewed by others.

Arrange a premier for the film, invite the young people and their families plus local dignitaries and possibly a celebrity to give out prizes.

Consider

Parental consent. You will need written consent for the young people to feature in the final film. You can achieve this with a simple form.

What your prizes will be. You will need to give them some incentive, but you may have a lot of people involved in the short film so cost could be an issue. You could get a local business to support the project to help cover costs.

Who will edit the final film. You will need someone with very good editing skills to make sure that the finished article is up to scratch. The young people will be expecting it to look professional.

Where you will have your premier. You need a location that you can make look nice but also project the film like a cinema. You need to think about who you would like to attend when considering the venue.

Media coverage. If you release some clips to local TV and radio you can give the project a wider audience.

How the film will be made available. You must decide how the final film will be viewed or purchased (either though a website or sale at the event). You could send copies to local schools and groups that were involved.

What Easter Means to Me

The Former Archbishop of Canterbury, Dr Rowan Williams

Good Friday brings us up sharp against the recognition that something is very wrong with the human heart. The cross on which Jesus dies reminds us of the countless places where human beings make other human beings suffer unspeakably - and of the fact that most of us most of the time don't notice, and, even when we do, can't do anything to stop it or make things safe. But Easter also reminds us that the whole weight of human failure cannot extinguish the creative love of God. Conflict and failure are part of the human condition, but Jesus' death and resurrection turns that on its head. We share one human story in which we are all caught up in a sad tangle of selfishness and fear and so on. But God has entered that human story; he has lived a life of divine and unconditional love in a human life of flesh and blood. If we can accept the unwelcome picture of us and our world that Good Friday offers, we are in the strangest way, set free to hear what Easter says. We can give up the struggle to be innocent and the hope that God will proclaim that we were right and everyone else was wrong. We can simply ask for whatever healing it is we need, whatever grace and hope we need to be free; then we can step towards our neighbour. Easter reveals a God who is ready to give you that grace and to walk with you.

God has entered that human story; he has lived a life of divine and unconditional love in a human life of flesh and blood

Agu Irukwu, Senior Pastor of Jesus House

Easter is a time when I feel incredibly weighed down by guilt yet weightless and free. It's a time when I reflect on the life of Christ and resolve to be more like him. My gratitude for the gift of his life stirs up a burning desire to emulate the life he led on earth. He gave us clear guidelines on how he expects us to live and if only for a period, I'm mindful of pleasing him, living like he did, mirroring his actions and words.

Easter helps me to appreciate the leadership of Christ. He was a leader of the people. He was no pen pusher; he got his hands dirty. He got involved in the lives of the people - he ate with them, drank with them, laughed with them and cried with them. He loved people deeply. He was no respecter of persons; he embraced everyone, from the greatest to the least. All were equal in his eyes. He was compassionate yet just. He provided for, healed and encouraged. He touched a man with leprosy and allowed a woman of the night to anoint his feet in public. He wasn't concerned with what the people thought about him, his primary concern was doing what was right. He was a man on a mission who did not relent 'til his mission was accomplished. He presented himself as he was and made no apologies for it. He wasn't a proud man, he was just a man who knew who he was and stood by what he believed in.

Easter makes me more mindful of Christ and his character; I can't escape thinking about what Jesus would do if he was living in these current times. He didn't twiddle his thumbs, he was a doer. He always got stuck in. As a 12 year old, his distraught parents who had been searching for him, found him in the temple listening to and questioning the teachers. He asked questions. He challenged the thought processes of the people. He stood up for those who were defenceless.

The death of Christ bought me freedom to be salt and light. His resurrection is a proof that he will return and I will have to account for how I have lived out his legacy. Impacting the world is not an option; it's a fundamental duty for me as a leader.

Bishop Wayne Malcolm, Founder of Christian Life City Church, London

As I reflect on the three days that changed the world I feel assured of the ultimate triumph of good over evil. As bloody and barbaric as the cross must have seemed to those who witnessed the crucifixion of Christ, the whole scene was really a triumph of love over hate. It serves as comprehensive proof that God's love is much stronger than our sins and that in the end his love will prevail. This fact should give each of us the assurance of God's total commitment to us in spite of our shortcomings and struggles.

It was also a triumph of God's plan over the schemes of men. King Herod, the Sanhedrin and the Romans all had a plan for Christ. They hoped that his crucifixion would put an end to his influence and that the rumours about him being the Messiah would be fully and finally squashed by a humiliating death. However, God's plan prevailed! Today Christ is adored by millions of people all over the world. He is worshipped as the Son of God and heralded as the saviour of the world. Quite clearly God's plan prevailed in spite of a conspiracy involving the most powerful minds in that day. This fact gives me hope that God's plan for me will prevail in spite of any plans to the contrary.

Easter is ultimately a triumph of life over death. Death is the king of terrors and is considered by many to represent the end of life. However Christ triumphed over death by rising from it on the third day. This was not a metaphoric resurrection, it was a real one; with an empty tomb and witnesses. His resurrection has taken away the sting of death by assuring us of a wonderful life hereafter.

EASTER IS ULTIMATELY A TRIUMPH OF LIFE OVER DEATH.

The three days that changed the world have given us all hope in the ultimate triumph of good over evil.

Rt Hon Stephen Timms MP

Easter is the answer to despair. We spend a lot of time worrying about problems and struggling to solve them but as we remember that Jesus rose from death, Easter puts our struggles in perspective. It's a crucial reminder that, one day, things which are obviously wrong today will be put right.

By highlighting that death is not the end, Easter confirms that we can afford to serve. Serving others may not appear to do us much good. There is a compelling argument for putting ourselves first instead. But Easter reminds us of the bigger picture: even death is not the end. Our long term future is secure, so we have the freedom to do what is right. If I didn't believe in the resurrection, I would have little alternative but to pursue my own, narrow personal interests.

People often say you shouldn't mix faith and politics. I don't agree. In fact, my view is the opposite – that faith is a great starting point for politics. Because faith is the source of the values that we need to make politics work – responsibility, solidarity, persistence, compassion, truthfulness. And it's the events of Easter which, above all, make those values real for Christians. Easter proves that it is worth doing the right thing, rather than the expedient thing or the selfish thing. It's the reason Christians changed the political climate in Britain 200 years ago to abolish the slave trade, or in the past ten years, in *Jubilee 2000* and *Make Poverty History,* to increase Britain's international aid. It's the reason Christians are working in every community in the land – for example, supporting young people, helping people trapped in debt, or enabling people without jobs to find them. Above all, working to tell the good news that, through the events of Easter, we can now all become friends with God.

Rt Hon Caroline Spelman MP

Easter is a special time for me as I was originally confirmed on Palm Sunday and the dynamic of Holy Week reminds me of that important decision I made in adult life to confirm the faith in which I was raised as a child. I always remember Good Friday being a day of reflection in the village in which I grew up. The parish church in which my Father was an usher was stripped of its ornaments and the mood of the 3pm service was sombre. When I went to work in France, I was astonished that Good Friday is a regular working day which demonstrates the power of secularism. It felt all wrong as it should be a day of remembering everything that Jesus did for us.

The contrast between Good Friday and Easter Day couldn't be stronger with the church transformed by the joy of celebrating Jesus' resurrection. The sombre mood is gone and instead churches are filled with spring flowers reminding us of life bursting forth from the grave. The whole dynamic is a microcosm of our individual journey from a certain death without faith to eternal life with it.

The contrast between Good Friday and Easter Day couldn't be stronger with the church transformed by the joy of celebrating Jesus' resurrection.

Go to our website www.hopetogether.org.uk to find small group studies written by Church Army to help people engage with the story of Easter in a fresh way and provide inspiration for mission. There are also free videos to download that tell the Easter story.

You'll also find material for four youth group sessions provided by Soul Action (a partnership between Soul Survivor and Tearfund) that introduce the themes of Easter and God's heart for mission.

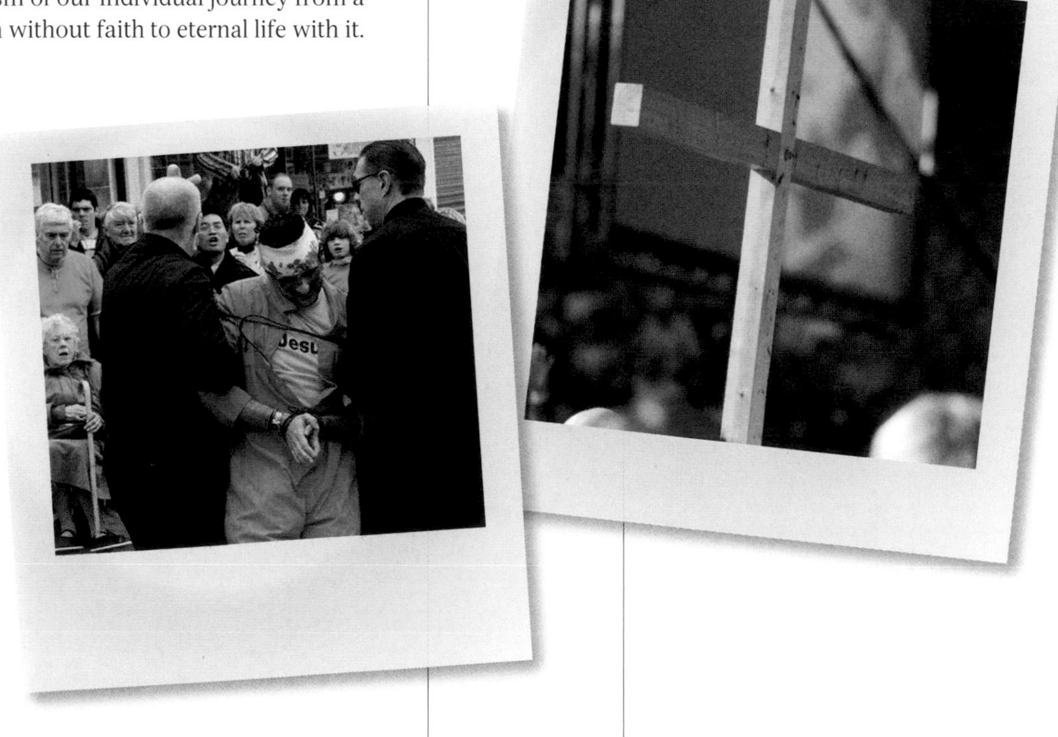

festivals & fun days

'Let's make the Pentecost weekend a time when we relevantly and kindly meet the needs of our local community, empowered by the Holy Spirit.'

Pentecost and Summer

Summer is the ideal time to get outside the walls of your church and to build strong links with your community.

HOPE on the Streets

Simon Nicholls

ONE When the Holy Spirit was poured out on the day of Pentecost, everything changed. Right there at the inception of the Church, in the first gathering of the followers of Jesus after his return to heaven, the Spirit came and empowered the disciples to go. Instead of staying hidden in their house in Jerusalem, or waiting for more power, the disciples were sent out. They left the building to tell people about Jesus and saw 3,000 added to their number that day alone; 3,000 people in one day!

That's one of the reasons we based our 'Noise' weekend around Pentecost – as a reminder that we are filled with the Holy Spirit to go and reach others in word and deed. The Bank Holiday weekend gives us a fantastic opportunity to get stuck in to some social action projects and meet some practical needs in our communities.

In 2012 thousands of churches joined the party as people of all ages celebrated the Queen's Diamond Jubilee. The Big Lunch (www.thebiglunch.com) continues to offer free resources about planning a street party for you to use on the first Sunday in June. The aim is to get as many people as possible across the whole of the UK to have lunch with their neighbours once a year in a simple act of community, friendship and fun.

COVERED IN PRAYER AND FUELLED BY WORSHIP, LET'S MAKE THE PENTECOST WEEKEND A TIME WHEN WE RELEVANTLY AND KINDLY MEET THE NEEDS OF OUR LOCAL COMMUNITY.

Covered in prayer and fuelled by worship, let's make the Pentecost weekend a time when we relevantly and kindly meet the needs of our local community, empowered by the Holy Spirit, that we might see thousands come to know Jesus.

Where to start

There are lots of questions that it's good to ask before you start planning:

Where in your community do you want to do your activity? Where is the greatest need?

- Defining the area in which you want to work will allow you to be specific about the needs.
- Dependent upon the size of your project, this might be more than one area, with entirely different demographics.

How long will you do it for?

- Is this going to be a full weekend or just a day? Will there be specific events on different days?
- Importantly, will this continue longer term?

Who are you trying to serve?

- Is there a specific demographic of people that you would like to reach? Young people or the elderly? This will dramatically change the projects you undertake!

Do you have local residents who know and understand the needs?

- All of this should be done in the context of relationship. Never just parachute something in and do it TO people. Build relationship, so that you are doing it WITH them.
- Are there local people who know what is going on in that area? Once relationships are established locally, you will be able to identify the actual needs rather than the perceived needs.

- What's already happening?
- Can you partner with or join projects that are already happening? Can you find complementary projects?

What resources do you have?

- Do you have access to gardening equipment or painting gear?
- Do you have equipment to fix bikes or cars?
- Do you have relationship with local police or businesses that could give or loan you equipment?

What are the strengths within your church?

- Is there something you are great at as a body of people? Are you good at cooking or fun days or something else? Play to these strengths.

Who is getting involved?

- Who is in your church? What skills do they have? Do you have trades people who can do specific quality work or people who could lead a team?
- Is this going to be a youth-led project or will it be the whole church?

Can you do this together?

- Would you be able to join together to do the Noise with other churches to make a bigger impact?
- Can you all do it at the same time, but in different areas? Can you come together at the end of each day and have a celebration or maybe eat together?

Can this go forward as a longer term project?

- Will this be just the weekend or can it be that ongoing relationships are formed with the community which allow you to keep going with projects long term?

Whatever you plan, make sure it is truly beneficial to the community and can be done well within the time frame you have. If you're going to set up a long-term project, use the Pentecost weekend as a chance to launch it and make a splash.

Simon Nicholls is Soul Action Project Manager at Tearfund

Whatever you plan, make sure it is truly beneficial to the community and can be done well within the time frame you have.

50 ideas to get you started!

1. Summer play schemes/holiday clubs/Saturday morning Kids Club
2. Playgroup for children, e.g. parent and toddlers' group, crèche
3. Training schemes for young people, life skills e.g. IT, CV writing
4. Repairing damage caused by vandalism
5. Free car wash
6. Clubs and groups for people with special needs
7. Arrange a community party/festival
8. Soup kitchen for homeless people
9. Open a community shop e.g. second hand children's clothes
10. Give a facelift to a derelict property or a paint job to a local school
11. Toy exchange
12. Pets corner/city farm for kids on estates
13. Food delivery or a foodbank
14. Activity week/sports week during summer holidays
15. Teach English
16. Offer pensioners' pedicures
17. Community audit for local churches
18. Sports activities e.g. running club, walking etc.
19. Crafts/painting activities
20. Run a dads and kids club
21. Hold a pre-school breakfast club
22. Litter collection
23. Decorating/painting
24. Senior citizens' banquet
25. Work with homeless people (with associated Christian agencies)
26. Produce a community newsletter
27. Community radio – in a local hospital

28. Hospital visits
29. Set up a recycling unit
30. Turn wasteland into a garden
31. Remove graffiti
32. Ironing service
33. Help elderly people in practical ways – gardening, repair and maintenance to the home, collecting groceries
34. Start a nearly new clothing depot
35. Visit residential care homes
36. Give practical help to lone parents
37. Offer a furniture collection and delivery service
38. Painting murals
39. Soft drinks bar/hangout for young people
40. BBQ
41. Bicycle hospital
42. Repair broken furniture
43. Constructing new play/leisure equipment
44. Laundry service
45. Outdoor barber shop
46. Shoe-cleaning service

Find out the prayer needs in your community by placing a prayer box in a prominent place (e.g. a Post Office, a pub or shop where the management is happy for you to do so), and provide slips of paper for people to leave their prayer requests. Local churches could then pick up the box each week and pray for the requests. Or you could drop leaflets to local shops and businesses and ask them to email you with their prayer requests.

IF YOU'RE GOING TO SET UP A LONG-TERM PROJECT, USE THE PENTECOST WEEKEND AS A CHANCE TO LAUNCH IT AND MAKE A SPLASH.

47. Free hedge cutting service
48. Health awareness campaign with a local doctor's surgery
49. Assist local residents in crime prevention measures
50. Fit smoke detectors in homes in conjunction with local fire brigade

Festival fun in Sheffield

ONE

Sheffield churches ran not just one, but 20 events over a week ranging from a bacon butty drop-in to a rock night for bikers and a fun fiesta for children.

In the months leading up to Whitfest the churches were mobilised in prayer, with at least four key prayer initiatives taking place. Then 40 people attended workshops on how to share their faith so that by the time of the festival, people had a confidence to share their story.

More than 100 people were mobilised from local churches to engage in mission activity and well over 1,000 people attended the different events. During the week, church members had the opportunity to pray with people from the area and young people joined pre-existing youth projects. Most importantly, people were reached with the gospel for the first time.

The festival also opened up new doors into the community and one of the highlights for the organisers was new relationships formed with local businesses. One church had been praying about how to have an impact in their local pub. At the end of the evening the pub owner approached one of the Christian bands for their details, to invite them back for further events.

The Noise in Bristol

The Noise in Bristol first started in 2001 when 30 people from a few local churches got together to see what they could do by working together and pooling their resources. The most recent Noise event saw 870 people from around 50 different churches/groups serving in eight different communities in North and East Bristol!

What does a Noise weekend look like?

For three days over the May Bank Holiday weekend, people from all over Bristol and beyond, get together to serve the urban estates of North and East Bristol in a lot of very different ways. The day starts with registration, a bit of admin, and being given a blue Noise t-shirt. Then there is time for sung worship, an opportunity to think about what we are about to do and why, and a time to pray together in teams before everyone is sent out to various different projects and locations.

Over the whole weekend there are Community Transformation Projects which involve anything from teams completely re-vamping the gardens of vulnerable adults/lone parent families, to massive rubbish clearance in public spaces, to painting murals and maintenance in local schools and community centres.

As well this, there are local Family Fun Afternoons that happen in each community The Noise works in, community BBQs, senior citizens' banquets, sports activities including football coaching and tournaments, and car washing. There are also teams of volunteers out praying on the streets over the whole weekend too.

What happens the rest of the year?

Although The Noise focuses on a high profile weekend of activities in May, we are keen to emphasise that this is not just a one-off event. We aim to encourage individuals, groups and churches to get involved doing this kind of thing all year round. For example we've built a link with a secondary school in North Bristol which has led to students working regularly on a Friday afternoon at a nearby community centre helping to clear ground and put in some allotments. These students have also regularly helped serve and wash up at a local senior citizens' event which has been a massive success and enjoyed by everyone involved.

It is always a real buzz to see so many people of all ages, and from very different church backgrounds, united by the same desire to get stuck in and serve the local community. It has been especially encouraging to see a big growth in the number of 11-18 year olds taking part in the last couple of years, and it is awesome to hear how The Noise weekend has inspired them to go on and run similar initiatives in their own schools and communities.

IT IS ALWAYS A REAL BUZZ TO SEE SO MANY PEOPLE OF ALL AGES, AND FROM VERY DIFFERENT CHURCH BACKGROUNDS, UNITED BY THE SAME DESIRE TO GET STUCK IN AND SERVE THE LOCAL COMMUNITY.

Local residents' comments:

'Thank you so much for the lovely dinner and entertainment at the senior citizens banquet. I enjoyed the whole afternoon very much. Thank you for giving everyone in the community such a great time on Saturday afternoon. God bless you all for showing God's love in practical ways working so hard here.'

'Thank you so much for doing my back garden. It gives me great pleasure when I look out of my patio doors, not looking at brambles and long grass. A great big thank you to all the volunteers - you were brilliant. Keep up the great work. You have helped a lot of grateful people who couldn't have done it themselves.'

Ignite Hope

Ignite Hope gathered 700 young people who undertook 10,500 hours of social action projects and acts of kindness throughout Cardiff, the Vale of Glamorgan, the South Wales Valleys and Caerphilly. Over the weekend, the good news was preached and 150 young people responded to the gospel for the first time.

Pentecost prayer

TWO Churches in North Devon got together at Pentecost to offer prayer to the entire town of Barnstaple as part of a month-long outreach. They printed postcards encouraging people to phone a 'prayer hotline' and visit their local church, prayed through the streets and set up a website.

Fun Days

ONE A free Fun Day puts the church right at the heart of the community and is a brilliant opportunity to work with other local churches to make a really big splash.

Hosting an event is easy! Pentecost Festival have pulled together a whole array of easy-to-use downloadable info sheets which give you a step-by-step guide to putting on an event. There are a number of different types of event so you can find what works for your community - some are very easy to replicate, whilst others will require more time and effort to pull them off well. The sheets have been given a difficulty rating, so that you know what you are getting into!

If you're interested in doing a whole week of festival of events then this requires lots more planning, but around 50 groups of churches across the UK have successfully pulled it off! Pentecost Festival have written a 'How to run a Community Festival' Guide that explains everything you need to do from how to liaise with civic authorities through to how to write a press release to publicise your event.

For £125, you can order the Party Host pack which includes banners, bunting, follow-up material and party bags! To order, or to download free information sheets, visit www.pentecostfestival.co.uk.

The festival also opened up new doors into the community and one of the highlights for the organisers was new relationships formed with local businesses.

'Open Crowd' Community Festivals

'It is a wonderful opportunity to see churches working together. It broke down barriers between us. Our town is buzzing that these crazy Christians are doing this for nothing!'

Open Crowd Festivals began 40 years ago in Australia by Fusion Youth and Community and have now spread to 27 countries across the world, with over 400,000 people across the UK attending one last summer. They provide a taste of 'the way life was meant to be' - a picture of heaven on earth giving people a place to belong and combating social isolation.

This style of festival is a fun community celebration that brings people together but behind the fun and games are ...

- A prayerful commitment of a core group in their local community and a larger group of volunteers who have caught something of the vision
- A trained team skilled in face-painting, balloon sculpting, circus activities, crafts, community building games, dance, activities and hospitality

Each event is provided free of charge, offering generous hospitality and activities that are aimed at helping people relax, engage, connect and become free to be who God has made them to be. It's not about entertainment but developing authentic community.

NB: After the festival make sure there is an invitation to attend something else that local churches are running so you can maintain the connection.

South London Festival

We first met Patricia when she turned up to a festival we organised for the local community during the opening night of the London 2012 Olympics. She had just wandered down with her mum and two young children. She was being temporarily housed at a council housing unit just around the corner from where we gather as a church community.

Several people from our church community made conversation with her and the girls.

It was a great joy to see her at our Sunday morning gatherings over the following weeks, initially a little cautiously standing at the back, but as she felt welcomed and became more confident she started trusting people with her children.

We found out she was being moved by the council to alternative accommodation and so we offered to help her move. On the morning of her move, more than 30 people from the church turned up at the housing unit ready to help. She only expected a few people to turn up and burst into tears when she realised how many were there just for her! The move created quite a stir amongst other residents as they watched the Church in action. In just over an hour her flat was emptied and cleaned and we were on our way to unload her belongings into her new place.

Since then she has been coming to our Sunday gatherings regularly and more recently has been inviting some of her friends to come, all of whom are completely un-churched. The comments they have made over the weeks they have been joining in have been familiar and very encouraging:

'Thank you so much for helping me today. You are my family now. Thank you for giving me hope again. My kids will be privileged to grow up and be part of this church.'

The Pastor says, 'It is as if the "woman at the well" has turned up to our church with her friends coming along to find out more.' Her Social Worker, a Muslim lady, couldn't believe what the church community had done for Patricia.

The festival we ran with Fusion marked a break-through into being a part of our community. We had some youth clubs already running but the festival gave us a vision for more. It wasn't just for more groups (we now have lots more) but also for the church to be right at the heart of the community. God has amazed us in the doors he has opened.

Richard Colbrook, Oxford Community Church

THANK YOU SO MUCH FOR HELPING ME TODAY. YOU ARE MY FAMILY NOW. THANK YOU FOR GIVING ME HOPE AGAIN. MY KIDS WILL BE PRIVILEGED TO GROW UP AND BE PART OF THIS CHURCH.

Grants available
see www.cinnamonnetwork.co.uk for details

To ensure your festival is inclusive and accessible to disabled people see www.throughtheroof.org/inclusive-festival-guide

Find out more, view inspirational and training videos, obtain all the materials and job descriptions you need to run a festival and find out about training opportunities on the Fusion Youth and Community website www.opencrowdfestival.com.

Prayer

Why not have a prayer tent set up as part of your fun day? People could come in for a chat and to be prayed for, there could be a reflective space if they'd like to pray quietly alone, and an opportunity for some to write down their requests and leave them in a box if they prefer.

Lunch

'Before I came to Lunch I was isolated and lonely. Now I feel like I have found family and it has also made a big difference to my money.' Single mum of three

In 2011 it was estimated that 3.5 million children were living in poverty in the UK, with one in five sometimes going without food. School-aged children from struggling families are offered free school meals during term time, but during the holidays there is no provision. Lunch wants to see the 1.2 million children who receive free school meals fed during school holidays by local people. It works by encouraging churches and community groups to partner with local schools to set up Lunch during school holidays, providing safe, accessible places for these children to come to receive a healthy meal.

Benefits

As well as ensuring children are being fed well during the school holidays, and taking some financial pressure off hard-pressed parents, Lunch also offer something to do during the long days of school holidays, and a safe place to meet with other children and people from the community. Most Lunch projects ask parents to stay with their children, some offering meals for the adults too as long as supplies allow.

Many Lunch projects invite parents to get involved preparing and serving the food, or running activities for the children. One mum helping in the kitchen commented that she'd learnt some great recipes and was looking forward to being able to cook for her daughter at home.

Lunch is a great opportunity for churches to build strong connections with the schools and communities in their immediate neighbourhood.

Challenges

You may find the demand is high (in one area a school of 600 had a list of 300 pupils receiving free lunches) so you might need to start small. Better to support a few families rather than letting large numbers scare you off doing anything at all!

Local supermarkets are often keen to give once they hear about the project.

There can be a stigma attached to being a "Free School Meals kid" so try to find ways of offering lunch to those who need it without singling people out – i.e. either by offering meals to anyone who comes, or by creating an exclusive invite-only club without publicising your selection criteria.

Money can be a challenge but Lunch are keen to help with that wherever they can, either by helping find grants and funding sources, or by contacting local businesses to ask for donations of food or money. Local supermarkets are often keen to give once they hear about the project and one even sent a couple of staff members to help serve the food. Some churches have asked members to 'sponsor' lunches (£5 feeds one child for a week).

How easy is it to replicate this idea?

This is a really easy idea to replicate! You can download a 'How To' pack at www.makelunch.org.uk which takes you through all the necessary steps to get started, including making contact with the school, risk assessments, menu planning and building a volunteer team. Training is also available if required.

Contact details

www.makelunch.org.uk
E: hello@makelunch.org.uk
T: 07793 433013

Emma's story

Emma is a single mum with a daughter Anna, 13, and a son Jamie, seven. Since her marriage broke down, Emma has been struggling to support herself and the children on benefits, having barely enough to cover the mortgage and bills. She supplements her benefits with a few hours of childcare work with a local child minder. Emma told us, 'Even with careful budgeting and keeping an eye on spending, money is tight. We really appreciate the Free School Meals during term time but the holidays are a struggle.' Having a good meal at Lunch every day meant that the usual additional financial pressures of the summer holidays were reduced. The family also found that to going to Lunch together gave them gave them something to do during the day and the children enjoyed playing with other children after they'd eaten. Emma and Anna plan to get involved in the kitchens next year.

Jen's story

Jen and her partner moved to a new town just before the start of the summer holidays. Their daughter, Ellie, is due to start nursery in September. They stumbled across the Lunch café that had opened on the high street near their new home and attended almost every day while it was open. As well as getting a good meal each day, the family appreciated the opportunity to eat together and to meet others from the community. After one particularly quiet day, Jen said 'Please keep doing this, even if nobody comes sometimes. It's important.'

EVEN WITH CAREFUL BUDGETING AND KEEPING AN EYE ON SPENDING, MONEY IS TIGHT. WE REALLY APPRECIATE THE FREE SCHOOL MEALS DURING TERM TIME BUT THE HOLIDAYS ARE A STRUGGLE.

Weddings and christenings

Many people make their first contact with their local church when they are looking to get married or have a child christened. This is a fantastic opportunity for us to provide a warm welcome and demonstrate something of Christian love and acceptance to the couple or family, and to their guests. As these inspiring stories show, weddings and christenings can bring people into the church family. Let's make the most of every opportunity that weddings and christenings provide, going the extra mile to make couples and families feel welcome and supported.

Congregation's kindness won our hearts

'I felt different from the moment I walked out of church,' said Pauline who married Richard at St Andrew's Church, Glaston, Rutland, in August 2007. She had always intended to have a church wedding, believing it to be the 'proper' place to marry; the solemnity of the service had been important to her.

Following several meetings with the vicar, the Revd Jane Baxter, a date was arranged for Richard and Pauline's wedding. The vicar recommended the couple got to know the congregation before the wedding and so they attended services leading up to the wedding date. 'I couldn't believe how kind and welcoming everybody was,' said Pauline, 'and as the wedding drew near, villagers came to clean the church, someone volunteered to cut the grass and polish the brass. The Churchwarden even arranged a barbeque for all those who were helping to spruce up the church!

'With everyone joining in to help us, we began to feel part of their community. Despite the hour's drive from our home to the church, we still want to continue to see them and be involved in the church and community; it's such a special place. Everyone has been fantastic.'

The Revd Jane Baxter said: 'Richard and Pauline had such a special day - they and their family put so much into the occasion. They made considerable efforts to travel here and to become part of the community. People in our church were only too pleased to welcome them and help them out for their wedding.'

A christening that led to a wedding too

Mel and Richard Tilling thought getting married would be too expensive for them. But they did want to christen their son Joseph, who has a life limiting genetic disorder.

Mel described how their plans to christen Joseph snowballed; 'a small thing got bigger' and they decided that since they were going to get their whole family together for the christening they would get married too.

'The Revd Felicity Walters made it possible,' said Mel, 'as well as Richard's granny, Margaret, who paid for the church ceremony and made it to the church despite breaking her pelvis three weeks before the wedding.'

The couple got married at St John the Baptist Church in Huntley, Gloucestershire, with their family and friends surrounding them. Joseph was christened and Mel's daughter Erin, who was a bridesmaid, was blessed with the whole family at the end of the service.

Friends and family also helped to make the wedding possible; friends from work decorated the pub where the reception was held, an auntie made the wedding invitations and Mel arrived at church in her dad's car.

Joseph, whose illness doesn't allow him to walk or sit up on his own, gave Felicity a big grin as he was christened. 'We are lucky to have him and make memories where sometimes others, who lose a child, can't,' said Mel.

Felicity said, 'I had first met Richard and Mel shortly after Joseph was born, before anyone knew that there was anything wrong. Over the months I'd prayed with Margaret as the news got worse, and it was an incredible privilege to baptise Joseph at the same time as marrying Richard and Mel....the highlight of my year.'

We fell in love with our 'football club church'

As an Aston Villa fan, Colin Howells had always noticed St Peter and St Paul in Aston, Birmingham, which was opposite the football ground, but he hadn't thought about marrying there because he didn't really go to church. But one day as he drove past the church with fiancée, Flo, he said to her, 'It would be nice to get married there.' They decided to stop by and found the Revd Andy Jolley in his church office. The couple said Andy made them feel so welcome, they decided to go to the church service to see what they were like. They received a warm reception at the church. 'Everyone opened their arms and welcomed us,' says Colin.

> We were so glad that Colin and Flo chose us for their wedding service and that they have become such a vital part of the church family.

Sadly Colin developed cancer shortly after deciding to get married, but he and Flo were able to carry on going to church and became more and more involved in church life. On their wedding day, when their vows were exchanged, the promise to stay together 'in sickness and in health' was particularly poignant. Colin had already undergone chemotherapy before getting married and surgery was imminent after the honeymoon. Thankfully Colin has been in remission for some time now and the couple have carried on going to church long after their wedding day.

The Revd Andy Jolley said, 'We were so glad that Colin and Flo chose us for their wedding service and that they have become such a vital part of the church family, as honorary treasurer and leading an Alpha course which helps people find out more about the Christian faith. They have helped to welcome many other new people to the church.'

For more inspiring stories and to find out what support is available to churches in your diocese, please see www.yourchurchwedding.org.

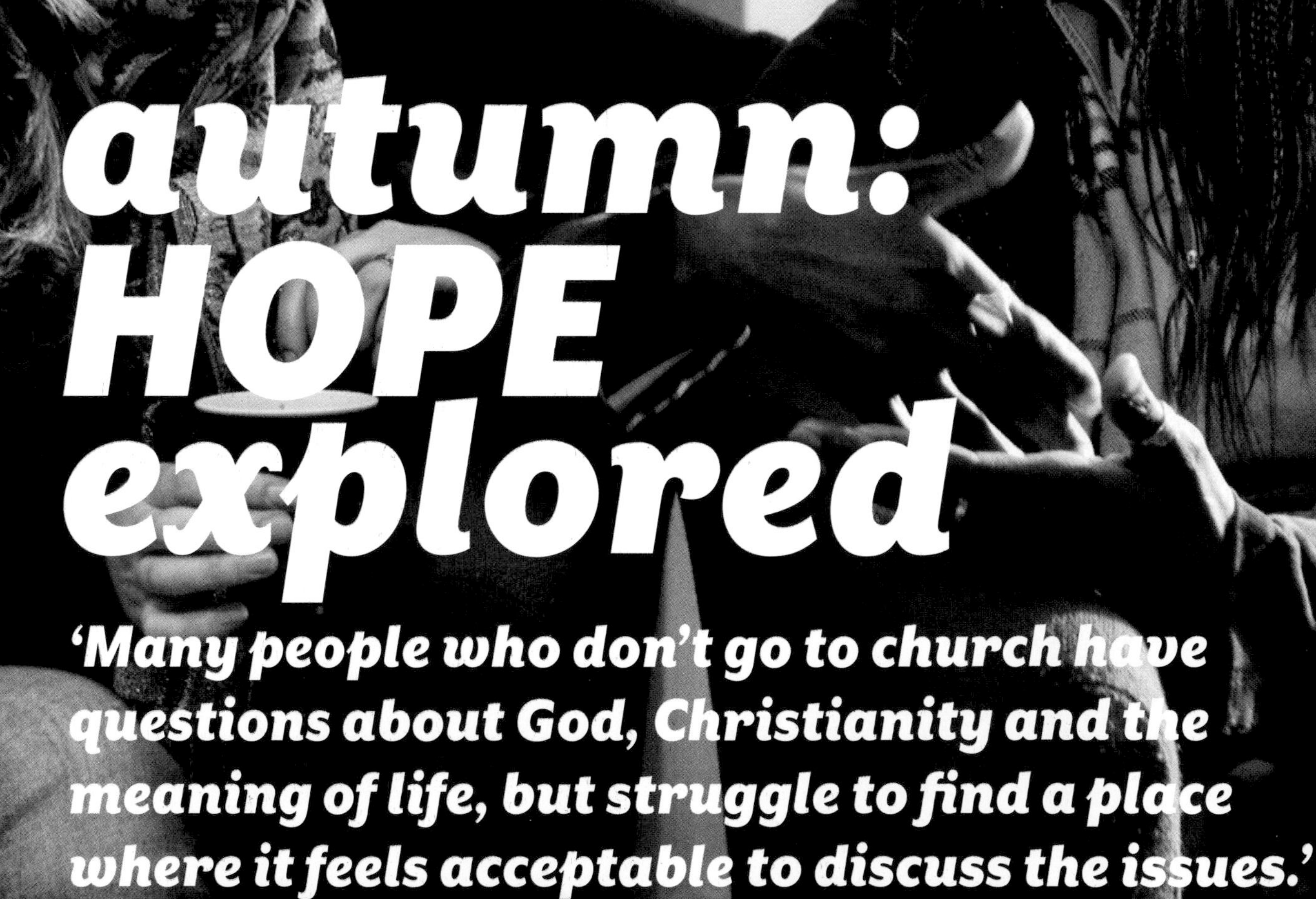

autumn: HOPE explored

‘Many people who don’t go to church have questions about God, Christianity and the meaning of life, but struggle to find a place where it feels acceptable to discuss the issues.’

Autumn

Many people who don't go to church have questions about God, Christianity and the meaning of life, but struggle to find a place where it feels acceptable to discuss the issues. We have nothing to fear in inviting people's questions; our faith stands up to examination and debate! Over recent years courses like Alpha and Christianity Explored have become extremely popular, with millions [3] taking the opportunity to find out more about the Christian faith in a relaxed and friendly atmosphere. These courses provide a way to present key elements of the gospel, whilst allowing opportunity for people to respond and discuss their own views.

Courses work well at any time of year but the new school year, starting in September, works particular well within the church calendar. It also means you have something to invite people to that you meet during your summer outreach programmes.

'What Alpha offers... is permission, rare in secular culture, to discuss the big questions.

Alpha Course

THREE The key elements that bring success to courses such as Alpha seem to be:

- Providing a relaxed and informal atmosphere, usually aided by refreshments or a meal.
- An encouragement for conversation where there is no pressure to have to agree, but a genuine opportunity to engage in an exploration of the Christian faith.
- The conversations are open to all, whether they have faith or not.
- The Christian faith is presented in a clear, accessible and relevant way.

Courses can be run in churches, bars, coffee shops and homes, and typically include food, a short talk about the Christian faith and an opportunity for everyone to share their thoughts. There's no pressure, follow up or charge.

Over 7,000 Alpha courses are currently running in churches in the UK and it is designed so that anyone – whether a church leader or someone brand new to church – can run it. The talks can be given by a live speaker (there are talk notes and transcripts) or watched on DVD or online at alpha.org. There are also guest manuals, team training materials, posters and invitations – all the kit you need to run a successful course.

The Guardian wrote about Alpha: 'What Alpha offers, and what is attracting thousands of people, is permission, rare in secular culture, to discuss the big questions – life and death and their meaning.'

[3] Alpha has reached 20 million people since its inception, with 66,000 courses in 169 countries and in 112 languages.

Alpha is a ten-week course including a weekend. Some of the topics covered are:

Is there more to life than this?

Who is Jesus?

Why did Jesus die?

How can we have faith?

Why and how do I pray?

Why and how should I read the Bible?

How does God guide us?

Who is the Holy Spirit?

What does the Holy Spirit do?

How can I be filled with the Holy Spirit?

How can I resist evil?

Why and how should I tell others?

Does God heal today?

What about the church?

How can I make the most of the rest of my life?

Sam's story (age 23)

I would say I was a militant atheist; I really associated with those people and would have debates on Facebook about it. My first day on Alpha I was really gunning for Christians. Something happened though, over those ten weeks; something amazing really. I discovered that my understanding of the mechanics of evolution and natural selection does not eradicate the need for an agent, and now I study the universe, but I study it within the realm of God and to me, I'm free; I'm free from my previous life.

I was a slave to a lot of things: I was a slave to society, I was a slave to my peers, but now I'm free to live my life, and I'm just excited to see what God's got in store for me.

I WAS A SLAVE TO A LOT OF THINGS: I WAS A SLAVE TO SOCIETY, I WAS A SLAVE TO MY PEERS, BUT NOW I'M FREE TO LIVE MY LIFE.

Darrell Tunningley's story (age 33)

I was using drugs from the age of 11. By the age of 16 I was selling drugs and dealing for some hard hitters. We were debt-collecting, giving punishments and some pretty nasty stuff. We hit a wages depot and came away with £40,000, but I was caught and sentenced to five and a half years. While in prison I carried on the same way I behaved outside – getting into fights. I assaulted prison officers and spent a lot of time on the segregation block where you are in your cell 24 hours a day, seven days a week.

I was invited to Alpha by another prisoner who said we'd get a free afternoon, coffee and biscuits. We gave the two nuns that ran it a lot of grief, but they never got angry, they only ever showed love and compassion. It came to a point where I realised they deserved a little bit more respect. They were saying that the whole point was about a clean slate. It was smashing up your old slate completely and getting a new one, a complete fresh start, being forgiven. They said, 'God loves you exactly as you are, but he loves you too much to leave you that way. He wants to take the best of who you are and get rid of the worst of who you are.'

It just made sense to me. Something clicked. That night in my cell I thumbed through the Alpha leaflets and came across 'The Sinner's Prayer'. It didn't really make sense to me at all. Then I picked up the Bible they had given me and it opened at Job. It was a modern translation, so I started having a read and I kept on reading and reading. This story gripped me and it made me ask a question: this guy lost absolutely everything, but it would not shake his faith in God. I thought, 'What made God so real to him that he would not move no matter what? I sat there on my bed and I picked up the pamphlet again and I looked at 'The Sinner's Prayer' again and it still didn't make sense to me. So I sat there and said my own version. The gist of it was: 'God if you're real, prove it. I've tried to stop with the drugs; I've tried to stop with the violence. Nothing I do works. If you're real, prove it. Take away my drug addiction. Take away all this anger that's inside me and if you do that for me, I'll live the rest of my life for you.' And that was it. There were no bright lights, there was no shaking cell door, no visitations from angels... I just went to bed. But when I woke up the next morning, a series of weird events started to happen.

I felt physically sick at the thought of smoking my cigarettes or weed. I threw it all out of the window, and as soon as I'd done it, I stopped feeling sick. I went to get a wash and I almost couldn't recognise the reflection in the mirror because I was beaming. It was as if someone had washed away every bit of anger and guilt and frustration. I haven't touched drugs, smoked, drunk, or had a fight since. On my release I started working for Hope Corner Church in Runcorn. I've now been married to the pastor's daughter for six years and have a little boy and a baby girl. I'm an Assemblies of God minister and I have written my biography called Unreachable *(Sovereign World). Before Alpha, Jesus was an irrelevant historical figure who did and said a lot of good stuff, and now he's my everything. He's my lifeline, he's my strength, I couldn't live without him and everything I do is through him and for him. My life wouldn't be the way it is if he wasn't exactly who he said he was. He is alive.*

He's my lifeline, he's my strength, I couldn't live without him and everything I do is through him and for him.

Tips

- Join with other local churches to hold your courses or to advertise them together.
- Try a new venue – sometimes people feel more comfortable in a café than a church.
- Encourage your church members to run an Alpha-style course in their workplace.
- Consider making a big splash for your first week of each new course with a guest speaker and a special meal or venue.

Other courses available

The Y Course

This eight-week evangelism course helps people face life's biggest questions and introduces them to Jesus.

- Guests need no knowledge of the Bible or Christian language.
- It includes issues like 'Why does God allow suffering?' and 'What about other religions?
- It talks today's language, uses stories that relate, and doesn't rush people to a decision.

The resources for The Y Course include –

- 16 chat-show style DVD segments (six minutes each) featuring Peter Meadows and Joseph Steinberg with Gemma Hunt
- A guide for course leaders
- A guide for small group leaders and over 100 questions to stimulate discussion
- *The Book of Y* – the core content for the course

Full details at www.ycourse.com or call 01903 241975 for a free sample DVD and product brochure.

Christianity Explored

Christianity Explored is an informal seven-week course for people who'd like to investigate Christianity, or just brush up on the basics. It can be held in a church, a pub, a prison, a curry house, a coffee shop, or even in your own home. Each evening usually starts with food or drinks, then participants take a look at Mark's Gospel to consider who Jesus is, why he came and what it means to follow him. Then there's an opportunity to ask any questions. A short talk is given by a speaker or by using the Christianity Explored DVD, then there is a chance to discuss what has been heard.

The course is primarily for anyone who wants to investigate Christianity informally with a group of other people.

Christianity Explored offer all the resources you need to run a course including a handbook, a leader's guide, and a DVD, plus additional resources for those who would like to explore the questions raised further.

If you are interested in running a course, visit the Christianity Explored Ministries website www.christianityexplored.org for more information about the course materials and other resources.

Jo's story

I grew up on a council estate in South East Essex. We were a single parent family as my dad was an alcoholic and died when we were young. It was a difficult environment and I think my mum was worried we'd be taken into care.

I got into tai chi and yoga and then into things like Buddhism and all different kinds of prayer–really New Age things. I was just taking all the nice bits of all the different kinds of religions. I went to an interfaith seminary where you learn about the five major religions. You try and put them all together and see if we can all live nicely together. While I was there I made a friend who had breast cancer and was dying. As we began to speak about her funeral, we realised we just couldn't make all these different religions hang together.

While I was looking at all of the New Age things, my brother was a Christian, and he went to a church in London. I would go with him and he would listen to all the things I had to say about my New Age things. He was really patient with me and he would just say: 'I think there's more.' I began to realise that he knew Jesus as a real person, and he had something that I didn't.

WHEN I WAS ON THE CHRISTIANITY EXPLORED COURSE I REALISED THAT JESUS WAS A REAL PERSON, AND HE COULD SEE ME AND HE COULD KNOW ME.

So I went to a course in London called Christianity Explored, where you can talk about that, and start to ask questions. And it was great. When I got there, the people were normal and we had some fun together. Then I started reading the Bible and I realised that whilst I had an opinion about it, I'd never actually read it. It was great then to be able to take all my questions and start firing them at the people who were there as leaders, so I could work out what I believed.

I'd spent all of my life really worrying about appearances, and trying to cover up the difficult things from my past. When I was on the Christianity Explored course I realised that Jesus was a real person, and he could see me and he could know me. He knew everything and he loved me. It was such a relief. I knew that I had to choose to accept what Jesus was saying about him being the way and the truth, and just give my life to him: to follow him and read the Bible and learn more about what he wanted for me in my life. I couldn't ignore it anymore.

So that means that I can really live my life openly. I'm not defensive all the time; I'm not so worried about 'Do people like me or do they not like me?' I can just accept that some people will, some people won't. I'm able to be more genuinely who I am, even though I know some of that is not very good. And I know that I'm still loved.

harvest

‘Harvest is a fantastic time to be thankful to God for all the good things he brings to us through our work and to look at all the opportunities our workplaces bring as mission fields.’

Mission Ideas

In many rural churches harvest is a well-celebrated season, but for those in towns and cities we've lost some of the emphasis on this season as an opportunity to thank God for the ways he provides for us. Harvest is a fantastic time to be thankful to God for all the good things he brings to us through our work and to look at all the opportunities our workplaces bring as mission fields. It also gives us a chance to reflect on God's generosity to us and to try to express that same generosity to others, as well as being good stewards of what has been entrusted to us.

HARVEST IS A FANTASTIC TIME TO BE THANKFUL TO GOD FOR ALL THE GOOD THINGS HE BRINGS TO US THROUGH OUR WORK.

Harvest Festival Services

TWO Many churches hold a Harvest Festival, providing an opportunity to thank God for all that he has provided. This is a great chance to involve the wider community in your church service, perhaps by inviting local businesses or how about holding your celebration outside of the church walls so it's easily accessible for all? You could:

- Hold an outdoor Harvest Festival at your local allotments and invite local schools to come along.
- Hold a celebration at a local supermarket.
- Build a bread oven as a church community project and invite local residents along for a bread - or pizza-making afternoon before or after the Harvest Sunday service.
- Consider calling it a Thanksgiving Service in order to make it more accessible to members of urban communities.

How about using your Harvest Festival service as a chance to get people thinking about a lasting harvest? Ask people to consider what the harvest from their life will be, and to bring a symbol of this to the Harvest service.

Idea for small groups

ONE Hold a meal at your house, inviting friends from outside church, and giving everyone an opportunity to say what they are thankful for.

Prayer idea for Harvest Festival

Encourage everyone to bring a picture of either someone or something for which they want to give God thanks, or to bring a short prayer of thanks. Invite them during the service to come up and put their pictures or prayers on a prepared wall or boards, then spend time in thanksgiving and prayer, using scriptures and songs.

Food collections

For many, harvest is traditionally associated with ONE collecting non-perishable food items and donating them to people in need in the community.

Make the most of your food collection by:

- Speaking to local charities to ensure your collection goes to those in need. You might want to support projects working with people who are homeless or living in women's refuge centres. Speak to the local council who will know about families that might be in need of a care package.

- Find out what your chosen charity would find most useful to receive and give suggested shopping lists to your congregation a few weeks ahead of Harvest.
- Encourage your congregation to change their thinking from 'buy one get one free' to 'keep one give one away' in the run up to Harvest.

Alternatives

- Instead of bringing food you could ask people to donate the money they would have spent to support a project either close to home or overseas. Make sure people are clear about where the money is going and how much of a difference it will make to the lives of those in need.
- Ask your congregation to donate pieces of fresh fruit, make them into small gift baskets, then give these out on the local streets as an act of kindness.
- Donate your time to local projects instead of giving money or food.

Grants available see www.cinnamonnetwork.co.uk for details

The Trussell Trust Foodbank Network

When 13-year-old Sophie's dad died, the cost of funeral expenses tipped the family over the edge and they were forced to turn to the foodbank: 'It was such a massive help and the people there were really kind,' said Sophie. She added that the food parcel helped them to get back on their feet and that without it 'it would have been impossible to cope'.

'It's very hard to look at your baby and not be able to feed him, but with your help today I was able to, so thank you very much.'
Young working couple struggling on low income

Barbara's husband Steve took pleasure in being the breadwinner for the family until the bones in his neck began to crumble. He was left unable to work and forced to live on statutory sick pay. A family crisis meant finances went from bad to worse leaving the couple with no money for food. Barbara said, 'We were going to bed hungry every night. If it wasn't for the foodbank Steve and I would be in a box.'

Vision

The Trussell Trust's UK Foodbank Network provides emergency food to people in crisis through local, church-led foodbanks. Their vision is to launch a foodbank in every UK town, creating a nation where no-one goes hungry.

What does a foodbank do?

Foodbanks provide three days worth of non-perishable emergency food to support people who are in crisis and cannot afford food. Foodbank clients are usually low income families hit by an unexpected crisis. They are people who have been made redundant; victims of domestic violence; people experiencing benefit delay or those hit by illness. Many face decisions between eating and paying the rent. Others are so desperate that they consider stealing to feed their children. The Trussell Trust partners with churches across the UK to open foodbanks to help stop men, women and children from going hungry. Each foodbank engages the whole community in donating food, funds and time, as well as partnering with care professionals to identify people in need.

Benefits

The Trussell Trust Foodbank Network gave emergency food to over 128,000 people in crisis in the UK in the 2011-12 financial year. In the six months from April to October 2012 around 110,000 people received foodbanks' emergency food Foodbanks are a lifeline for many. One father of two was considering suicide before coming to his local foodbank and he said 'the foodbank saved my life'. Every week people say that the kindness received at the foodbank gave them 'hope' and 'a reason to go on'.

Foodbanks also help to resolve the underlying cause of the problem by signposting people to additional services. Responses from care professionals and beneficiaries confirm that the foodbanks' interventions at times of dire need prevent the escalation of short term crisis into crime, housing loss, family breakdown and mental health problems.

For those working at foodbanks

Coventry foodbank Manager Gavin Kibble gave up a six figure salary to start a foodbank but he says he wouldn't change it because of the 'wow' factor. He says: 'If you want to see God at his most powerful start a foodbank, it is an absolute eye opener.'

START SMALL AND EXPAND THE PROJECT AS YOU GO AND IT'S A GREAT IDEA TO PARTNER WITH OTHER LOCAL CHURCHES SO YOU CAN POOL YOUR RESOURCES.

Volunteering at foodbanks also has proven benefits: 96% of volunteers at Welsh foodbanks said that volunteering increased their sense of wellbeing and helped them to make friends, whilst 92% said it helped them to understand people's needs and 73% said their self-esteem increased.

Foodbanks help communities to understand local poverty better and to work together across social divides to become part of the solution. Thousands of churches, schools, care professionals and volunteers help at foodbanks every year. One 13 year old boy said 'It's shocking that people go hungry in Salisbury but it's nice to feel part of helping a family to get food.'

Challenges

With 13 million people living below the poverty line in the UK and over one million children living in households where there is not enough food, there is a great need to be met. To give UK-wide access to emergency food, there is a need for over 1,000 foodbanks nationwide. The challenge is to start enough foodbanks to meet the growing need.

How easy is it to replicate this idea?

The Trussell Trust has developed a tried and tested foodbank model that is very easy to replicate in any community, though it does require time, effort and resources. It has been designed so that you can start small and expand the project as you go and it's a great idea to partner with other local churches so you can pool your resources. The Trussell Trust will provide you with a complete toolkit for running a local foodbank project for £1,500. This includes: a business model, business plan, operating procedures, health and safety procedures, on-site training, website design, website hosting, design work for promotional material, access to a network of more than 270 other foodbanks for support, fundraising and publicity advice, as well as general guidance and advice.

Tips

- Building relationships with the whole community is vital to the success of the foodbank.
- All food given out is donated by schools, churches, businesses and individuals and every client coming to the foodbank must be referred by a frontline care professional such as a doctor, social worker or schools liaison officer.

Contact details

Contact The Trussell Trust's foodbank network office on 01722 580171 or foodbanknetwork@trusselltrust.org and get an information pack. They will also put you in touch with a Foodbank Development Officer for your region who will work closely with you as you seek to set up a foodbank.

www.trusselltrust.org
E: enquiries@trusselltrust.org
T: 01722 580171

One delighted family

During the coldest week of winter, Anne-Marie and Danny, 22, were forced to choose between eating and heating after a delay in benefits hit at the same time as Danny was off work with flu. He received no sick pay and finances got so tight that they were faced with eviction as well as having no money for food. The couple and their 18-month-old daughter, Tia, were living and sleeping in one room to reduce heating bills. They resorted to borrowing a tin of soup from their neighbours to stop little Tia going hungry. When the foodbank delivered an emergency foodbox to the delighted family there was ice on the inside of their windows. Danny said: 'I don't know what we would have done without the foodbank.'

Turn some local wasteland into a garden which not only looks good but where food can be grown to give to local people in need. You could run simple teaching sessions alongside this on how to grow your own vegetables.

Harvest Suppers

ONE

Harvest is a brilliant time to bring your community together for a celebration. There are countless different ways you could make your Harvest Supper special as you welcome in members of the community; here are some things to consider:

Food

- You could grow the food yourselves, suggesting a menu and things for your congregation to plant ahead of the event.
- Why not eat a typical meal from the developing world but charge the typical price of a Western meal and donate the money to charity?
- Hold a 'bring and share' meal so the responsibility is split between everyone who comes.
- You could have a multi-cultural food tasting festival, inviting people to bring unusual or exotic dishes reflecting their cultural roots.

Costs

You may want to make the meal totally free as a blessing to your community or you could ask for donations and then split them between charities (e.g. a local Christian charity, a local project run outside of the church and an overseas project).

Venue

You could use your church, hire the village hall or make it an intimate event in your home and invite your neighbours. If the weather is warm and dry, you could have a picnic or a party in the local park.

Entertainment

- Play games or run a quiz.
- Have a live band.
- Hold a ceilidh or barn dance.

As an alternative you may want to hold a café-style event with coffee, cakes, quizzes and games.

Community survey of thankfulness

Go door-to-door in your neighbourhood and ask residents what they are thankful for and what they most need.

- Use the data to inform future outreach projects.
- Use the opportunity to invite the people you speak to along to church.
- Use the data as part of your Harvest service, giving an overview of what people in the area are thankful for and praying for their needs.
- Ask people if they have any prayer requests that you can intercede for during Harvest. You may want to leave them a postcard to fill in and drop back to you.
- Or how about visiting local shops, businesses and schools in your community and asking individuals what they are thankful for about your area? Take photos of them and then create a display in your church of the photos and sound bites as a way of celebrating the harvest of the local area. You could also leave the people you speak to with an invitation to come to see the display and attend a Harvest service.

Random acts of kindness

Why not take the opportunity to bless your friends, family and neighbours with an act of kindness?

- Leaf raking for neighbours.
- A week before the clocks change, drop cards round to local houses reminding them to change their clocks. You could also attach a small gift or offer to pray for them and their needs in the extra hour.
- Make cookies and cakes and hand them out in a public space. Also give out a bookmark giving thanks to God for all he gives us at Harvest time and details of church services/Alpha courses running in the town.
- As a church take a market stall and donate money raised from produce sold to a local charity.

Ask people if they have any prayer requests that you can intercede for during Harvest.

- Publish a free mini-magazine and distribute locally with good-quality goods that members of the congregation are willing to give away for free.
- Open up your church for an afternoon so people can come and see the harvest flower displays and share a cream tea.
- Offer to wash people's cars free of charge.

Prayer and food!

Each day we eat foods from all around the world. Why not take up the challenge to count how many different foods from different places you eat in a day? Perhaps as a small group you could share your findings and pray for the places the food came from. Give thanks to God for all the people represented in the chain bringing that food to your plate. You could share the idea with colleagues and friends, or do the project with children.

You could hold a special night of prayer for areas around the world experiencing drought and for UK farmers whose crops have been ruined by floods. Find out more about where food is produced in the UK using www.goodfoodnetwork.com. You could use a map to trace where all your food comes from and use it as a prompt for prayer.

Ideas for kids

Harvest musicals

TWO There's a range of Harvest musicals with catchy songs and readings, aimed at different age groups from Key Stage 1 through to older teenagers. All are available from www.redheadmusic.co.uk and are ideal for schools. Choose from:

- Harvest Praise!
- Harvest Rock!
- Harvestsong
- Harvest . . . It's a Little Bit CORNy!
- Lord of the Harvest! (great for older children and teenagers)

You could stage one of the musicals with your Sunday school and take it out into the community – perhaps to a shopping centre, a hospital, a retirement community, a local park or even a service station. Hand out song sheets so that everyone can join in, and perhaps give away something to eat or drink. You could have collection buckets to raise money for charity at the same time.

Further ideas

- Go on a nature walk and collect as many seeds as you can (conkers, acorns, berries, grasses, etc.). Identify them with the children and talk about sowing seeds and harvesting.
- Write prayers for those in need on fruit and vegetable cut-outs.
- Support a charity that works overseas but also learn about how the charity helps people, where it works and the food and farming methods of the country.
- Squash berries and use the juice to dye pre-cut banners to be hung in the church. (Make sure you know which berries to avoid!)
- Make bread.
- Try flower arranging.
- Make collages with autumn leaves, etc.

SUPPORT A CHARITY THAT WORKS OVERSEAS BUT ALSO LEARN ABOUT HOW THE CHARITY HELPS PEOPLE, WHERE IT WORKS AND THE FOOD AND FARMING METHODS OF THE COUNTRY.

- Put on a drama such as the one below discussing the importance of saying thank you:

Zac does not like getting up on a Saturday morning (. . . who does?). Mum calls him several times to come and get his breakfast. When he appears he refuses to say grace.

'Why should I say "thank you" to God for my toast? God didn't make my toast; Mum did.' Then [very begrudgingly] 'Thank you, Mum, for my toast.'

Mum refuses to accept the credit saying, 'All I did was to put the bread into the toaster. It's no good thanking me; you should thank the people at the Co-op [or any other outlet] for the bread.'

So Zac goes to the Co-op and says thank you to the baker who works in the bread department, who says, 'It's no good thanking me; you need to thank the delivery man who brings the ingredients to make the bread'. . . who says, 'It's no good thanking me; you need to thank the miller who makes the flour' . . . who says, 'It's no good thanking me; you need to thank the farmer.'

Now the farmer goes to Zac's church. When Zac appears and makes his little speech, the farmer takes Zac to a field and tells him that all he does is sow the seed. God sends the sunshine and the rain, the day and the night, and God makes the seed grow. So, really, he needs to say 'thank you' to God . . . at which point you can explain that harvest is saying 'thank you' to God for all that he provides . . .

Community prayer treasure hunt

A 60-minute adventure outside the walls of your church building, praying for your local community.

- Begin inside the church building. Prepare your hearts and minds before you start.
- Put people into small 'family teams' of different ages. Give each team a colour.
- Explain that there are clues hidden in plastic boxes around your local community. Colour-coded envelopes, one for each team, are inside these boxes. No stealing or tampering with other teams' envelopes!

- Explain each team will be on a different route around the game, so their first clue will take each team to a different prayer box to start.

Select from the following prayer box ideas to design your own prayer time or make up your own! Five or six boxes will probably be enough for a 60-minute prayer walk. Teams will need time to walk between prayer stations. Choose the geographical area to be used with care. Walk and time it ahead of the event!

Box 1: Faith like mustard seeds

Put this box outside a school or key building of influence. Inside, place mustard seeds in small bags, one for each team participating. Put an instruction sheet that says: 'Take the packet of seed for your team and divide it equally among yourselves. Jesus told us all we needed was faith the size of mustard seeds to remove obstacles to the kingdom! Examine the seed. Now each person should spend five minutes sowing their prayers of faith for the school [or other place]. Plant the seed or throw it to the wind. What will you dare to pray?'

May the God of hope fill you with all joy and peace as you trust in him.

Box 2: Jesus, the Bread of Life

Place this box in a place like a park or piece of grass. Put in enough slices of bread for each team with the instruction: 'Either scatter bread in your local park for the birds or eat it yourself! Spend five minutes praying that there would be a growing hunger for truth in your community and for knowing the purpose of life. Ask God for opportunities to share this bread (hope) with others.'

Box 3: The Lord's Prayer

Make a photocopy of the prayer that Jesus gave his disciples. Write the instruction: 'Each person must choose a phrase or a line from The Lord's Prayer. Turn this line or phrase into a prayer as you walk to the next box. Teach the younger ones how to do this. For example, "Our Father" – "Thank you for being our Father, for being the Dad who loves the people in the home I am walking past. Bless them, Father..."'

Box 4: Prayer shapes

In this box write the instruction: 'Your task as a team is to make the word HOPE with your bodies! (Take a photo on your mobile to prove it later to the other teams!) Read out loud the scripture from Romans 15:13, *'May the God of hope fill you with all joy and peace as you trust in him, so that you may overflow with hope by the power of the Holy Spirit.'* You could say this scripture a few times and make it a prayer for your community, changing the word 'you' for the name of your town, village or city.

Box 5: Egg-timer blessing

Place this box close to another church in the town or community. Write a note that says: 'Use the egg-timer! Turn it over to start the prayers. Pray all together as one, for as long as the timer lasts. Pray heaps of blessings upon that other church (the leaders, youth, families, children, etc.). '

Box 6: In the bag!

In this box place two or three pairs of rubber gloves and one black bin liner per team. Place this box in a street where there will be some litter to pick up. Instruction note: 'For five minutes use the gloves and bin liner to pick up litter from the street. As some of the team do this everyone is to ask the Lord to send the Holy Spirit to convict the community of the rubbish in our lives and to make people aware of their conscience and God's wonderful gift of repentance and new life in Jesus!'

Idea provided by Andy Kennedy of King's Kids, YWAM England.

Harvest Labyrinth

A labyrinth reshapes a 12th-century ritual for the 21st century. It is an ancient symbol which combines the imagery of the circle and spiral into a winding path, inviting anyone to walk slowly along the path, stopping at different points for personal reflection, interaction and prayer about their spiritual journey and their relationship with God, their community, our planet, etc. This could be laid out in a church or church hall, or set up alongside any community activity, e.g. a harvest supper. It can be done just for those within the church family or it can be modified to be used by anyone in the community.

COULD BE DONE IN SMALL GROUPS.

You could create your labyrinth based on the journey of a grain of wheat to a loaf of bread, having stopping points which include a tray of soil, seeds to plant, watering and shining light on the soil, a growing plant, harvesting the wheat, grinding the wheat into flour, and a loaf of bread. At each point provide something to interact with, something to reflect on, something to do and something to pray. Use Bible texts to draw out the parallels between the seed and our spiritual journey.

Connecting work and harvest in non-rural churches

Since most people don't make their living by farming, traditional displays of bringing food into the church as offerings may remind us of God's provision of our daily bread, but they don't connect visually to the way that God has chosen to meet many urban people's material needs. A suburban child does not look at a display of potatoes and make the connection to their father's job in IT.

A contemporary harvest display might involve a range of objects that represent how people are engaged in work such as a hard hat, a baby's bottle, a set of keys, a spade, a computer or a syringe. In one church, the whole congregation were invited to bring an object that represented their work. Then they were invited to lay it on the altar as a symbolic dedication of their work, their co-workers and their workplaces to God. Children were involved and brought text books or pencils and one unemployed person laid their UB40 form on the altar – a moving reminder of their lack of paid work but also of God's provision through the wider community.

Another church asked people to bring in pictures of themselves in their workplaces then displayed them around the church, as a way for the community to get to know and appreciate the variety of places in which God has given them work.

Working with Rural Communities

Jerry Marshall

Mission is about making a difference to people and their communities through actions and words. Rural churches are already good at knowing the communities of which they are a part and are often already deeply involved in community life. These existing relationships with rural communities give an advantage over many churches in towns and cities that have to work hard even to be known in their areas.

For some rural congregations, especially small ones, mission can seem like an impossible task, or one that needs to be done by someone else, but it is not. Everyone has some skill or gift that they can contribute to making a difference for the Kingdom of God as effective mission in the countryside is based around the whole community. So what can you do?

Some things to think about first.

What do you already do that can be extended or developed further?

Do you run a regular coffee morning or lunch club, a social evening or other special event? Who is it for? Can the invitation be extended more widely? Can they be used as an opportunity to reach out to people who are isolated or who have no contact with the church? Have you thought of creating an opportunity for people to talk and ask for prayer as part of the event?

What is already being done in the community that you can join in with?

Are there other organisations present in the community that need help and volunteers? Consider if local schools, uniformed organisations for children and young people, the youth club, sports club or pensioners group needs volunteers.

RURAL CHURCHES ARE ALREADY GOOD AT KNOWING THE COMMUNITIES OF WHICH THEY ARE A PART.

Make use of existing contacts and relationships?

Many people in a community are involved in more than one activity in that place so that each person is at the centre of a web connecting lots of different people. These networks of contacts and friendships are lifelines for communication of information, hope and love. Local organisations can be where church members work out their response to Christ's call, making a difference through word and service.

Pray for the community regularly?

Do you pray regularly for your community, its people, groups, businesses and activities? Make a list to be used regularly in public and private prayer. Can you organise a special service to celebrate the work of different groups and activities?

What resources can help?

The Arthur Rank Centre has produced a simple toolkit to help you understand your local rural congregation and the community you serve before thinking about community-based mission. The toolkit will help you to get an accurate picture of the local community and its needs, identify the gifts and skills of the congregation, investigate the possibility of working in partnership with others and asses ways of developing further.

www.arthurrankcentre.org.uk/publications-and-resources/profiling-tools

Other good publications for rural mission

The Arthur Rank Centre – a wide range of resources on rural churches including on mission, evangelism, community engagement, worship and church buildings.
www.arthurrankcentre.org.uk

Country Way: life and faith in rural Britain – a magazine for rural churches to share ideas information and inspiration.
www.countryway.org.uk

Making Connections – a resource book for mission in rural churches www.arthurrankcentre.org.uk/publications-and-resources/making-connections

SHAPE – your SHAPE for God's service – material to help identify the gifts God has given, specifically for rural churches
www.carlislediocese.org.uk/ministry-training-and-vocation/growing-as-christians/Shape.html

Caring for All – a pastoral care course
www.urc-eastern.org.uk/td-locall-church/focus-booklets

Growing in Welcome – a resource from the Episcopal Church of Scotland to help churches review the quality of their welcome and outreach
http://md.glasgow.anglican.org/wp-content/uploads/2011/01/Growing-in-Welcome-Workbook-January-2011.pdf

Rural Ministries – an evangelical mission agency committed to planting and growing rural churches in the countryside www.ruralministries.org.uk

Jerry Marshall is Chief Executive Officer at The Arthur Rank Centre

Youth Groups and Harvest

On our website at www.hopetogether.org.uk you will find two youth group sessions designed by Urban Saints to help young people engage with Harvest, thankfulness and generosity.

Mission ideas for young people

HOPE Revolution is all about seeing young people get out of their comfort zones for Jesus and expressing his love through what they say and do. We want to see young people take risks for Jesus, becoming agents of change in their communities and living the radical adventure that is being a disciple of Jesus Christ. Here are some Harvest mission ideas particularly suitable for young people to use to express God's love and our thankfulness on the streets and in the heart of our communities.

'Give us this day our daily bread'

A great idea to meet a practical physical need over a lunch-break

What's the idea?

The land is satisfied by the fruit of his work… wine that gladdens human hearts, oil to make their faces shine, and bread that sustains their hearts (Psalm 104:13,15).

Create an opportunity for a group of young people to take to the streets one lunchtime where they set up a stall to make sandwiches to be given away. This can act as a reminder of God's provision and goodness to us; that he does indeed provide our daily bread. The stall could display scriptures such as Psalm 104:13,15, and young people can use this as an opportunity to express God's love that is made free to all in a practical way.

WE WANT TO SEE YOUNG PEOPLE TAKE RISKS FOR JESUS, BECOMING AGENTS OF CHANGE IN THEIR COMMUNITIES AND LIVING THE RADICAL ADVENTURE THAT IS BEING A DISCIPLE OF JESUS CHRIST.

A GREAT IDEA TO MEET A PRACTICAL PHYSICAL NEED OVER A LUNCH-BREAK

Consider

- Prepare clear signs for good visibility.
- Hygiene: ensure antibacterial hand wash is used and visible as well as catering gloves and aprons worn by all.
- Utilise cool boxes to keep fillings fresh.
- Provide ample table space for sandwich preparation.
- Pre-prepare all sandwich fillings, grated cheese, ham slices, egg mayonnaise, sliced cucumber, sliced tomato, shredded lettuce, and make salad cream and dressings available. Provide sandwich bags and napkins.
- Provide information on Harvest services or church activities, such as Alpha, to customers.
- A number of young people could be available for conversations whilst others are preparing sandwiches.

Expressions of thankfulness

ONE An opportunity to encourage the community to reflect on the things for which they are thankful, and to remind them that all good things come from God.

Praise the Lord 'who satisfies your desires with good things so that your youth is renewed like the eagle's' (Psalm 103:5).

What's the idea?

Get your young people together for an afternoon, where they take to the streets with a 'thankfulness' sign and flipcharts. They can ask passers-by to write on the flip chart something for which they are most thankful, allowing participants to consider being thankful to God.

Consider

- Have publicity to hand out for youth clubs and church events.
- Give out flyers which provoke thought about God's goodness to us.
- Offer to pray a blessing upon people, that they might know more of God's goodness and the fullness of life.
- Find creative ways of displaying suggestions. Perhaps have the word 'thankfulness' written in large letters, with participants' suggestions being written on Post-it notes and stuck on to the letters.
- Give out sweets as a 'thank you' for participating.
- Have Gospels available for those who want to engage at a deeper level.

THE FRUIT OF THE SPIRIT IS LOVE, JOY, PEACE, PATIENCE, KINDNESS, GOODNESS, FAITHFULNESS, GENTLENESS AND SELF-CONTROL.

Harvest 'Fruits of the Spirit' stall

TWO *The fruit of the Spirit is love, joy, peace, patience, kindness, goodness, faithfulness, gentleness and self-control* (Galatians 5:22-23).

Challenge your young people to offer prayer to passers-by who recognise their need for differing fruits of the Spirit.

What's the idea?

Set up a Harvest 'Fruits of the Spirit' stall with nine different sections of fruit labelled love, joy, peace, patience, kindness, goodness, gentleness, faithfulness and self-control. Ask passers-by if they would like a free piece of fruit, and to choose one which represents something they would like more of in their life at this time. Offer them the chance to receive prayer to know and receive more of their particular chosen fruit of the Spirit, and let them know that this is something that God gives to us.

Consider

- Perhaps a local supermarket or grocer would be prepared to discount or even supply you with some free fruit.
- Present your stall well, with the fruits clearly shown and labelled.
- Involve young people as market stall traders, calling out 'Amazing fruit that can last for ever! Come and get some life-changing fruit here!'
- Use sweets such as rosy apples and lemon sherbets instead of fruit to save space and money.
- Pray blessings over the passers-by.
- Give fruit to people who are homeless and talk about the fruits of the Spirit with them.
- Invite people to a Youth Alpha course where the Holy Spirit is explained in more detail.

£5 Giveaway

An opportunity for young people to be creative in ways to bless others.

What's the idea?

Get your young people into groups of two or three and challenge them to bless members of their community by spending £5 in the most creative and beneficial ways. Use this as an opportunity to direct any thankfulness for the actions to God.

Consider

- Asking God to guide and lead those taking part so they know who to bless and how to bless them.
- Buying cards to thank people in the community for the things they do.
- Giving away 'Love Heart' sweets to let people know they are loved.
- Buying £1 umbrellas for those are getting wet when it's raining.
- Buying a meal for a homeless person.
- Completing a full risk assessment and putting clear boundaries in place for the young people.
- Approaching the church to back this event financially.
- Getting the young people to do a fundraising event to raise the money to be given away.

Invading the community during Harvest

Love the Lord your God with all your heart and with all your soul and with all your mind. .. Love your neighbour as yourself (Matthew 22:37–39).

An opportunity for young people to be challenged to love and serve their local communities through what they say and what they do.

Harvest 'Mowing and Reaping'

An occasion for young people to do a random act of kindness for the residents of their local community.

Love the Lord your God with all your heart and with all your soul and with all your mind.. . Love your neighbour as yourself.

What's the idea?

For young people to offer a free lawn-mowing service, emphasising our call to care for God's creation and using it as an opportunity to bless their local community.

Consider

- How could the people most in need of help be targeted?
- Wearing T-shirts profiling the initiative for maximum visibility in the community.
- Using this time to pray for the occupants of the house, and to chat to them about church activities.
- Risk assessments should be completed to ensure all the necessary safety precautions are taken, e.g. using circuit breakers; giving safety training for using lawn mowers; providing adequate supervision and ensuring that the activities are completed in small groups.

Further ideas

How about offering fence painting, raking up leaves, garden clearing and general garden maintenance?

Harvest sports competition

An opportunity to celebrate our health and give thanks for our bodies, involving young people in community sports challenges and competitions.

What's the idea?

Hold a half-day sports event, giving young people the opportunity to engage in a variety of sports and competitions. Use this as an opportunity to build relationships and bless young people in the community, whilst empowering your youth to lead and facilitate these activities.

Consider

- In addition to football, hockey or rounders competitions, consider having some Harvest-themed challenges that could utilise food, e.g. food eating challenges, relays involving a variety of foods, etc.

- Conclude the activity with a barbecue (for a small fee if necessary to cover costs).
- Give away trophies, medals, prizes and/or certificates.
- Utilise sports that can draw in all ages and both genders.
- Have a prayer team praying for the young people who participate.
- Develop a regular sports activity for the community.

Other community activities could involve litter picking and graffiti clearing which could serve local community centres, schools, residential homes as well as individuals and families in the community.

Invading your school during Harvest

Why not use Harvest as an opportunity to thank our schools and teachers for all they do to support young people? Additionally, how about expressing gratitude for God's creation and all of the earth's provision in our schools, using it as an opportunity to bless those less fortunate than ourselves?

School food hampers

What's the idea?

Challenge your young people to invite pupils in their schools to provide hampers of non-perishable foods for vulnerable people in the community.

Consider

- Think about how you can get teachers and the school involved with this initiative.
- Prepare a letter for the school to send out to all students following an assembly devoted to Harvest asking for their help with the hampers.
- Get your Christian Union to deliver the assembly, or involve local youth leaders in the project.

Why not use Harvest as an opportunity to thank our schools and teachers for all they do to support young people?

- How about consulting with the local authority to identify suitable projects to support, such as a women's refuge centre, a local project for homeless people, or a local project reaching out to elderly people.

24-hour fast

A 24-hour fast could be a great way to raise money for a local, national or international project that helps to feed people who are in need.

Participants could fast for just one meal if they aren't able to do the full fast, or could fast from another activity for a longer period (e.g. not buying chocolate or fast-food for a week and donating the money saved).

If you hold the fast through a school, consider putting on an activity over the lunch break such as a prayer time for people who are starving in parts of the world.

As alternatives to a full fast, young people could:

- eat half portions of their meals and donate the money saved.
- exchange their dinner money for a piece of fruit or a protein bar.
- be encouraged to donate their change from their lunch.

Bless your teacher

Use Harvest as an opportunity to thank your teachers for their investment in you, to show your respect and appreciation for all that they do.

- Buy them some chocolate or flowers.
- Write them a card of personal thanks.
- Get the whole class to present a gift, flowers or card, explaining that Harvest is a time of thanksgiving.
- Ask if there is a task that your class could do to help them.
- Leave an anonymous gift on their desk.
- Get your homework in on time!

Thankfulness, Generosity and Mission

Tearfund

Whenever we consider the nature of God, we cannot get far without encountering a powerful reminder of God's incredible generosity. From the dawn of creation, through centuries spent nurturing his chosen people, right up to the birth, death and resurrection of his only Son, we are reminded that God's nature is pure generosity.

Just as John 3:16 reminds us that *'God so loved the world that he gave…'*, in the rest of Scripture we find plenty of reminders of the driving force behind human generosity. And what better illustration than Jesus' encounter with the 'sinful woman'? (Luke 7:36-50) Her act of lavish generosity was caused by love – a direct response to the knowledge that her sins had been forgiven. Jesus himself underlines the truth, stating that when we become aware of the power of God's love to cleanse us, we cannot help but feel full to overflowing with gratitude.

This remains relevant for us today. Christ's feet may have stopped leaving fresh prints on our soil – and our backgrounds may be different – but haven't we all been rescued by the loving forgiveness of God? Don't we all have reason to weep at his feet in gratitude for what he has done for us?

The answer is 'yes'. But to whom should we show that gratitude? Towards the end of his ministry Jesus declared that 'whatever you did for one of the least of these brothers and sisters of mine, you did for me' (Matthew 25:40), making it clear that the search for opportunities to express our gratitude to God should be conducted with eyes wide open out beyond the walls of the church.

> Christ's feet may have stopped leaving fresh prints on our soil... but haven't we all been rescued by the loving forgiveness of God?

James is beautifully direct when tackling this subject (James 2:17-19). It's no use our making grand statements if our faith and love are inert. If we want to show gratitude to God there's no better place to start than among those on the margins of our society.

This theme of being motivated to reach out beyond ourselves by Christ's love for us is echoed in the parable of the Good Samaritan (Luke 10:25ff). The story has been drilled into those of us who grew up in Sunday school, yet the lessons it offers can take a lifetime to absorb. Who is the good neighbour, we are asked? The outcast, we reply, the one despised by those with status and power. The parable reminds us beautifully that in seeking to uphold the first commandment to love God with all our heart, soul and strength we must not forget the second: to love our neighbours as ourselves. These 'neighbours' are not defined by clan, creed or country. Instead they are simply those who are in need of our help. Where there is need, there are neighbours. Do we have the vision to see them?

Be thankful for where you are

It might not be the first thing that springs to mind, but being thankful for where we live is an important attitude for churches to adopt. In spite of the headlines and falling red lines on statisticians' graphs, churches still have incredible potential when it comes to local communities. And, like the little boy who gave up his lunch of fish and bread, our decision to respond in generosity to those around us can so easily be multiplied by our Lord God.

In 2008, ICM Research was commissioned to find out how much people on the same street interact with each other. Amongst other things, the survey discovered:

- More than a fifth (22%) of Britons believe that the UK's neighbourhoods have become less friendly in the last five years.
- Half of Britons said hello to fewer than six people in their street during the previous week – *and one in ten of those questioned had spoken to no-one.*
- Some now think there is a serious decline in everyday interaction – *and argue that this leads to needless disputes.*
- 36% of us would not trust anybody on our street with our keys – *among 25- to 34-year-olds this figure is almost half.*

With that in mind, here are a few ideas which might help your church connect in new ways with what it means to be good neighbours and to be thankful for where God has placed us.

GET OUT AND ASK PEOPLE IN YOUR COMMUNITY WHAT THEY LOVE ABOUT WHERE THEY LIVE AND WHAT COULD MAKE LIFE IN YOUR AREA EVEN BETTER.

Photo collage

Get together in groups – with friends, neighbours and people from church – and take some cameras out and about in your community. Take photos of the good things you see and the positive changes that have been made. Come back together and create a positive community collage.

Hit the press

Gather all your local papers and cut out any pieces that you think show actions that are worth celebrating. Compile all your cuttings into a collage and display it in – or outside – your church.

Monthly dinners

If you are able to, you could invite a new neighbour to dinner each month, starting with a Harvest meal.

Celebrate your community

Get out and ask people in your community what they love about where they live and what could make life in your area even better. You might be surprised by what you hear. Find ways to share your results so that everyone can see the positives.

And Finally, Pray . . .

A Liturgical Prayer

Our Father, who brings heaven to earth,

Merciful and mighty Son who guards our hearts,

Compassionate and counselling Spirit who walks with us,

We stand in prayer with our Christian brothers and sisters around the world,

In places where food is scarce and hunger powerful.

And with them we pray for your light to burn brightly on their work.

As we pour out our prayers, pour out your mercy to answer us.

Merciful and mighty Son,

Sender of good gifts, bringer of life, worker of miracles,

You have given your church your own heart.

Help us, through our prayers and actions, to enable local churches to lift the broken.

To release the potential which resides in even the poorest communities.

As we pour out our prayers, pour out your mercy to answer us.

Compassionate and counselling Spirit,

We commit ourselves, as part of your global church movement,

To play our part in bringing a kingdom of justice.

In bringing spiritual and material transformation

Into the darkest places.

In being part of the church – and releasing its potential to be your agent of change in the poorest of places.

As we pour out our prayers, pour out your mercy to answer us.

We pray for strength to fulfil your call to us, to care for the orphan, to feed the hungry, to release the potential of poor communities so that they may find a better future.

Hear us, your servants.

Amen.

ENCOURAGE EVERYONE TO HAVE A THANKSGIVING WEEK WHERE THEY TAKE TIME EVERY DAY TO THANK GOD FOR ALL THAT HE GIVES.

Prayer idea for small groups

Choose an evening and ask everyone to bring two or three favourite scriptures from the Bible on giving thanks. Next, start to ask everyone to make a list of the many things we receive from God, covering all the spiritual, physical, emotional, intellectual, material and relational blessings he gives. Share some of those with each other then have a time of prayer inviting everyone to share short prayers of thanksgiving: 'Lord, I thank you for . . .' and see how long you can keep going! Encourage everyone to have a thanksgiving week where they take time every day to thank God for all that he gives.

Then when the group next meets, take time to share and pray into all that has been learnt.

Remembrance

Laurence Singlehurst

Remembrance Day and Remembrance Sunday fall into the harvest period so it's worth considering some activity focused around this memorial. Churches have historically been very good at Remembrance Sunday, with most respecting a two-minute silence within their Sunday service. However, increasingly, local communities are taking note of the '11th of the 11th' as well, which often falls midweek and tends to focus around the village, town or city war memorial site. In my town at ten minutes to 11am there is very little happening around the war memorial, but over the last few years, as it creeps up to 11 o'clock, several hundred people appear as if out of nowhere and stand respectfully in silence as the Last Post is played.

Let's think of ways we can stand with our community as we remember those who have fought in past wars, and those who continue to risk their lives in conflicts. The sad reality is that many members of our churches and communities are still touched by the worry and pain of having loved ones in the armed forces. Let's stand with them and show our respect for the sacrifices they are making.

We asked churches around the country how they honour Remembrance Day and these were the ideas they gave us:

- Participate in the civic remembrance parade service and wreath laying.
- If there is no civic event, hold your own parade, joining with local groups and representatives of the armed forces to take a walk of remembrance. You may need to talk to the police about shutting roads on the route to traffic. Lead the parade towards your church and hold a service of remembrance there, before holding a two-minute silence at the local cenotaph.
- Take Armistice Day services in local schools.

THE SAD REALITY IS THAT MANY MEMBERS OF OUR CHURCHES AND COMMUNITIES ARE STILL TOUCHED BY THE WORRY AND PAIN OF HAVING LOVED ONES IN THE ARMED FORCES.

- Have a live link to the remembrance service at the London Cenotaph beamed onto a screen for five minutes during morning worship in your church.
- Hold a special service to remember people from your community who have died in armed conflicts during the last 12 months.
- Give an opportunity in your church service for people to speak about their own experiences in the armed forces.
- Remember those who have 'fallen' by reading their names and lighting a candle for each of them within the church service.

- Hold a remembrance service in the local primary school, using information from research on the children's ancestors.
- Use the breaking of bread and sharing of wine in remembrance as Jesus taught us. This could be extended to having a community meal where there is an opportunity for the community to talk about their own experiences or share memories of service men and women.
- Give financial support to relevant charities who care for wounded service men and women, and who care for the bereaved.
- Hold a service in the Police canteen on Armistice Day.
- Explore what it means to be peacemakers today with testimonies or stories of people working for peace throughout the world.

Resources

British Legion: www.britishlegion.org.uk

National War Museum: www.cwgc.org/education/rememberme.htm

Churches Together in Britain and Ireland website www.ctbi.org.uk and the book ***Beyond Our Tears: Resources for Times of Remembrance***, (CTBI, 2004)

Defenders - a church pack for Remembrance Day and Armed Forces Day from www.cvm.org.uk

Give financial support to relevant charities who care for wounded service men and women, and who care for the bereaved

The cycle of mission

We hope that as you plan your year of mission for 2014 you will see the successful activities as a cycle that can be updated and repeated year after year in the future. So as you come to the end of the autumn ideas, turn again to the Christmas chapter. Revisit what worked last year and what could be improved. Could you take on an additional activity? Could you work with other churches to make your outreach bigger and better? Let's keep the momentum of missional activity flowing, so that we might see our communities blessed in the name of Jesus.

On our website you will find Bible study materials from Stewardship, looking at Harvest in the Old and New Testament. Download for free at www.hopetogether.org.uk

These studies are also available in the HOPE For Harvest resource book which is available from the HOPE website. The book features many more ideas for mission around the themes of Harvest, generosity and the workplace.

work

'There are loads of ways churches can celebrate God's provision of work for the various members of their congregations, so the workplace becomes a place for mission.'

Supporting Your Church At Work

There are loads of ways churches can celebrate God's provision of work for the various members of their congregations, supporting them on Sundays, or in their small group, so the workplace becomes a place for mission. The following ideas show what it can look like when a church is supporting members to be missional in their working lives. Many of the ideas don't take very long, and cost absolutely nothing, but could make a real difference to how supported and encouraged people feel in their work.

TTT – This Time Tomorrow

During a normal Sunday worship service, perhaps once a month, the church leader interviews one of the congregation for two minutes. They ask the interviewee a few questions about their daily occupation, about what they will be doing TTT – 'This Time Tomorrow'. The questions can be really simple:

- What do you do?
- What are your challenges/the things you are thankful for?
- How can we pray for you?

The interviewees do not need to be the Chief of Police, the Chief Executive of a major multi-national company or the England fly-half. In fact, even if you have some members with extraordinary roles, it's usually best to start with people doing ordinary work in ordinary places, and to include people whose daily occupation may not be paid, such as a housewife, a retired person involved in a variety of purposeful activities, and those who are unemployed.

Ordinary Christians doing ordinary things are important to God

This simple practice tends to have a range of transformative benefits:

- It acknowledges, affirms and honours the interviewee, telling them that what they do every day is important to the leader, important to the church and important to God.
- As TTT follows TTT month by month, the whole congregation recognises more deeply that ordinary Christians doing ordinary things are important to God – even if some people never get to share from the front. These stories and prayer requests become part of the way the church does life together.
- TTT creates new conversations. It gives people who didn't know the interviewee an easy way to talk to them, and perhaps to share similar challenges or pertinent insight or encouragement.

- TTT triggers a new *kind* of conversation. Issues that are often considered to be off the spiritual agenda (work, futility, failure, success, daily relationships, mission in daily life) are validated as legitimate topics for conversation and prayer.

Consider

- Once you've done the interview you could ask others to stand who share the same issues or pressures so they can also be prayed for.
- Be creative in the way you do the interviews. One church arranged for members to use a small video camera to record their interviews in their workplace, which helped people understand each other's everyday contexts much better.

Provide an opportunity for people to report back in future services on how the congregation's prayers have been answered.

Commissioning and thankfulness

When someone gets a new job or is promoted it is something to be thankful for and perhaps to acknowledge as a whole church. Furthermore, a new job is not just a source of provision; it is an opportunity for mission and ministry so, in the same way that a church would pray for a new pastor, it is hugely encouraging to commission someone for their new job or their new role.

Ideally, the prayers would have three main thrusts:

- Reflect an understanding of the job to be done and how it contributes positively to others, the place it will be done and the skills required.
- Reflect the conviction that the Christian goes into the workplace as a representative of the Lord Jesus carrying his commission and confident in his promise to be 'with' his disciples 'to the very end of the age' (Matthew 28:19–20).
- Reflect the conviction that the Christian goes into the workplace as the individual representative of your church. Thank God that he has given your community an opportunity to make an impact in that place.

WHEN SOMEONE GETS A NEW JOB OR IS PROMOTED IT IS SOMETHING TO BE THANKFUL FOR AND PERHAPS TO ACKNOWLEDGE AS A WHOLE CHURCH.

Opportunities for prayer

After the offering

Most churches take up an offering every Sunday so you don't have to change anything in a service to begin to enrich people's understanding of God's generosity and the variety of ways he may bless his people in, at and through work, and other mechanisms of provision. Across a year you could probably teach and pray a whole theology of work, divine provision, money and generosity, just through offertory prayers. Themes might include:

- Gratitude for work.
- Gratitude for being created with skills.
- Recognition of the need for stewardship.
- Recognition of God as the source of money.
- Gratitude for money.
- Gratitude for the privilege of being able to give.
- Gratitude for our workplaces, our bosses and colleagues.

General prayer

The simplest way to build mission-consciousness is to include a reference to the world of work and school within general prayers. Take, for example, a confessional prayer like:

'Lord, we bring to you our relationships – our relationships at home, our relationships with neighbours, our relationships at work or at school. Show us where we have failed to love as you would have us love.'

The simple addition of seven words 'our relationships at work or at school' instantly transforms this prayer into one that encourages the whole congregation to recognise that their life cannot be compartmentalised, that God is interested in the 9 to 5. It only takes another three seconds to say!

Prayer and the rhythm of the non-agricultural year

Plough Sunday, Rogation Sunday and Harvest were key moments in the agricultural year that everyone in a rural community shared. In a mixed economy, however, there are still moments we all share. So, for example, for the bulk of the population the tax year begins in the first week of April, so the first Sunday of April might be a good moment to ask for God's blessing on the work of our hands in the coming year. Similarly, May Day retains some of its historic connection with work and therefore might be a natural moment to give thanks for our participation in God's mission through work.

There is no obvious equivalent to Plough Sunday but it might still be marked as Technology Sunday, as a moment when we thank God for the liberating impact of technology on our lives and its helpfulness in limiting drudgery and producing goods and services that contribute to human flourishing to the glory of God.

Indeed, many of the advances in the widespread use of technology have emerged out of a biblical understanding of work that sought to limit the drudgery imposed on people and animals. It's true of the development of the watermill – long known in the East – but only brought into widespread use by Benedictines seeking to reduce toil. It's true also of the clock, of the iron horseshoe, of the crank . . .

Prayer and pressure points

Just as Plough Sunday and Rogation Sunday and Harvest represented key moments in the agricultural cycle – not least in terms of effort – so a church can connect its prayer for different people into the rhythm and pressure points of their working year – sheep farmers in lambing season, accountants at the end of the tax year, kids at exam time, teachers at the beginning and end of terms, shop assistants during sales, hospital workers during August when newly qualified doctors start. An example calendar is available to download from www.hopetogether.org.uk so you can ask people in the church to fill it in and then perhaps display it.

MAY DAY RETAINS SOME OF ITS HISTORIC CONNECTION WITH WORK AND THEREFORE MIGHT BE A NATURAL MOMENT TO GIVE THANKS FOR OUR PARTICIPATION IN GOD'S MISSION THROUGH WORK.

Praying blessing @ work

On the completion of each day's work of creation in Genesis 1 – 2 God blessed the living creatures he had made, bidding them increase and multiply and fill the earth. Blessing is powerful – our words matter! How can we bless our work?

Ask the congregation for aspects of their work that they would want to bless. Help them explore why it would be good to bless each aspect.

Possible areas:

- The privilege of having work.
- Relationships at work.
- The prosperity of the organisation for whom we work.
- Management and decision-making.
- Use of resources.
- The 'output' of our hands and minds.
- The godly aspects of the culture and values of the organisation.
- Conversations at work which point people to Jesus.

In groups of three or four ask the congregation to construct a short prayer (one or two sentences) to bless one aspect of work. Record and group these.

As a congregation, pray blessing on work as different people stand up and read out their short prayers.

Type up the prayer of blessing to be circulated for future use.

An example prayer of blessing

Thankfulness

Bless the Lord O my soul and forget not all his benefits. We bless you, Lord, for your gift of work – for the opportunity to co-labour with you and to provide for our families and communities.

Output

We bless the creativity and skills you have given which enable us to make goods and deliver services that others need.

Relationships

We bless every contact with another person, be they colleague, customer or supplier. We bless those we meet, speak to or email, that they may experience something of your love through us.

Resources

We bless the use and stewardship of all resources: financial, material and human. We bless ethical decisions in how we source our materials and how we dispose of waste.

Organisation

We bless the organisations for which we work; we bless them as employers and pray that job opportunities may multiply through them. We bless the management decisions to reflect Kingdom values.

Culture

We bless the culture of our organisations. May they be contexts for human flourishing – places where people feel valued. We pray for people's lives outside of work – that they will be honoured.

Evangelism

We bless our contact with non-believers through work. We bless every opportunity to speak of you, through both our words and actions, with fruitfulness.

Amen.

We bless every contact with another person, be they colleague, customer or supplier. We bless those we meet, speak to or email, that they may experience something of your love through us.

Demonstrating the love of God in the workplace

A colleague of mine that I have become close to over the years suffered a miscarriage eight months into her pregnancy. It was a hugely challenging time for her, and I could see her gradually sinking into the depths of despair. She was a Hindu and I knew that her gods would not be able to help her at this time of critical need. I am naturally a joyful person and I knew that I had something to give this woman that could not be bought with money. During one of our discussions I asked if I could pray for her and she said yes. I have discovered that people everywhere are searching for solutions, but it is only the living God who truly has the answers the world is searching for. Showing concern for her provided the opportunity for me to share my faith. Within a year she had conceived again and gave birth to a healthy child. She confessed that she believed that the God I had prayed to answered her prayers.

Demonstrating the love of God in the workplace is an open door to share the gospel. When people ask me about my weekend, I use this as an opportunity to tell them about going to Church on Sunday. I am able to tell them about the sermon preached and how it ministered to me personally. By doing this they are getting to hear the gospel.

Catherine, hospital pharmacist

Praying for businesses and workplaces in your community

Businesses are vital to alleviating poverty. People need help, food, medicine, shelter and stable honest government but they also need jobs.

One of the things a congregation can do is to thank God for the businesses, shops and organisations you have in your area. You could be proactive, telling local shopkeepers or businesses that the church will be praying for their health and prosperity (Jeremiah 29:7) and asking them if they have any particular requests. In one small town, the pastor went into the local shops to ask for their prayer requests – but you could ask individual members of a congregation to do this or to adopt a shop/business that they use or was significant to them. This is also a great way of engaging with a local community.

ALSO A GREAT IDEA FOR SMALL GROUPS.

Extra ideas

- Come to church dressed in your workplace clothes.
- Bring examples of your work to church.
- Visit your congregation in their workplace.
- Invite local industries to make a display in church over the Harvest weekend or celebrate what they do with a DVD about them, including things to celebrate and things to pray for. Or invite local business people to come and represent their industry, thank them for their contribution to the community and pray for them. You could link up with a number of churches in the area to make sure different industries are honoured within your community.
- Run clinics for people in your church and community who are looking for work, offering help with CV writing, job applications and interview skills.
- Develop a church CD library with resources for workers to listen to as they commute, or make your Sunday talks downloadable from your website and recommend other good podcasts.
- Have a map on the wall in your church, indicating where people are employed (much as you would a traditional missionary map of people around the world).

BUSINESSES ARE VITAL TO ALLEVIATING POVERTY. PEOPLE NEED HELP, FOOD, MEDICINE, SHELTER AND STABLE HONEST GOVERNMENT BUT THEY ALSO NEED JOBS.

for the workplace

Gateway Chapel is a ministry where young and seasoned professionals are trained to become urban missionaries in their careers and businesses. The Gateway Chapel passion for marketplace training propelled them to develop people through training courses and a mentoring programme. They even provide some of their training online to help those who are working 9-5 take part. Courses include: 'How To Do Well At A Job Interview', 'How To Turn Your Passion Into Profit' and 'How To Get Out Of Debt.

Tope Oso who attended a training programme said: 'Prior to attending GWC Training programmes I have always wanted to do more than my 9-5 job and also wanted to impact my local community, With the training received at Gateway Chapel, I was able to start a voluntary group in my local borough, providing housing and benefits advice to service users facing homelessness. I started the project in 2007, and since then, the project has been growing from strength to strength, with continued support from Gateway Chapel. The project is now a registered charity providing support and advice to an average of 50 service users yearly, preventing a lot of families and individuals from becoming homeless. Gateway Chapel Training Programmes have impacted my life in so many ways, and as a result, I have been able to be a source of blessing to my community.'

Find out more at www.gatewaychapel.org.uk or contact admin@gatewaychapel.org.uk if you'd like some help setting up a similar project.

I am a Christian woman and have been working amongst predominantly male, Muslim colleagues for the past ten years. Living as a Christian and practising my faith started as a challenge as I was not familiar with the outlook and fervent beliefs of the majority of my colleagues. Over time, I have been able to learn and understand these and live amicably. With increased understanding, it has been easier to forgive offences that come along in the course of the long days we spend together, and to allow for new beginnings each time. I have had to love indiscriminately and relate with my colleagues equally at all levels. Throughout the years I have seen that every human being responds to love, humility and kindness.

Treasurer, City of London

CAP Job Clubs

'I love running my CAP Job Club! In Edenbrige we have seen broken and downtrodden people loved back to life through a fantastic mix of practical support and care for their wellbeing. Best of all, I get an opportunity to present God's love to people every single week.'

Chris Neal, CAP Job Club Edenbridge

'I really like the sense of community in the Job Club and the friendly atmosphere. These Job Clubs are a breath of fresh air.'

Vision

Christians Against Poverty's mission is to empower the local church to lift people out of poverty in such a way that they can experience and respond to the love of Jesus. To find out how they do this through debt help and money management courses, turn to page 77.

CAP Job Clubs are a new and exciting initiative born out of the work CAP has done for the last 16 years helping people out of debt. Unemployment is one of the leading causes of poverty and debt in the UK and now with CAP, through the local church, we can bring an opportunity for the long-term unemployed to find work.

Alongside helping people to find work, the CAP vision is to give them a chance to know Jesus and to get them linked in to the love and support available from their local church.

Job Clubs meet once a week and are open to anyone who is trying to find work, but they are specifically aimed at the long-term unemployed. A Job Coach from the local church is there to facilitate practical assistance in areas such as CV writing and interview technique. However, their primary focus is to foster a sense of community, build delegates' confidence and self-esteem, vastly increasing the likelihood that they will find work.

Grants available see www.cinnamonnetwork.co.uk for details

You will get to meet people week in and week out and support them on their journey into employment.

Benefits

Establishing a CAP Job Club in your church will give you the opportunity to share the love of God with people that might never ordinarily find their way into a church. You will get to meet people week in and week out and support them on their journey into employment; this offers countless opportunities to pray with them and talk about faith and the love God has for them. You will be there for them as they go through the highs and lows of a job hunt, picking them up when they don't succeed and celebrating with them when they do find work. They will know that at their time of need, the local church was there to support them.

Challenges

Accessibility – A lot of Job Club delegates have never been in church before. This provides a challenge to make sure your church is welcoming and accessible to all members of society, while maintaining core gospel values and teaching.

Many of the people you will be trying to reach may have given up hope of finding work. You will need to find ways to let them know about the Job Club and inspire them to join in.

Resources

Ideally you need three or four people to run a CAP Job Club. This is so you can ensure that week-in, week-out your Job Club can open its door for new and existing members to come along. It will also give you enough people to have valuable one-on-one time, either for practical or spiritual reasons.

CAP Job Clubs will provide everything else you need to ensure you can run, manage and maintain a Job Club in your church. Further information around pricing and training days can be found on their website.

Tips

If your church is already involved with other community outreach, CAP Job Clubs are an ideal ministry for you. Unemployment is often a symptom of other problems and so an active church is the best place for clients to find a complete solution to their unique situation. Churches already running foodbanks, rehabs, parents and tots groups or providing other practical help, find great synergy between CAP Job Clubs and these ministries.

Getting started

Visit www.capuk.org

'It's brilliant getting back into work, but even nicer knowing I've got people at the Job Club supporting me when both in and out of work.' Job Club Delegate

It's brilliant getting back into work, but even nicer knowing I've got people at the Job Club supporting me when both in and out of work.

The Salvation Army in Ripon recently started an employment and resource centre aiming to bring both ministry and practical help to people affected by unemployment. One of the first people to attend was called Neil. He had lost both of his parents that year and was in desperate need of love and care as well as a job. Within a week of attending the employment centre, Neil began to attend church on a Sunday. Since that day, Neil has seldom missed a Sunday and a few months after starting the job club he gave his life to the Lord.

Working Everyday with Purpose

Ken Costa

Most people want to make a difference with their lives. To do this, we have to identify our part in extending God's Kingdom and find out how we can bring blessing to the world. For many of us our part in extending God's Kingdom takes place in the workplace, an environment which often leaves us unclear and confused about how God could value our daily activities and how our office space could possibly be seen as a mission opportunity. As an investment banker in the City of London, I have read the *Financial Times* and the Bible almost every day for the last 30 years. People often ask how I reconcile being a banker and a Christian. There is a widespread view that God and business simply don't mix: the competitive, cut-throat demands of the marketplace are seen as the obvious enemy of Christian compassion and love. But I have found that the God who created and sustains the world is also the God of the workplace. The world of work doesn't belong in the slipstream of 21st century Christian spirituality, but in its mainstream. That's how God meant it to be. If the Christian faith is not relevant in the workplace, it is not relevant at all. Finding purpose in our work is one of the greatest challenges we face but taking the time to understand how God values our work, and how we can be a light for Christ in our work, enables us to view our day-to-day world very differently.

All work has two main opportunities. The first is an opportunity to worship because our work stations are our worship stations. Worship is the total submission of our whole person to the glory of God as we recognise our dependence on him. Our workplaces should therefore be places of worship.

If the Christian faith is not relevant in the workplace, it is not relevant at all.

Indeed, the Hebrew word for work and worship is the same – *avodah*. God is our real employer. Second, work is also a witness opportunity. It is important to remember that our primary purpose at work is to do the job that we are being paid to do. Yet, when we do this to the best of our ability and with the utmost Christian integrity, then opportunities for evangelism will probably follow. Every Christian can be a missionary in their workplace, and workplaces are often in just as much need of God as the far-flung countries that missionaries traditionally go to.

The workplace is also where faith is tested and sharpened by day-to-day encounters with the ambiguities and stresses of modern commerce. Our faith is tested when we recognise our weaknesses at work and we learn more about our hard and soft spots in our working relationships precisely because we cannot always choose the people with whom we work. For the most part, I have had the privilege of hugely enjoying my work, but there are moments when a sense of depression seems to hover over me at work. The causes are often deep-seated, but the triggers go off unexpectedly – a failed transaction, a disappointing pay review, unpleasant relationships, fear of the future. These times of trial happen to everyone. They are, however, opportunities for God to be glorified. Paul said, 'When I am weak, then I am strong' (2 Corinthians 12:10). I have come to see that weakness is very hard to show in the workplace unless we remember its object is strength – our dependence on God.

Over the past 20 years I have battled with many of the big questions often asked by Christians in the workplace and spent many an hour discussing these issues with trusted friends and members of my church at Holy Trinity Brompton. It was through these discussions I was encouraged to write the book *God at Work* which has since developed into a course. The course can be run in any church and uses six sessions to cover why work matters, the place of ambition, tough decisions and choices, stress and work-life balance, failure, disappointment and hope, and money and mission. Read on for more details and information on how to get hold of the course materials.

The light of our work

I am often struck by the fact that Jesus did not just say that he was the light of the world (John 8:12), but he told all his followers that we, too, are to be the light of the world, following his example:

'You are the light of the world. A town built on a hill cannot be hidden. Neither do people light a lamp and put it under a bowl. Instead they put it on its stand, and it gives light to everyone in the house. In the same way, let your light shine before others, that they may see your good deeds and glorify your Father in heaven' (Matthew 5:14–16).

Jesus calls us to be radiant for him in our workplaces. We are to shine brightly for our Father in heaven with whomever we come into contact with. Yet we can conceal the light in at least three ways.

GOING TO THE PUB WITH A COLLEAGUE AND CHATTING ABOUT THE BIG QUESTIONS OF LIFE IS JUST AS MUCH A MINISTRY AS LEADING A COURSE AT CHURCH.

The first way we can conceal the light is *physically*. The solution to this is interaction. The danger can be that, while we spend time in the workplace, we never truly rub shoulders with anyone. Sometimes we put our head down and do our work as fast as possible so that we can get out of work as early as possible, leaving little time for interaction with others. The reality is that interaction with our colleagues is a good, important and godly thing. As we begin to spend time with colleagues, particularly over lunch or after work, we can begin to share our lives with them and, with our lives, the gospel. Going to the pub with a colleague and chatting about the big questions of life is just as much a ministry as leading a course at church.

The second way that we can conceal the light is *morally*. When Jesus speaks of our light shining, he is primarily referring to our 'good deeds' (v16). Yet so often we let the culture of our workplace transform us, when Christ longs to use us to transform our workplace, and for us to be people of integrity. Of course, we will not live perfect lives at work and it is good to be honest and admit our failures and apologise to others when we are wrong. But we should aim, empowered by the Holy Spirit, to live and work with as much integrity as we can.

The third way we can conceal the light is *verbally*. If we never mention our connection to Jesus, then people will end up praising us, rather than 'praising our Father in heaven' (v16). As the American pastor, John Piper, writes, 'Thinking that our work will glorify God when people do not know that we are Christians, is like admiring an effective advert on TV that never mentions the product. People may be impressed but they won't know what to buy.' One of the most natural things we can do is to invite our colleagues to 'come and see', just as Philip encouraged Nathanael to 'come and see' Jesus (John 1:46). This may be through our discussions or we might invite them to church or an event where they can hear about Jesus. For example, I once invited a colleague to come to an Alpha supper at my church. Amazingly he came, and I did little else but pray for him, but he became a Christian and he now heads up Alpha across all of Asia. At HTB we have increasingly realised that it is often easier to encourage others to 'come and see' Jesus whilst physically remaining in your workplace, rather than dragging them all the way to your Sunday church. That's why we have specifically tailored the Alpha course for the workplace, and many workplace Christian groups now run their own courses. The content is similar to the Alpha course but sessions are shorter so groups can meet before or after work, or during a lunch break. Read on to find out more about Alpha in the Workplace and how to get hold of materials. It continues to excite me when I hear about the many ways people are using Alpha in the Workplace to share their faith. There are courses running from boardrooms to factories and from local coffee shops to those run through virtual online networks. I personally found running a course in my workplace to be a fun and rewarding experience and one I look forward to repeating in the near future.

I personally found running a course in my workplace to be a fun and rewarding experience and one I look forward to repeating in the near future.

Resources

God at Work course

The God at Work course aims to equip Christians to live out their Christian calling at work and find purpose in every aspect of their working lives. The course provides a Christian perspective on how to face challenges at work, as well as teaching on how to support our family and friends in the difficulties we all inevitably face. The six sessions cover: why work matters, ambition, tough decisions and choices, stress and work-life balance; failure, disappointment and hope; money and mission. For more information and all the resources you need to run the course visit www.godatwork.org.uk.

Alpha in the Workplace

THREE This course provides a practical introduction to the Christian faith over 7 to 15 sessions. It is an opportunity for people of all backgrounds to explore the meaning of life in a familiar and convenient location and is designed to fit into a regular working day, e.g. over a lunch hour or after work. There are courses running from boardrooms to factories and from local coffee shops to those run through virtual online networks. All the materials for running a course are online, downloadable and easy to use. Find out more at http://alpha.org/workplace.

Small groups in the workplace

Over the years there have been a number of experiments on how Christians in the workplace can be supported and support one another in bringing purpose to what they do to earn a living..

One idea that has been tested over the years is called Bands where three or four people gather together (friends or acquaintances) with a loose structure based around three Ps.

The first P is **Presence**, they read a Bible verse and tell a story of what God has done in their lives since they last met and anything that brings a sense of Jesus into their gathering. They then go on to the second P which is **Pressure**. What pressures do they face as Christians in the workplace; what are their challenges at work, with family and in life? They then pray for one another about the issues raised. The last P is **Purpose**. What are each of them trying to do in terms of being transformational, 'salt and light', in the way they work? They then pray for each other about their purpose and what they are hoping to see happen as they live out their Christian faith in their workplace.

These groups can meet weekly, fortnightly, monthly or whatever suits the people involved. Using this easy format means they don't really need a leader and they can take place anywhere they can find a quiet corner whether that's in an office, a meeting room or a café.

Find out more at www.celluk.org.uk/bands

Ken Costa is Chairman of Alpha International. A former City banker, he is the author of *God At Work* (Continuum International Publishing)

Living it out

Recently my long-held view that operating in business and the market place as a Jesus follower is a great privilege and opportunity, has been reinforced by these three things:

- ***The Bible teaches that there is no such distinction between what is secular and what is sacred – everything is within God's economy. Therefore I must choose to be the same person in every facet of my life. I must recognise the sacred in my ordinary day to day living. I should practice virtue in work, at home, and when out and about in the ordinariness of life!***
- ***Business leaders recently agreed that to succeed in our current 'driven' world you need to be authentic and demonstrate integrity in all aspects of your life and do it with passion so that you communicate inspirationally.***
- ***The typical church culture is disconnected from everyday culture to some degree. There can be a sense of unreality in the church experience because my Monday to Friday world is all about the cut and thrust of the market place. So I must strive to make my everyday culture better not a Christian sub culture.***

Paul Lindsay is a chartered surveyor who owns/manages a project management consultancy.

Salt and light in the workplace

James Featherby

Salt that brings some flavour, but does not dominate. Light that brings some clarity, but does not judge.

Yes, but how?

After 30 years of working in the City of London, for one of the world's greatest law firms, one might be tempted to look for evidence of tough battles won against injustice; of precious souls snatched from the noose of greed; and of courageous stands taken over ethical dilemmas. But actually it's not been like that at all.

For the most part it's been about valuing the temporal and the material as much as the eternal and the spiritual. It's been about the companionship of good friends, the pleasure of doing a good job, and the satisfaction of providing for family and others. It's been about explaining to clients why it's best to be legal, empowering others to fulfil their potential, and writing contracts that are clear and fair. It's not often been about doing the extraordinary. It's more often been about doing the ordinary, but differently.

It's been about recognising a worldview of individualism, materialism, utilitarianism and pragmatism, and trying to live out the opposite.

It's been about forgiving those who have hurt me, praying for those who have frustrated me, and accepting the lessons that arise from my shortcomings. It's been about trusting only who God says I am.

SALT THAT BRINGS SOME FLAVOUR, BUT DOES NOT DOMINATE. LIGHT THAT BRINGS SOME CLARITY, BUT DOES NOT JUDGE.

It's been about valuing the imprint of God to be found in everyone, of looking to see where God is working both sides of the street and following his lead to seek a more human working environment. And yes sometimes of sharing my innermost beliefs.

And latterly, but only as the season has become right, it's been about speaking truth to a community I love.

It's been about straining and praying for the Kingdom of God, then resting in the knowledge that the timing is his, then standing in amazement as his plans unfold.

But mostly, it's been about faithful presence.

James Featherby chairs the Church of England Ethical Investment Advisory Group and is a former partner of Slaughter and May.

Resources

Supporting Christians at Work, Mark Greene (LICC)

A concise guide for pastors which sets out the vision, the theological foundations and provides a host of practical ideas for everything from preaching to groups to décor that can help create a worker-friendly church without distorting the rest of the church's work. Available from www.licc.org.uk .

The Heavenly God of Earthly Work, Darrell Cosden (Authentic)

A genuinely original book which makes the case for the eternal significance of our daily work. A tightly argued, important theological reflection.

The Christian Medical Fellowship (CMF) works to unite and equip Christian doctors, students and healthcare professionals. The fellowship brings together more than 4,000 doctors and 1,000 medical students, and links with around 70 similar bodies worldwide.

They run a one day course called the Saline Solution which is designed to help Christian healthcare professionals bring their faith into their every day work and recognise God-given opportunities to demonstrate Christian love and concern without being pushy. The course has helped hundreds of doctors, nurses and other healthcare workers to become more comfortable and adept at practising medicine that addresses the needs of the whole person.

If you are interested in holding a *Saline Solution* course in your area please contact CMF at info@cmf.org.uk. To find out more about CMF visit www.cmf.org.uk.

THE BIBLE TEACHES THAT THERE IS NO SUCH DISTINCTION BETWEEN WHAT IS SECULAR AND WHAT IS SACRED – EVERYTHING IS WITHIN GOD'S ECONOMY.

Thank God it's Monday, Mark Greene (SU)

A fun, popular level book which includes material on the theology of work, vocation, ministry, evangelism, ethical challenges and work-life integration.

Small group resources

Christian Life and Work, Mark Greene (LBC)

A six-part, two-hour film, it includes a leader's guide linked to *Thank God it's Monday.* Topics include: theology of work, evangelism, relating to the boss, truth-telling, pressure, spirituality at work and work/life integration. Each session includes a creative Bible reading, teaching, group exercises and commentary on the issues raised from a check-out lady, a mechanic, a housewife, an IT clerk, a teacher and a company director, www.licc.org.uk.

Life on the Frontline (LICC)

With six short films and discussion material for groups, the series explores how we can help one another live fruitfully and faithfully for Christ in the ordinary places we live our daily lives, www.licc.org.uk.

I Love My Work, Robin Scurlock and Steve Goss (Terra Nova)

Six studies for small groups preceded by a helpful exploration of the key issues for leaders. Can also simply be read. Topics include: God's view of work, calling, success and failure, time, money and stress.

For more materials on whole-life discipleship and work, including free resources and downloads, go to www.licc.org.uk.

Celebrating Work

Mark Greene

Thanksgiving, harvest and work

Harvest was traditionally a time to celebrate the first-fruits of crops that had been grown. Here in 21st century UK the first-fruits of most of our labours are no longer new potatoes in March, bushels of barley in August or boxes of Bramleys in late September. Around 530,000 people are still involved in farming but, for the rest of us, work means things like cleaning offices, making deliveries, writing software, serving meals and delivering lessons. The rewards of our labour and the provision God makes for us are usually the wage that comes weekly or monthly, and we may see this as the main fruit of our work. Biblically, however, work, cannot be reduced to just an instrument for provision. God's intentions for work are much richer and broader. Work is central to his mission – a key component in fulfilling the Abrahamic promise to bless others, a key context for seeing God's ways lived out – 'thy will be done on earth as it is in heaven'. In sum, a primary arena for mission in the broadest sense.

Thanking God for work

It can be hard, it can be exhausting, it can be exhilarating, it can be fun . . . but work is one thing everyone has to do whether it's at home, in school, at church, in the office, in the field or in a factory. In fact, as Genesis 2:15 tells us, we were created to work. God, the worker God, who planned, implemented, finished, reviewed and celebrated his own work of creation, gave humankind purposeful, creative work to do: 'The Lord God took the man and put him in the Garden of Eden to work it and take care of it.'

PURPOSEFUL, PRODUCTIVE WORK IS STILL PART OF GOD'S PLAN FOR US AND WORK CAN STILL BE THE SOURCE OF MANY, MANY JOYS AND SATISFACTIONS.

Tragically, Adam and Eve rebelled against God and that rebellion had consequences for work: enter toil, drudgery and futility. Nevertheless, purposeful, productive work is still part of God's plan for us and work can still be the source of many, many joys and satisfactions. There's the joy of getting a job done, of working with other people, using a skill, being creative, solving a problem, developing a product or service that makes someone's life just a little better, cleaning a street so that disease doesn't spread, serving a coffee with the kind of smile that makes someone want to come back the following day . . .

Thank God for such opportunities.

Of course, we all do a lot of work that isn't paid but which still contributes enormously to people's lives: babies fed, beds made, homes decorated, ingredients turned into nutritious, delicious meals, hedges cut, cars washed and so on. There is joy in that just as there is also joy in being paid so that we can feed, clothe, house, educate, treat those we are responsible for. There is the joy of having money to give to God, to give to those in need, to help someone along a good path, or up from a fall, or simply to put a big smile on someone's face . . .

Thank God for such opportunities.

God uses work in other ways too – to develop and hone our talents and skills in the service of others, to learn to do all we do in his strength, not just in our natural abilities, and to learn to do whatever we do 'with all your heart, as working for the Lord, not for human masters, since you know that you will receive an inheritance from the Lord as a reward.

It is the Lord Christ you are serving' (Colossians 3:23–24).

Thank God for such opportunities.

Work is a central part of God's mission. There are some 29.14 million workers in the UK. The workplace is the single biggest mission field we have, and for most of us it's the place where we spend the most time with people who don't know Jesus. It's the place where we already have relationships, and lots of them. The average person in work connects, talks to, writes to, meets with and emails at least 50 people a week. Some people – teachers, for example – may connect to hundreds in a week. Unlike some overseas mission fields, we don't have to figure out the culture, we don't have to learn the language or the jargon, we already know it. Furthermore, the workplace is the place where we see people in all kinds of situations – at their best and sometimes at their worst. It's the place they get to see us, too, and to see in what ways Jesus might be alive in our lives, to see what difference he makes to our work, to our response to rebuke and reward, to success and to failure, to pressure and to ease, to rivals and colleagues, to bosses and subordinates. It's the place we learn to grow in the fruits of the Spirit – love, joy, peace, patience, goodness, faithfulness, gentleness, kindness, self-control.

Thank God for such opportunities.

It's the place we get to bless people and minister to them in all kinds of ways – by doing good work on time, by going the extra mile, by encouraging others, by getting them a cup of coffee when they don't have time, or sharing a sandwich, by noticing if someone is down, by praying for them without them knowing, by offering to pray for them, by celebrating their successes and commiserating with their disappointments, by befriending the person no one else likes … In short, by showing love.

Thank God for such opportunities.

The workplace is also a place where God disciples us. Why wouldn't he? Why wouldn't he use our bosses and colleagues to teach us about pride and humility, about when to say 'yes' and when to say 'no'? Why wouldn't he use our everyday situations to prompt us to pray, to trust in his provision and in his timing? Why wouldn't he teach us to become people of our word in the workplace – to do what we say we will do when we say we will do it? Why wouldn't he teach us about learning to practise forgiveness and about learning to say sorry in the place where we spend over 40% of our waking lives? Why wouldn't he want to teach us, as he taught Joseph and Daniel, that he has wisdom for our work?

The workplace is the place where we see people in all kinds of situations – at their best and sometimes at their worst.

Thank God he uses such opportunities.

The workplace may well also be the place where we learn perseverance and resilience, the place where day by day we are sharply aware that our values are not the same as other people's, where we feel like aliens and exiles, as Peter puts it in 1 Peter 1. It's the place where some, maybe most people around us will regard our trust in Jesus as odd, quaint, ridiculous, weird, stupid. It's the place where we may suffer because we believe there's no other way, no other truth and no other source of life. It's the place where our gracious Father may teach us to thank him for such opportunities to suffer for him.

Thank God.

The workplace is the place we may get to stand up for truth and justice – to go to bat for a colleague who has been maligned, to challenge an unjust practice, to make sure that someone gets the bonus they deserve, or to nip some gossip in the bud.

Thank God for such opportunities.

It's the place we get to share good news as well as show it. It won't happen every day or even every week but over time, as trust grows, the Lord often provides opportunities to testify to the difference that God makes in our lives: that he helped me get through that really difficult patch, that he helped me not bear a grudge against that colleague, that he helped me say 'sorry' to someone I'd offended, or indeed to testify that he helped me in the work itself, to do something better or faster than I have

ever done it before or to do something really difficult – firing someone, going to tell a parent their child has been in an accident . . .

Thank God for such opportunities.

The workplace is the place where over time we may well also have an opportunity to share the gospel directly, to do some Bible study, to invite a colleague to Alpha or Christianity Explored or just out for a coffee with some Christian friends they may like. Again, it won't happen every day, but over time, as trust grows, as we pray and as the Spirit leads, God who is probably wooing our colleagues in a whole variety of ways may graciously grant us the opportunity to share the gospel.

Thank God for such opportunities.

There may be Christians from other churches in our workplace so there may be an opportunity to pray and work together in mission. Or we may be the only Christian but, either way, we should go to work as the individual representative of the body of Christ, supported, just like an overseas missionary, by the prayers, encouragement and wisdom of our brothers and sisters in our local church.

Thank God for such opportunities for God's people to work together.

In sum, the workplace isn't just a place where we can participate in God's rich and diverse mission; it's also the place where we can come to enjoy a richer relationship with him, to learn that he cares about everything we do and every aspect of our lives, to learn that he is interested in all of it and that we can talk to him about all of it, to learn that he is in us day by day, minute by minute, second by second and that he is with us. He is Emmanuel, God with us, day by day, minute by minute, second by second. May we have eyes to see and lips to testify.

Thank God for his lavish and extraordinary grace in, through and at work.

The workplace isn't just a place where we can participate in God's rich and diverse mission; it's also the place where we can come to enjoy a richer relationship with him.

A Prayer of Thankfulness

Father, thank you for:
a job to do
resources to use
people to celebrate
skills to create.

Thank you for:
a product to produce
a service to provide
a challenge to meet
people to benefit.

Thank you for:
a budget to honour
a boss to please
a deadline to beat
a standard to meet.

Thank you for:
the contribution I have made
the money I am paid
the reward of serving Christ
in all,
in all,
in all of this.

Mark Greene

Mark Greene is LICC's Executive Director
www.licc.org.uk

A High Value of People

Laurence Singlehurst

Over the last few years the importance of the workplace and how we as Christians can make a difference both where we work and how we work, has come back onto the church agenda. Many of us long to make a difference through our values and the way we work, and our Christian history tells us how. From the 18th century, pioneering Christians in the business world have made a difference by realising that people have a high value.

A high value of people is an extraordinary value. It is at the heart of the Christian message because Christ died for all (2 Corinthians 5:14). This gives us a very powerful picture of how valuable people are. In the Old Testament we see that we are created in the image of God; in the New Testament we are told that Jesus died for us. For us!

Samuel Budget, an 18th century trader during the rise of Methodism, bought from people in a ruthless fashion and sold to people making maximum profit. He was then convicted that people actually had value and therefore he should buy from them so they could make a profit, and sell his good products at a fair price. His approach to business was embraced by Methodism, his story was published and his principles began to impact the world of commerce far and wide. We also have the wonderful examples of Sunlight Soap and Cadbury where business owners began to treat their workers with value and provide good salaries and good places to work. However, in recent years, through the pressures of commercialism and our consumer society, some companies that once held to these values now feel under pressure to let them go. As individuals we can often get caught up in the competitiveness of our environments and we lose a sense of our colleagues' value and lose sight of the fact that the way we treat them is significant.

OVER THE LAST FEW YEARS THE IMPORTANCE OF THE WORKPLACE AND HOW WE AS CHRISTIANS CAN MAKE A DIFFERENCE BOTH WHERE WE WORK AND HOW WE WORK, HAS COME BACK ONTO THE CHURCH AGENDA.

Imagine it this way: gardeners recognise that in the south-west corner of your garden you can create a micro climate; there is more sunshine if it is protected and you can grow plants in that corner that will only flourish there. When we go to work with a high value of people we can influence maybe two desks to the left and the two desks to the right and create a micro climate. A friend of mine, Julie, started a new job and found the little corner she worked in wasn't very friendly. People only made cups of coffee for themselves, but when Julie made one, she asked if she could make a drink for anyone else at the same time. She brought in cakes for her birthday and, after one year, a relatively short time, a little bit more sunshine had come to that corner of her office. Julie's example changed the entire nature of that small community. Now everyone offers to make coffee, everyone brings cakes in on their birthday, and a little bit of the Kingdom of God has come to that previously lonely corner.

Property developers are often seen as the shark of sharks, the toughest and meanest of the big fish that live in the city. In the 70s and 80s there was a highly successful firm of developers and their work always seemed to be good for the environment. They created buildings that were great to work in and that were priced at a fair price, yet everyone made a profit. They were called Hazelmere Estates and they were famous because they seemed, in essence, to have a high value of people at the heart of their business. David Pickford, the MD at that time, was a Christian man who believed it was vital to treat people with value as well as making a profit and he did both.

Many people have commented on the changes in the way people are now made redundant. Previously it might have been done by your boss or the owner of the company but now it seems to increasingly be the function of the Human Resources department. It can be cold and clinical, and the human touch, the sense that each individual is valued, seems to have gone with it. This is a slow trend of seeing people as a widget in the system, with no value and dignity. Yet there are still companies that decide to do something different. I led a carol service a number of years ago for a famous merchant bank which placed a high value on employees. They made it clear that no one would ever be made redundant by the HR department or sacked by someone they didn't know. If, sadly, someone had to be let go, the news would always come from the people they worked for, redundancy or terms would be as generous as possible and therefore each person knew they were valued. Every Christmas, employees were given a free turkey and they could choose a small, medium or large one. If you chose large they suggested you bring a lorry! This company maintained, based on their Jewish tradition, that having a high value of people was a better way to do business. They could speak with some authority as they were, and still are, one of the most profitable banks in London. They did not find having a high value of people a problem but a bonus.

AS WE VALUE PEOPLE, WE SHOW THEM SOMETHING OF HOW GOD FEELS ABOUT THEM AND HOW MUCH THEY ARE WORTH TO HIM.

So as you and I go to work or meet our friends at the school gate, let us take this value with us. As we value people, we show them something of how God feels about them and how much they are worth to him. We may be the ones influencing company policy at a high level; we may be looking out for a friend or colleague who is having a difficult time, or simply offering to make others a coffee when we can. Whatever we do, as we value people, it will change everything.

Welcoming Disabled People

Our churches should be snapshots of our communities, reflecting God's love for all. With one in seven adults of working age being disabled, if disabled people are missing, then the church is incomplete.

Facts about disability in the UK

- One in seven families with disabled children is going without food.
- A quarter of disabled people say they have no choice or control over their everyday lives.
- One in three disabled people lives in substandard accommodation.

As Christians, we believe that God created everybody equally valuable – regardless of gender, race, ability or health. And when Jesus was here on earth, he went out of his way to spend time with people that society had rejected – involving them, loving and defending them. How are we following his example? Who are we spending time with? Are any of our friends disabled?

Things to think about

Is your building accessible?

Even though the law says that public buildings like churches must be accessible for disabled people, many churches are lagging behind. In many communities, it's easier for disabled people to enter the local library or leisure centre than a church. Wouldn't it be amazing if churches were at the forefront, setting an example on this issue?

There are many ways that we can make our buildings more accessible including reserved, convenient parking spaces and step-free access, using ramps or lifts. Although building work can be daunting, there are often simple, creative solutions such as hiring temporary wheelchair ramps.

As Christians, we believe that God created everybody equally valuable – regardless of gender, race, ability or health

Are your meetings inclusive?

- Some disabled people might need extra help to get the most out of church activities. Large print song and notice sheets, an induction loop or a sign language interpreter can help during meetings.
- Parents of children with autism can find it helpful to have a quiet chill-out area.
- The use of visual aids and practical activities in home groups will help to engage people who don't feel confident in traditional Bible studies.
- Are there ways for people with disabilities to play their part, use their gifts and talents in your church?

Are you a welcoming community?

If your church has very few disabled members, find out what's going on in your neighbourhood through support groups, care homes or sports clubs for disabled people. Perhaps they need some practical help, from gardening to driving, or even borrowing a venue. Some disabled people will struggle to get out of the house, so how might church come to them?

Where do we start?

If you don't know where to start, the best people to ask for help are the disabled people in your church and local area. Ask them what they would like from your church and how they would like to get involved. Don't be afraid to make mistakes! Misunderstandings may arise, people will get things wrong, or say the wrong thing. None of us is perfect, and mistakes give us the opportunity to demonstrate grace, humility and forgiveness.

For some practical advice, or to share your stories of welcoming and including disabled people, visit www.livability.org.uk/church or email communitymission@livability.org.uk.

community

'As the local church we are called to be Christ's hands and feet on earth.'

Researching Your Community

Before we kick start any long term outreach and community programmes, we need to understand the nature of our community, the needs there are, and the gaps in provision. The best programmes don't do things *for* the community but work *with* the community to resolve issues and provide solutions to local needs.

Community outreach will look different in every village, town and city because every area, and every church that serves it, is different. But when it comes to planning our activities, there are some common things we can all be thinking about and some great resources that can help you.

The best projects are ones that are sustainable over the long-haul so it is worth spending some time before you start making sure you are serving in the right areas and have the necessary resources to keep the work going. There may be times for increased and focused activities such as fun days or weekend social-action projects, but ideally think about ways you can serve your community on a week-in, week-out basis. That way we become integral to community life, build relationships and get to know people as well as helping to bring change that may not be possible in the short-term.

COMMUNITY OUTREACH WILL LOOK DIFFERENT IN EVERY VILLAGE, TOWN AND CITY BECAUSE EVERY AREA, AND EVERY CHURCH THAT SERVES IT, IS DIFFERENT.

Get talking

- Take to the streets with a quick questionnaire. It's also a great way to meet new people and to discuss your desire to bless the community (and will likely get a better response than dropping one through local doors). Or you could hold a community event and provide a way for people to feedback local issues there.
- Talk to the council and police. They will have loads of information about the area, its needs and ways you can be part of the solution.
- You could speak to local schools, health visitors, shopkeepers – in fact anyone involved in the community – to find out what they think the needs are.
- Look at the statistics for your local area. Try entering your postcode into www.neighbourhood.statistics.gov.uk or www.upmystreet.com. What does it say about public service provision in your area? What do you learn about crime, local schools, health and employment?
- Organise a focus group meeting. This involves gathering a sample of the community together in one place and chairing a discussion about needs in the community. To encourage people to come you might want to provide food and drinks. Also, make sure you keep to time and ensure that participants understand the purpose of the meeting and how you plan to use the information afterwards. Make sure someone is taking notes on the discussion and that key points are recorded. An alternative to this would be to go out and visit other community groups, such as lunch clubs for the elderly, mum and toddler groups, youth clubs, etc. and ask the organisers if you can conduct your focus group at their meeting.

Think about

When you know the needs of your community the next thing to think about is where you, as a church, are at. Think about:

- The number of resources available to you such as people, time, skills and money.
- The things you are currently doing, how they are going and how they could potentially be added to or improved.
- What links you have already with other churches and organisations in the area that could help you address some of the issues in your community.
- Consider using the resources detailed on the next page to help your church engage with the process of community research and mission.

We can all learn something from each other and can all bless one another if we're willing to work together.

Working together

One of the key messages of HOPE has been unity amongst churches and it has had a wonderful impact across the UK as churches have joined together to serve their communities. We can all learn something from each other and can all bless one another if we're willing to work together; so whether you're a big church or a small one, think about who you work with and begin to build relationships with each other. It may take time and energy to work out the common ground between you but it will be more than worth it for you and your community.

Resources

Tearfund Discovery

Discovery is a practical process to help churches understand the needs of their community and plan ways to become a transforming influence within them. It's suitable for your leadership or for your whole congregation, perhaps run through small groups. The course brings together biblical insights, training tools and Tearfund's experience in helping churches respond to needs in their community. The toolkits guide a core group through a creative and accessible training and development process. Within the process churches learn the spiritual foundations for community development, identify their gifts and talents and the needs in the community.

Discovery helps churches develop the capacity to address problems unique to a church's community and culture. It teaches how to research, develop, grow and monitor a project and is designed to be fun and hands-on.

DISCOVERY IS A PRACTICAL PROCESS TO HELP CHURCHES UNDERSTAND THE NEEDS OF THEIR COMMUNITY AND PLAN WAYS TO BECOME A TRANSFORMING INFLUENCE WITHIN THEM.

Tearfund supports the course by providing a team of experienced church in the community advisers who can provide advice on how to manage the process including, costs, training and ongoing support. You can contact the team by email at discovery@tearfund.org.

Livability – Getting to know your neighbours and Community Health-Check

Livability runs a course on getting to know our neighbours and working with them to transform the community. Find out more at www.livability.org.uk in their events section. They have also produced a 'Community Mission Health-Check' that you can download for free, to help you review where your church is at in relation to 10 core factors for sustainable mission. www.livability.org.uk.

Community Transformation Projects

These ideas will work at any time of year but you will also find additional community transformation projects throughout the calendar and in the following sections.

Cafechurch

'We have four or five regular attendees with no church background.... It works very well as an intergenerational meeting with young teenagers, through to people who are retired.' Nigel, cafechurch Trowbridge (run by Trowbridge Baptist Church)

'Cafechurch is an important witness in the heart of the city. We have had opportunity to engage with friends and passers by and we have had a number of good conversations.' Lesley, cafechurch Norwich

'One pair of "guests" has on a couple of occasions met up for Bible study and discussion with a couple of our team members.' Andrew, cafechurch Birmingham

Cafechurch provides a fresh expression of community, bringing people into the relaxed café atmosphere of a coffee shop to deal with issues from a faith perspective. At cafechurch you may tackle issues such as fair trade, the environment, stress, adoption, parenting, debt or divorce - with quizzes, interviews, round table discussions, live music, good coffee and great conversation!

What is the cafechurch network?

The cafechurch network was established in 2008, to train, resource and support churches across the UK to run a cafechurch in their community. Churches have connected or even reconnected with their community with this opportunity to deal with issues from a faith perspective in the relaxed high street coffee shop setting. Through this venture, churches have engaged with their community and built relationships with people who do not, and would not, go to 'church'.

The first cafechurch began in Costa Coffee in Welwyn Garden City and it worked so well that the founder was given permission to put a cafechurch in every Costa Coffee in the UK.

Cafechurches are places where people can come to be part of a community, discuss issues from a faith perspective and receive spiritual and practical help. Subjects discussed are topical issues that impact on our everyday lives, things like parenting, debt, fairtrade and stress.

Getting started

- ***First understand the context*** – who are you seeking to reach? Sit in the coffee shop or the shopping centre and take a look around you. See the kinds of people that come in and are around. This might be an opportunity to strike up a conversation with people and also to prayerfully reflect.
- ***Understand your purpose.*** What are you seeking to do? Do you want to make connections, link people to your church, make friends, start a new church or influence your community?
- ***Make a plan!*** Where will you host the cafechurch? How are you going to invite people? Find out more about training provided

by cafechurch network (www.cafechurch.net). cafechurch network will also provide you with publicity resources to invite people (though most people come because a friend invites them).

- ***Set up a team.*** You will need welcomers, table hosts, prayer co-ordinators, a media relations co-ordinator and admin help. Where will you advertise? In which local media? How can you encourage the church to invite friends? What subjects are you going to cover? Cafechurch network provides resources to develop subjects aimed at the group(s) you are trying to reach.
- ***Consider how you will review what you are doing.*** Set a timescale to review what has gone well and what needs doing better. Remember to celebrate small things that went well.

Contact details

www.cafechurch.net
T: 020 8664 8506
E: info@cafechurch.net

'We see cafechurch being an "outreach" from the churches. Many people can't easily make Sunday mornings or find the structure too rigid for them – this could be the place they meet with God in their week. We have already prayed for and seen a couple of people healed; staff love the evening.'

Ann, cafechurch Worcester

Caring for Ex-Offenders

Vision

ONE Caring for Ex-Offenders' vision is to reduce reoffending by reintegrating ex-offenders into society through the local church. They equip churches, through training and advice, to enable them to support ex-offenders live transformed lives.

Caring for Ex-Offenders (CFEO) coordinates a link between someone coming out of prison and a local church community in order to better assist the individual's successful resettlement into society. They do this by training a CFEO team in a church near to where an ex-offender is relocating, in order to mentor and support them. The mentor establishes a relationship with the individual whilst they are still in prison, visits them if possible, meets them at the gate on release, and helps them attend initial appointments and cover their basic needs.

Set a timescale to review what has gone well and what needs doing better. Remember to celebrate small things that went well.

Grants available see www.cinnamonnetwork.co.uk for details

The church CFEO team can then offer friendship, and help individuals recently released from prison to achieve their goals for resettlement, to be less likely to offend, and to live as a part of a stable community.

How does it work?

1. An individual who wishes to be linked to a local church on their release from prison completes a CFEO referral form.
2. CFEO obtains risk and needs assessments from a member of prison staff and the Probation Officer.
3. CFEO contacts a church on their network that is suitable for the individual and near to where they are relocating. They ask the church if they are in a position at that time to support the individual.
4. If the church agrees, CFEO passes on the individual's details to the church CFEO co-ordinator. If not, they try another church on their network in the area until they find one that can help. CFEO also informs the individual that they have been linked to a church, and provides them with their assigned mentor's name.
5. A member of the church CFEO team contacts the ex-offender whilst they are still in prison, tries to visit, and on release, meets them at the gate.
6. The mentor meets with the ex-offender regularly to help with any of the practicalities of resettlement. CFEO staff are available to answer queries and assist the church in any way to offer this support.
7. CFEO contacts the church at intervals to assess the progress of the relationship and check if they need any further support.

Benefits

Coming out of prison can be a daunting experience. Not only are there practical issues of finding accommodation, employment and meeting basic needs, it can also be emotionally and socially challenging as an ex-offender seeks to reintegrate into a community. Often ex-offenders have negative social contacts or are living in a completely new area, which can be isolating.

The benefits to someone being linked to a church for support upon release from prison are that they can immediately join a supportive and welcoming community; they have a support network of a mentor and befrienders who can walk with them through the difficult early steps, encouraging them as they work towards achieving their hopes and goals for the future.

As the local church we are called to be Christ's hands and feet on earth, and who better than the body of Christ to be demonstrating his grace and concern for those who've been in prison, and for their loved ones? CFEO offers churches the support, tools and advice to welcome and care for ex-offenders in their community.

Challenges

Supporting an individual who has been in prison can require persistence and a willingness to go the extra mile. This is why CFEO encourages a team based approach, rather than linking an individual to just one person within a church. This means the responsibility of support can be shared and there will always be an available point of contact for the individual.

Supporting an individual who has been in prison can require persistence and a willingness to go the extra mile.

Getting started

Join the CFEO network

The first step to getting involved is to contact CFEO to register your church on their network.

Once your church has signed up to the network, CFEO offers the following resources and services:

- They send you a complimentary CFEO Church Handbook and their latest newsletter which includes the details of upcoming events and training opportunities.
- The CFEO team is on hand to answer any questions you may have about the Church Handbook, or about recruiting, training and equipping members of the church to get involved.

Gather a team of volunteers

Once you've joined the network, CFEO would encourage you to start putting a small team of volunteers together who will be able to support an ex-offender.

The team must be integrated into and accountable to the church leaders. The different roles include:

- ***Church CFEO coordinator*** – this person heads up the team and is the key point of contact for everyone involved with the ex-offender(s), both church members and external organisations.
- ***Coach/ mentor*** – an individual who builds a sustained relationship with the ex-offender, offering practical help and coaching towards life goals. Ultimately a coach should be a 'friend with purpose'.
- ***Befriender(s)*** – individuals who provide friendship.
- ***Prayer team*** – a group who are dedicated to praying for the team and ex-offender(s).

There may also be others in the church who can offer specific expertise or additional practical support.

Whilst it is useful to have clarity on who within the team is fulfilling certain roles, the roles are not necessarily distinct (for example a mentor is also likely to take on a befriending role) and roles will vary as to the support the individual needs and the size and resources of your church. Smaller churches might like to partner with other local churches to pool resources and support somebody together.

Training, Resources and Support

CFEO will let you know about training days in your local area, or can partner with you to run them at your church.

CFEO Coach Training is a two-day training event usually held on two Saturdays, a fortnight apart. The first day covers the need to care for ex-offenders, where to start, risk management and the practicalities of supporting ex-offenders. The second day looks at mentoring skills including communication, boundaries and the process of coaching an individual to meet their goals.

CFEO also offers suggestions of ways in which you can be involved in supporting those in and out of prison, through prayer, letter-writing and other volunteering opportunities, whilst you are waiting for a CFEO link. They also provide information about other tools which can help to support ex-offenders, e.g. the Marriage Course, Addiction Recovery, Bereavement Course, and Debt Counselling.

WHEN I CAME OUT, SOMEONE FROM THE CHURCH MET ME, WHICH WAS QUITE PROFOUND. HE BROUGHT ME INTO A FAMILY.

During the linking process, CFEO serves as the liaison between the church and the ex-offender and can offer guidance as you draw up an agreement and put support in place.

After a link has been made, they will check in with the church periodically to hear how the link has gone. You can also contact the team at any time for support and advice.

CFEO can link you with other churches in your area involved in this work, for sharing experience and expertise.

There is no cost and never any obligation to accept a CFEO link if you feel unable to offer the necessary support at that time.

Contact details

To find out more or to join the network, please contact the CFEO team at:

www.caringforexoffenders.org
E: info@caringforexoffenders.org
T: 0207 052 0332

Testimony from Tom, an ex-offender. He has now been out of prison for over 10 years and is still attending church and going strong in his faith.

'The most critical or vital part in an inmate's walk with God is that moment of release. If there's no one there to take them in and give them a chance, or a blessing, they have no hope. When I came out, someone from the church met me, which was quite profound. He brought me into a family. Lots of these guys inside have no family but relationship is what it is all about. It's not just me getting to know the church, it's the church getting to know me.'

Church Leader, London
'When the formal reopening of our church took place, one of the passions of our community that became clear was to be a church for all people. From the early days of our existence as a congregation, various members of the congregation had a desire for us to be a church that cares for ex-offenders. We organised an evening's training for prison ministry and caring for those on the fringes of society, and it was there that an initial enthusiasm was fanned into flame.

'We spoke about it, met a few times and have put in place what is required for us to care for those who have been released from prison, so we do it in a way that cares for our fledgling congregation as well as integrating the ex-offender into the life of the church. A few of our community have taken advantage of the CFEO training and we are putting things in place that will enable us to welcome an ex-offender into the life of our community. The team at CFEO HQ have been great, providing advice and training where needed. I love how CFEO looks for the right fit on both sides and takes the timing into account. It is only in the last month or so that we have really been in a position, practically and pastorally to welcome an ex-offender, and CFEO simply maintains a dialogue with us. I am really looking forward to our community being enriched by our partnership with CFEO as we seek to serve God in this way.'

Grants available see www.cinnamonnetwork.co.uk for details

Prospects

ONE

'I don't mind people knowing that I struggled with church because of my learning disability. I just couldn't understand what people were talking about. Then I started going to a Prospects Ministry Group. They helped me to learn about Jesus, how he died for us and about forgiving everybody.'

Sarah, Lincoln

Sarah became a Christian, then helped to start a group in her home church. Now she helps lead the group and is a regular member of a Prospects ministry team at a major Christian celebration event in Lincolnshire.

Vision

Prospects is a Christian not-for-profit organisation that values and supports people with learning disabilities so that they live their lives to the full.

This is achieved in two main ways:

- Through managing supported living, domiciliary or residential services for people with learning disabilities in partnership with local authorities.
- Through encouraging, training and supporting churches to welcome and include people with learning disabilities.

The latter has led to the development of an accessible model of discipleship group that works well for adults with learning disabilities. It is run by churches and facilitated through Prospects advice, training and resource materials.

Benefits

The key issue for people with learning disabilities is access to truth. Limited vocabulary, comprehension and concentration span make it difficult for people to grasp the gospel as it is generally expressed in churches. Complex words and abstract ideas together with figures of speech like metaphor and simile combine with the length of sermons to render much of a church service meaningless to many people with learning disabilities. The principle benefits of Prospects Groups is that people are able to participate effectively in Bible teaching, worship, prayer and Christian fellowship despite the communication and intellectual barriers created by their learning disability.

The benefits for the people serving

The majority of people who get involved in Prospects Groups are not only encouraged and excited about the spiritual growth they see in group members, but feel that they get more out of being involved than they put in. The leaders get truly blessed as they give their time and gifts to serve people who are so special to God.

No professional background is needed, nor experience of working as an evangelist; only a heart for seeing people with learning disabilities grow spirituality and a willingness to be led and equipped by the Holy Spirit. The groups need teachers and worship leaders, and many people have found that as they get involved in these roles, God uses their offering and develops gifts of communication that are a real blessing to the group.

The key issue for people with learning disabilities is access to truth.

Challenges

For some people the thought of working with people with learning disabilities is scary. Ignorance in society has led to confusion between learning disability (formerly mental handicap) and mental illness. People may be afraid of being attacked, of not being understood, or of not being able to make themselves understood. People may be hesitant about starting a conversation with a person with learning disabilities because of any of these concerns. Churches may be reluctant to consider undertaking this ministry because they consider it 'specialist,' and they don't know how/where to begin. Let's start by remembering that every person with a learning disability is loved by God and is made in his image. Often finding the first words is the hardest bit of a conversation but you may be surprised at how much you have in common with someone with learning disabilities once you get chatting. If you have any concerns or would like to get some advice, please contact Prospects.

How easy is it to replicate this idea?

Prospects Groups are easily replicable and groups can start small, growing as word spreads of what's happening. There may only be a handful of people with learning disabilities in a church or a nearby supported-living house. When those people begin to attend and enjoy the group they will start inviting their friends.

The essential elements of a group are really no different from a regular house group with worship, Bible study, prayer, fun and an opportunity to develop supportive friendships. The differences are that worship and teaching need to be interactive, songs need to be carefully chosen and introduced, the language used must be thought through, and things should be done for shorter periods than in other settings.

Resources needed

Prospects can advise your church on the process of preparation and training needed prior to getting a group going. Prospects has a wide range of resource materials that can be used for groups and by individuals. Among these are the Easy-to-Read Bible together with a series of 12 books of daily Bible Reading Notes, each of which is available in audio format on CD. Five CDs of specially written songs add to the range of worship material that can be used in a group, or for individuals to enjoy at home.

Bible study material for teaching in groups and Makaton resources are a great help for people who use signing as a preferred means of communication.

Costs

The cost of establishing a group is relatively low if a church room is provided free of charge. The initial teaching and worship materials would cost around £50-100, with a training day run locally by Prospects costing about £15 per person.

Contact details

www.prospects.org.uk
E: info@prospects.org.uk
T: 0118 9516 977

'I live in Llandudno, North Wales, in my own flat and I am supported by Prospects to lead an independent life. Last year I became a Christian. I had been thinking about going to church for quite a long time and talked to my support workers about it. I went along to Emmanuel Church, which is near where I live, and is where some of the support workers go. I had a lot of questions about God and people from the church helped me. They really welcomed me and made me feel part of the church. I feel I have changed a lot since becoming a Christian. I know right and wrong and I know about good discipline and bad discipline. I find it easier to ask for help now. I have a Good News Bible which my support workers help me to read and understand. I think more about other people and like to tell people about Jesus. I go to a home group in Llandudno which is great; it's easy to talk there and to pray for each other. You don't know how much Christianity has helped me; I pray and take advice from the Lord.'

Darren

Grants available
see www.cinnamonnetwork.co.uk for details

Refugee Support Network

ONE Jahan arrived in the UK two years ago due to his family's political involvement in his home country. He was alone and just 15 years old, missing his family every day. Due to recent unrest in his home country, Jahan is not even able to call or email his family as all communication to the country is being monitored.

Jahan is extremely bright and his teachers say that he has real potential to excel academically in the UK. However, as a result of the on-going violence in his own country, Jahan's mental and physical health are deteriorating due to stress and anxiety.

He is an example of a young asylum seeker with amazing potential who is in desperate need of support and encouragement in order to realise his potential. The Refugee Support Network has been supporting him through an educational mentoring programme. His mentor reports back on a weekly basis that Jahan is focusing in his mentoring session and he says that having a mentor is helping him to progress. In particular, Jahan has told us that he appreciates the encouragement from someone he respects, and that this helps him to study hard and not give up, despite his difficult circumstances.

'Every day I thank God for my good teacher and my mentor. I ask myself "why me?" why do I have such good people in my life?'

17 year old Somali refugee

Vision

The Refugee Support Network (RSN) supports young people affected by displacement and crisis, through an educational mentoring programme for unaccompanied refugee and asylum-seeking young people in the UK. This helps the refugees to access and progress in education so that they can achieve their potential. Investing in education creates hope for the future, both for the young refugees in the UK and for those who return to regions of the world affected by conflict.

The educational mentoring programme links up recently arrived young asylum seekers and refugees with a member from their local community who spends one hour per week with them, helping them with an agreed aspect of their education. In addition, mentors offer social support, providing a stable adult relationship, and help with understanding their new culture and local area, as well as accessing local services.

Benefits

For many of the young people that the RSN supports, the UK is the first place where they have been able to access education and they tend to be very keen to succeed and progress in their studies. An educational mentor gives them a much better chance of doing well and progressing in their education. In addition, for many their mentor will be the only adult engaging with them who is not paid to do so, which is often very meaningful to them. Most of them have social workers, solicitors and teachers, but often no adult who spends time with them simply because they want to. The young people have had to leave their home countries because of conflict, persecution and oppression, and many have lived through significant trauma. They may have been separated from their families to flee to the UK, meaning that they have little social support here. Through the support of educational mentors they can know some comfort, care and encouragement.

Benefits for the people who serve

Those who mentor often report that spending time with refugee and asylum seeking young people helps them to gain refreshing perspective on life and how privileged we are in the UK to live in freedom, safety and peace.

'It's been such a pleasure getting to know each other. We meet in a café one evening a week to go over any schoolwork she's finding tough, with lots of laughter and a humbling insight into some of the struggles she faces. She is such an inspirational young lady who is determined to overcome the barriers she faces to succeed at school and build a better life for herself. I love the opportunity to get alongside her and provide support in such a practical way.'

Mentor

IT'S EASY TO START A MENTORING PROGRAMME IN YOUR AREA – ALL YOU NEED IS SOMEONE IN YOUR CHURCH WHO IS COMMITTED AND PASSIONATE ABOUT ISSUES FACING YOUNG ASYLUM SEEKERS AND REFUGEES.

Challenges

The young people referred to the educational mentoring programme have often been through extremely difficult experiences in their country of origin. In addition they, like teenagers the world over, are going through a tumultuous and often confusing stage of life. Whilst some young people are easy to mentor, others require patience, perseverance and lots of encouragement!

How easy is it to replicate this idea?

It's easy to start a mentoring programme in your area – all you need is someone in your church who is committed and passionate about issues facing young asylum seekers and refugees in your local community. They would need to recruit volunteer mentors, help conduct CRB checks and organise training (which is provided by RSN). In addition, the mentoring coordinator would need to build relationships with local colleges, assess all referred young people and introduce each young person to their mentor. The coordinator will also need to oversee the progress of each pair, reporting back regularly to the RSN central team.

RSN envisages that each community franchise will oversee ten mentoring relationships, meaning that the mentoring coordinator would not need to spend more than one day a week running the programme. (This could be a paid or voluntary post depending on the church.) Each church will need to make an annual contribution towards the central running costs of RSN to ensure that the management and oversight role which the central RSN office will provide is sustainable.

RSN will provide training for the coordinator and the educational mentors, as well as ongoing management and support of the mentoring coordinator. They will also give you all the help you need with systems, processes and resources, including child protection policy and training, in order to make setting up the programme relatively straight forward.

Tips

- It is important that you identify someone in your local church who would either be willing to run the programme voluntarily one day a week, or raise the appropriate funds to employ a member of your church to do this.
- It would also be advisable to discuss this project with the wider church to ensure that there are at least ten individuals who would be interested in becoming educational mentors.
- A needs assessment of which services in your local area are already available to young asylum seekers and refugees would be helpful to ensure that you are serving your community in ways that address the real gaps and needs.

Getting started

Contact the RSN office to arrange a time for their team to meet your church leadership team.

Contact details

www.refugeesupportnetwork.org
E: via website
T: 0776 9695 377

My mentor helps me to stay strong and stay in college. I have a lot of things in my life which make me sad and sometimes I want to give up. It's good to have someone to help you stay focused.
18 year old Syrian asylum seeker

Sunday Night Live

Our SNL has been established well over a year now and has matured into more than just an evening with excellent music, coffee and company. Different monthly themes have captured the imaginations of the local families and churches and we've seen people's lives healed and transformed as they hear about how much Jesus loves them.

Mike, Merseyside Christian Fellowship

Vision

Sunday Night Live (SNL) provides the ability, training and resources to host live entertainment with a twist of faith in high street coffee shops. Each event is hosted by a group of local Christians and features top quality artists and inspirational speakers from across the UK. SNL and its spin off events, such as Live Lounge for weeknights and Live and Loud for 13-18 year olds, aim to build a community of people who enjoy coffee, cakes and live entertainment with a twist of faith.

SNL's Mission Statement: To see communities brought together from whatever background or ethnicity, to provide live entertainment in the form of artists and speakers, free of charge, to inspire those present and highlight the Church (its values and beliefs) in such a way that people see God and Christianity in a new light.

Benefits

SNL is a great way for Christians to take their friends to a neutral venue, giving them the chance to hear the amazing good news of the gospel during a professional and fun event. SNL will provide all the information, advice and guidance you need to run an event every month and they provide a ready-made outreach team of dedicated people to do all the initial work required.

Costs

The average initial cost is around £500, with a further £50 per month subscription but costs can be trimmed if your budget is low or you are a church plant. SNL will provide you with banners and flyers to advertise your event, training for event hosts, and use of iConnect – a service enabling you to keep in touch with people who attend your events. You can also book artists from an extensive database by getting in touch with the SNL team.

Getting started

Download an info pack at www.sundaynightlive.org.uk

You don't need to approach the store you'd like to host the event directly as the SNL team will do that on your behalf (they already have relationships with the main coffee shop chains and many independent ones too).

Contact details

www.sundaynightlive.org.uk
T: 07445 957632
E: admin@sundaynightlive.org.uk

WOW is all I can say. This is a GOD thing and I am so glad that we are a part of it. We were packed out with more chairs having to be brought in from one of the churches. The band was great and the lady who spoke (who also does Thought for the Day *on Radio Nottingham) just hit the right spot. We are very excited and just concerned that we were so full; what will we do as we continue to grow? But what a great problem to have!*

Rob, Eagle's Nest Church, Nottingham

In the early days Christians didn't worship in churches... 2,000 years on Johnny Kinch (founder of Sunday Night Live) has re-kindled the idea, but with a modern twist.

Diane Louise Jordan, *Songs of Praise*

Open Doors

Princes Avenue Methodist Church in Hull began their Open Doors Project in 2000 to welcome asylum seekers and refugees. The church had found many were fleeing to the city from Africa and the Middle East, so they developed a Thursday afternoon Drop In session to meet with them. They also provide pastoral support visiting clients at home and in hospital, putting clients in touch with relevant agencies and organisations, helping provide furniture and household items/food and helping with language barrier issues.

WOW is all I can say. This is a GOD thing and I am so glad that we are a part of it.

Parish Nursing Ministries

Parish Nursing is a way for nurses to reach the local community and provide holistic health care. Parish Nurses do not perform clinical tasks but fulfil other aspects of the wider nursing role, such as being health educators. They are able to identify the health needs of those they serve, either providing support or making sure appropriate care is sought. Find out more, including training details, at www.parishnursing.org.uk

Street Pastors

Street Pastors is an inter-denominational Church response to urban problems, engaging with people on the streets to care, listen and chat.

It was pioneered in London in January 2003 by Rev Les Isaac, CEO of the Ascension Trust, and has seen some remarkable results, including reduced crime in areas where teams have been working. There are

now some 9,000 trained volunteers in around 250 teams around the United Kingdom.

Street Pastors is designed to provide a reassuring presence in local communities. Individual street pastors seek to listen to and talk with people in their local community, to provide information on local agencies, help and services, and to discourage anti-social behaviour.

Practical help provided by Street Pastors includes handing out space blankets outside nightclubs, and flip-flops to clubbers unable to walk home in their high-heels; giving out water, chocolate for energy, personal alarms and occasionally even condoms; carrying bus timetables, and ensuring that vulnerable people are safe. Street Pastors remove bottles and other potential weapons from the streets, in order to discourage violence and vandalism.

Street Pastors is also supported by 'Prayer Pastors', who do not patrol but who provide support to street pastors by praying for them.

'Street Pastors is about Christians rolling up their sleeves and getting involved in practically responding to the problems of crime and safety. They are like beacons on our streets and I want to see them shining brightly in every constituency.' David Burrowes, MP

Find out more at www.streetpastors.co.uk

Beyond the Streets

Beyond the Streets exists to see a world where people are free from the chains of prostitution and sexual exploitation. They want to help women who have been forced into prostitution to rebuild their lives.

Their work started as an informal network of grassroots projects in the 1990s aiming to help people caught up in prostitution find a way out. They uncovered some shocking truths:

- 68% of women in prostitution meet the criteria for Post Traumatic Stress Disorder in the same range as victims of torture.
- 75% of women in prostitution became involved when they were children.

'Street Pastors is about Christians rolling up their sleeves and getting involved in practically responding to the problems of crime and safety.

Since the 1990s Beyond the Streets has helped 75 local initiatives in the UK, involving over 800 volunteers, and has worked with 6,000 people caught up in prostitution. As a result many of the women have been empowered to change their lives for the better. As the only national Christian charity working to provide real options and ways out for those who want to leave prostitution, they are also providing an increasing number of direct services to those still caught up in abusive power structures.

A difference made

The message they hear over and over again from women and girls who have found their way out is that without support they would not have been able to leave prostitution. They say 'we would not have been able to be where we are if it was not for the love, care and continued support we received'. It is so great to hear stories of women who have been able to rebuild their lives. They have become nurses, authors, teaching assistants, and are in managerial positions in high-end retail outlets and restaurants.

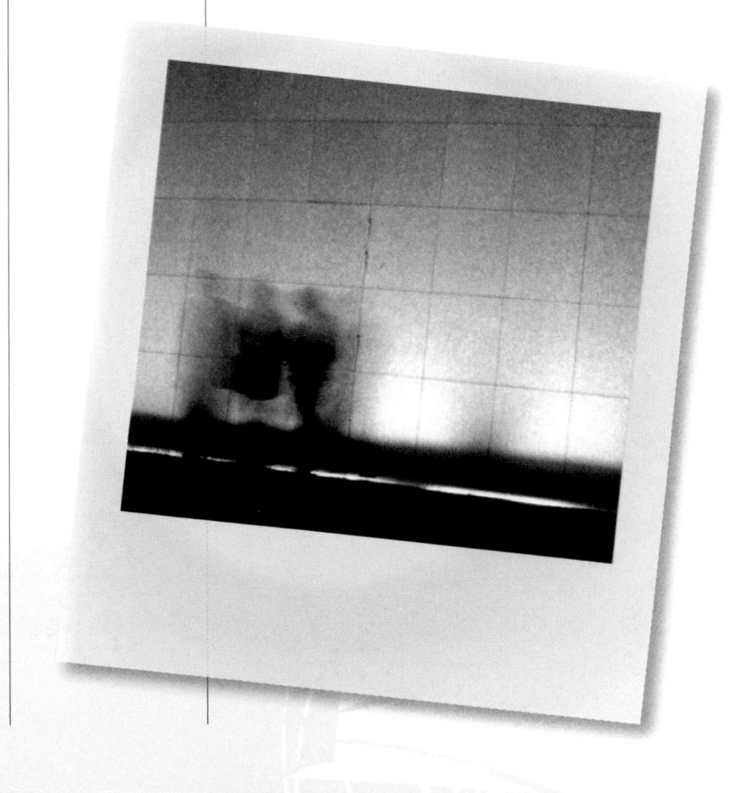

Take Maria for example. She made contact with Beyond the Streets through their telephone support line and was desperate for help. She lived in a violent environment: a brothel, where she was constantly sexually exploited and monitored. After a few phone conversations and some advice, Maria decided to escape and got out, leaving the city she was in and moving to another part of the UK. Woman are incredibly vulnerable when they leave prostitution so Beyond the Streets referred her to a safe house. Together with the safe house staff, Maria was able to explore her options. Despite fearing being found by her previous 'employer', Maria settled in well and eventually moved into her own flat. Beyond the Streets supported her, made referrals to other help services, and enabled Maria to have the space to think and dream of what she wanted to do with her life. Maria has now started her own business and is attending college.

Beyond the Streets has a rich history of providing high quality support to a diverse range of initiatives supporting women to leave prostitution through training, conferences, resources and direct provision. They have also been a consistent source of developing and disseminating good practice nationally through training and resources, always with the highest of standards and integrity.

Ours is the story of what can be achieved when a small number of people come together with a heart to make a difference.

Contact details

Whether you are a church leader or an individual you can contact Beyond the Streets to find out how you can get involved. They can connect you with local projects or discuss providing training for you to start a project of your own.

www.beyondthestreets.org.uk
E: office@beyondthestreets.org.uk

Ours is the story of what can be achieved when a small number of people come together with a heart to make a difference and, with God's help, change what they can: a lot! Beyond the Streets worker

Working in Schools and with Families

If you're looking to engage with young people then schools are a great place to start as that is where they spend the vast majority of their time. Many schools also appreciate extra help and support and there are numerous ways you can get involved.

GREAT IDEAS

Take a lesson

Schools are increasingly being asked to provide a wide range of curricular activities for all pupils but don't always have the specialist staff to deliver it. What specialism do you have? Can you give an hour a day or a week to help out in your local school? Whether it's RE, Geography or PE, an expert in the field is often welcome in any school. Find out who is already involved in your local school and seek to work with them and support them. If there is no obvious involvement, approach the school via a teacher you know or a letter to the head of the department you are keen to work with.

Book a team

Lots of organisations offer teams who could come and add impact to your current schools programme. A team could visit for one day or for a whole week, working with you to arrange a full timetable of activities including assemblies, lunch clubs and after school clubs. To make sure this isn't a 'hit and run' activity, it's best to have a local team who are able to follow up after the event by running a drop-in club or a discipleship course. Organisations like Youth For Christ, Christians in Sport and Message Trust offer a number of different teams.

Many schools also appreciate extra help and support and there are numerous ways you can get involved

Start a club

The extended schools programme has increased opportunities to run after school, lunch time and holiday clubs for all ages. Looking for ideas/material? Scripture Union and Youth For Christ offer good resources you can use.

Easter, Harvest and Christmas

Use the key events in the Christian calendar as an opportunity to engage with local schools and help young people understand the spiritual significance of the celebrations. See the Calendar section for ideas and inspiration.

Help children learn to read

Many schools welcome helpers who can offer even one hour a week to sit and listen to children read. It can boost a child's confidence and skill, whilst blessing over-stretched schools.

Painting, gardening and more!

Offer the services of your church to help the school with its upkeep by doing any painting, decorating, gardening or clearing jobs. Contact the Parent Teacher Association Chair or the school's Head to see what practical needs you could meet.

Prayer Space

Scripture Union Associate Trust, Graceworks, in partnership with 24/7 Prayer has started an initiative to create prayer spaces in schools helping hundreds of young people engage with prayer for the first time.

A Prayer Space turns an ordinary school classroom into a place where pupils are encouraged to try out different forms of prayer, expressing their feelings about themselves and their world to God in creative ways. A small team spends a full week in school, inviting every Year 7 to 10 class to experience the Prayer Space at least once as part of their RE timetable.

'We usually do a short lesson to introduce the kids to the different zones in the room, but then we let them just get on with it,' explains 21-year-old Sam Fowler, an intern with the SU South East regional team and a volunteer with Prayer Spaces for the last few years. 'There are spaces to think about forgiveness and letting go of past hurts; places to express thanks for things in our lives; an area to consider the hurdles and obstacles we are facing; and time to think about the wider world,' says Sam. 'Afterwards we wrap up and ask them how they felt about praying. Some don't even realise that's what they've done and we say "Congratulations – you've just prayed for the first time!"'

A Prayer Space becomes a place of peace and safety in the middle of a busy school day. The room is kept open during lunch and break times for those who want to use it again in their own time. Volunteers are always on hand to talk, answer questions and even pray with young people who ask.

'Prayer Spaces definitely change the spiritual temperature in a school,' reflects Sam. 'We see people more open to talk about faith issues. Teachers say that young people seem more relaxed and engaged while we're around, and behaviour gets better all round the school. 'We've seen some cases where the Christian Union group in the school has just exploded after we've been in for a week.'

You can pray anywhere, in any way. It's not boring, it's awesome.

Even though the team are careful not to proselytise in school hours, they were delighted when last term, one pupil came back in over lunchtime saying she had thought carefully about what she'd heard and she wanted to give her life to Christ. 'What we try to communicate is that prayer is simply about being real with God,' says Sam. 'You can pray anywhere, in any way. It's not boring, it's awesome. And prayer can change your life, so just give it a try!'

Primary to Secondary

LifeMatters is a Scripture Union initiative to help pupils make the transition from primary to secondary school. It is organised by local churches and run in partnership with schools, taking place for one day in the Autumn. Find out more at www.scriptureunion.org.uk.

School Pastors

In February 2011 a sister organisation to Street Pastors called School Pastors was launched nationally after several trial projects. School Pastors aims to reduce bullying, anti-social behaviour and drug use, and to remove barriers to learning. They mentor young people within a school setting, and patrol outside to break patterns of negative behaviour at the end of the school day.

www.schoolpastors.org.uk

Top tips for working in schools

- Build a relationship with schools first.
- Ensure the team perform 'professionally'.
- Follow any guidelines given by the school.
- Ensure you are thoroughly rehearsed.
- Be prepared for the unexpected – including heckling!

To my shame, I used to see our church toddler group as unimportant, even trivial. I saw it as just a few mums gathered together to natter about kid's stuff – as a man I stayed away. Somehow I had segregated the group from the rest of the life and mission of the church.

It took me some years to realise that every week in my church some 50-60 unchurched parents with toddlers not only gathered, but were happy to be there, and were not only willing, but eager, to do Bible crafts, hear Bible stories, sing Christian songs and even say prayers! With 52% of under-fours in England attending a church-led Parent and Toddler Group (bringing with them a multitude of adult carers) this is an amazing opportunity for the church!

I was amazed to find that though most who attended our group weren't yet believers, they considered themselves part of our church. I began to realise that the Parent and Toddler Group was not some fringe group but, in the economy of God, a central plank in his mission to our community. More people from the surrounding area attended this group every week than any other in the life of the church.

We began to ask ourselves how we could deepen the relationships and draw those who attend further into the life of the church. We knew part of that was supporting, valuing, encouraging and resourcing the Parent and Toddler Group Leaders to be more effective in their ministry, and we decided we wanted to do this, not only for our own leaders but also for other groups in the UK.

WE BEGAN TO ASK OURSELVES HOW WE COULD DEEPEN THE RELATIONSHIPS AND DRAW THOSE WHO ATTEND FURTHER INTO THE LIFE OF THE CHURCH.

We set up 1277 which aims to bring together all who have a heart to see Parent and Toddler Groups make a difference in our society. 1277 seeks to represent the views, concerns and interests of church-based toddler groups to those in authority both in Westminster and around the country. By registering your group and receiving information from 1277, you will become part of a movement that together will make a difference to our society, by reaching one parent and one toddler at a time.

Rev Richard Hardy

Director of the Entheos Trust.

www.theentheostrust.org

Messy Church

TWO THREE

A year ago we thought that we would give Messy Church a go. With a word from God to 'cast our nets over the other side', we continue to catch. Through this Messy Ministry God excites us, challenges us, surprises us, refreshes us and, through simplicity, disciples us. Messy Church: what a mighty powerful tool for outreach, gathering and renewal!

Vicky, Maidenhead

Messy Church began in an Anglican church near Portsmouth as a way to run church that would appeal to the whole family, and that would give families an opportunity to grow in faith together rather than in isolation from each other.

Though Messy Church varies, it usually happens once a month on a day and at a time that suits families and team. It begins with a warm welcome then an activity time which runs for about an hour and may have up to ten Bible-themed crafts, activities, competitions, games and experiments. For each activity there are one or two team members to explain it and its link to the theme of the day, and to grow relationships with old and young who come to try things out. Families are free to do as much or as little as they like. At the end of this time, everyone takes part in about 15 minutes of more explicit worship: usually story, song and prayer, then they enjoy a meal together before everyone leaves. The values are creativity, hospitality, celebration, being appropriate for all ages and being Christ-centred.

Families enjoy being in a church where they don't need to keep their kids quiet; and where they can experience the generosity and goodwill of Christian community. It's fun for the teams too and they relish being part of a team that is doing effective mission in their local church, growing in faith and confidence as they see God at work.

Whilst Messy Church could be run anywhere, the key is to contextualise it to make sure it works for what your community wants and needs. There is a network of support from BRF (Bible Reading Fellowship) who resource Messy Church across the world, making sure all the health and safety issues are dealt with. Plus there are plenty of practical resources to help you get started and to sustain the momentum, ranging from books and a DVD to face to face training, local networks and national events. See www.messychurch.org.uk for details or call 01865 319700.

'It's brought new life to our church'

From mums at Messy Church

'You don't have to be religious to come – we're not!'

FAMILIES ENJOY BEING IN A CHURCH WHERE THEY DON'T NEED TO KEEP THEIR KIDS QUIET; AND WHERE THEY CAN EXPERIENCE THE GENEROSITY AND GOODWILL OF CHRISTIAN COMMUNITY.

Resources

Scripture Union aim to equip and support those who work in schools and help churches share the good news with children in schools. Find out more at www.scriptureunion.org.uk.

ExploRE is a new resource to use with 11-14 years olds as part of their Religious Education lessons in school, giving students the opportunity to investigate the Christian faith in a way that is fresh, engaging and relevant to their everyday lives. Each lesson plan unpacks key areas of Christian beliefs and practices by providing an exciting array of activities: games, drama, art, discussion and interactive illustrations. The pack also includes a DVD that incorporates vox pops, short films and testimonies from Christians themselves. To find out more see www.exploreforschools.co.uk.

Pure Creative Arts uses theatre in education productions, interactive workshops and ongoing projects to work in schools and youth groups across the country to tackle subjects that young people find hardest to talk about. They have resources available for assemblies, lessons, workshops and an 'Impact Programme' – find out more at www.purecreativearts.co.uk.

Saltmine Theatre Company presents the gospel in churches, schools, colleges, prisons, youth clubs and universities, touring with a wide range of productions. They also run summer holiday initiatives. For more information visit www.saltminetrust.org.uk.

Superbook is supported by Superbook.TV which provides an online community for the entire family to learn more about the Bible. Christian Broadcasting Network (CBN) is updating these hugely popular animated programmes for children age six and upwards, to help them engage with Bible stories. Parents can download special resources to help them guide their children as they grow in their faith. For more information visit www.superbook.TV

Kidz Klub

'We have a graphic design apprentice called Andy who first came to Kidz Klub when he was four. He has a brother who is in prison – yet he is working hard on achieving his dream of being a designer. Another young man from Toxteth has trained to become a sound engineer – he wants to use his trade to bring God's hope to others, and he does so regularly on mission trips overseas.'

ONE

Kidz Klub Liverpool

TWO

Kidz Klub is a weekly children's club that can be run by any church in their local primary school. Their heart and passion is to bring hope to the UK's inner cities through high quality, sustainable children's work.

The government has a scheme called 'Extended Schools Provision' which requires schools to put on breakfast clubs and after-school clubs based on syllabus subjects. There are many Art Clubs, Maths Clubs and PE Clubs, and Kidz Klub adds to this with a free RE after-school club.

There are some huge advantages to working within a school as part of the school day:

The school gets to offer a free after school club, open to all their pupils.

Parents who send their kids get an extra hour of free childcare as part of the school day.

Your church gets to build long term, sustainable relationships with many pupils and their families (usually averaging 50 children per school - with a volunteer ratio of 1 to 10!)

The challenge of running Kidz Klub like this is commitment. To have an impact on your community requires a committed team who are passionate about Kidz Klub. As you work in schools, cancelling the club for a week because you are short staffed isn't an option.

However the benefits far outweigh the challenges. Kidz Klub have many stories of former Kidz Klub members - young people from inner city areas who have family members who are in gangs or are in prison, but who have chosen to live a different way. Using this approach of working in schools is a low-cost way of connecting with children on a weekly basis, bringing them hope and showing them the way God wants them to live their lives.

If half of the churches in the UK ran a Kidz Klub in a local school with only 50 kids attending, together we could reach 1.2 million Kids!

Kidz Klub has the experience and the resources to help your church reach your local community through schools work and they would love to share their experiences with you and give you the tools you need to transform the lives of children and families in your community.

Getting started

Visit www.kidzklub.biz to find out more and to see all the resources available. A Kidz Klub starter pack is £100 and contains resources for an assembly, a term's worth of sessions, two t-shirts and an advertising banner.

Contact details

www.kidzklub.biz
E: jonny@frontline.org.uk
T: 0151 733 3373

If half of the churches in the UK ran a Kidz Klub in a local school with only 50 kids attending, together we could reach 1.2 million kids!

Christian Victory Group – I Care Projects

ONE

Christian Victory Group (CVG) aims to provide quality and affordable childcare services for the people in their local community in Brixton, London.They offer a high quality pre-school education that boosts a child's development. The nursery understands that children are complex and have inter-related needs which can be best met by people who care in a professional and safe environment.

Their pre-school curriculum consists of maths, language and literacy, personal and social development, creativity, science/technology, and

Bible knowledge. These subjects help prepare children for the transition to upper school and help to develop the confidence and self-esteem of the child as they play alone or interact with other children.

'When we first came from Germany to London about 15 months ago, Jonas did not speak English at all and he missed home, especially his grandparents and the children from his previous nursery. The staff at the Victory Nursery welcomed him with their 'big family' like atmosphere. Jonas settled in quickly and he really enjoys going there. Jonas has not only learnt to speak English, but has now started spelling and writing.As parents, we feel confident to say that Victory Nursery provides excellent childcare. A great variety of activities are offered to the children, providing a balance between playing and learning. We believe our son will be well prepared to start school next year.'

Mrs Jenny Geyer

If you'd like to run something similar, contact your local council (Early Years Department) to find out what resources exist in your area and the gaps in their early years provision. Your church can then decide to fill the gaps in service provision in the local community and you may find there is funding available to help you do so.

CVG would be happy to show you round their nurseries and give you some advice on your own project. Just contact Victory Nursery Angel Town on 020 7274 6263 or Victory Nursery – Brixton Road on 0207 733 5626 or visit www.victorynursery.org and www.cvgicare.org.

Grants available see www.cinnamonnetwork.co.uk for details

Safe Families for Children works by supporting parents through a crisis; this then has a significant impact on the lives of children in the local community.

Safe Families for Children

Overview and aims

ONE

Safe Families for Children (SFFC) is a new initiative offering churches a great opportunity to transform the lives of children and families by offering hospitality, befriending and practical support to local families in crisis. It provides an informal but structured way for the Church to work with families who don't have anyone else to turn to. With this support families can stay together, avoiding breakdown and children being taken into care.

This early intervention approach has operated successfully in the United States for over 10 years and has recently been brought to the UK by the Vardy Foundation.

Mission statement

Safe Families for Children extends community support by hosting vulnerable children and strengthening their families in crisis through a network of volunteers motivated by compassion.

The SFFC movement is based on the perspective that the safety and health of the children of our communities are the responsibility of each one of us and that parents are the key to providing a long term safe environment for their children.

How it works

Safe Families for Children works by supporting parents through a crisis; this then has a significant impact on the lives of children in the local community.

The support is voluntary and unpaid and may involve agreeing to host a child temporarily to enable the parents to focus on a short-term crisis (such as homelessness or ill health). It is based on the principle that providing a little support at a key time can alleviate the build-up of stress and may prevent family breakdown and the need for children to be taken into care. It provides an opportunity for the local church to play a vital role at a significant stage of a family's life which could make all the difference to the wellbeing of the child, the long-term stability of the family and ultimately benefit the whole community. Specific voluntary roles such as host family, family coach and family friend enable clear boundaries to be established and support to be given. The whole initiative is backed by rigorous safeguarding, training and a range of policies and procedures. The wider church community is encouraged to get involved by offering time, skills or household goods.

What difference does it make?

SFFC has been working in the USA since 2002 and now operates in 14 states. It has already led to a clear reduction in the number of children taken into state care, as well as demonstrating a range of benefits such as increased immunisation rates and improved child development. Parents also report less stress and better parenting. Besides this direct impact on children and families, SFFC US has also seen a number of states amending their policies to allow volunteers from faith communities to host children. Meanwhile churches have discovered the challenge and satisfaction of living out their faith, making a long-term difference for families and children and playing a significant role in the local community.

In the UK, hard-pressed and under-resourced local authority staff have welcomed the potential of SFFC's early intervention model to support and stabilise families, recognising and valuing its ability to meet a huge need.

How can you get involved?

Because SFFC is a brand new approach here in the UK, please check their website or contact their office to find out how you can work with them:

Contact details

www.safefamiliesforchildren.com
T: 0191 374 4777
E: info@safefamiliesforchildren.com

'Safe Families for Children is a significant and timely initiative which will help transform the lives of children in need of love and security. I encourage churches everywhere to get involved.'

Nicky Gumbel, Vicar, Holy Trinity Brompton, London

'With our teenage children becoming increasingly independent, life was busy with responsibilities at our church in the Tees Valley, and in other situations. With a degree of curiosity, and in a state of open mindedness we went along to hear about Safe Families for Children. Not too long into the talks, and even without having to discuss what we had heard with each other, we both knew that this was for us. We have just completed the initial Host Family training and our assessment is well underway – we are both excited and a little daunted at the prospect of becoming a Host Family.'

Rich and Marcie Costello

'I passionately believe the Church should be at the forefront of responding to the social issues our country is facing at the moment and that this is a great way to do it. The proof is obvious where this project has taken off - there is a real excitement to be involved. We have seen it work, and it is a blessing to both the people who do it and those who receive help. We are not going to solve all the problems of families in crisis but we can come alongside them, showing God's love when they need it most.'

Sir Peter Vardy, founder of Safe Families for Children in the UK

I PASSIONATELY BELIEVE THE CHURCH SHOULD BE AT THE FOREFRONT OF RESPONDING TO THE SOCIAL ISSUES OUR COUNTRY IS FACING AT THE MOMENT AND THAT THIS IS A GREAT WAY TO DO IT.

Working with Young People

Phil Timson

HOPE Revolution

Can our nation truly be transformed for Jesus? We believe it can. Not only that, but we believe that young people should be at the heart of this and can lead the way! HOPE Revolution is a national movement of young people daring to live out their relationship with Jesus, responding to his call 'to go and make disciples of all nations'. We dream of seeing young people, throughout the UK, join together to bring change to their communities, boldly sharing the gospel through words and actions. Being part of the Hope Revolution is to live radically, be different, and choose to completely step out of our comfort zones. It's about young people using their energy and passion to share Jesus and demonstrate his unending love to the world around us.

HOPE Revolution is a powerful expression of unity between many of the UK's leading Christian youth movements including Soul Survivor, Youth for Christ, Urban Saints, Scripture Union and the Message Trust. The vision is to mobilise and empower a movement of young people to live out mission day-to-day, having fresh confidence in the gospel, and daring to share it boldly in word and action. Through this we believe we will see lasting change amongst a new generation of young people.

HOPE Revolution exists to see young people join in with thousands of others to bring Jesus' truth, hope and life to the broken world in which we live. We seek to empower young people to be creative as they communicate their faith relevantly in today's ever-changing culture. May God transform the lives of many young people through a movement of their peers who dare to live a lifestyle of mission, and daily risk getting uncomfortable for Jesus.

Can our nation truly be transformed for Jesus? We believe it can. Not only that, but we believe that young people should be at the heart of this and can lead the way!

Jesus' last words to his disciples were: *'All authority in heaven and on earth has been given to me. Therefore go and make disciples of all nations, baptising them in the name of the Father and of the Son and of the Holy Spirit, and teaching them to obey all I have commanded you. And surely I am with you always, to the very end of age'* (Matthew 28:18-20). Praise God we do not go in our strength! We go in his strength and in the assurance that Jesus, the one in whom we can do all things (Philippians 4:13) comes with us. This is amazing news. Jesus, the ultimate radical revolutionary started the Hope Revolution and now, through us, Jesus is continuing it. As we 'Go', in unity, may we see a HOPE Revolution sweep across our land.

To explore ways in which you can be part of the HOPE Revolution, visit www.hope-revolution.com

Andy Hawthorne: *'We'd love to see hundreds of local groups step out in word and action and grow in faith. We will do whatever we can to encourage them, pray for them and invest in radical next-generation disciples. Thousands of young people will be changed by the gospel building up to 2014 and into the future.'*

Gavin Calver: *'HOPE is all about encouraging more mission together, through our words and actions. See new things happen in your community, be part of churches working together, and see folks in your area come to know Jesus for themselves. God is doing something amazing among young people. Start praying believing and dreaming of all that can be done and be a part of the change you long to see!'*

Mike Pilavachi: *'Let's be obedient to the Great Commission and share God's love with hurting*

people, serving our communities. Let's grab hold of the truth, live a radical life of worship and follow God's call to mission. Most importantly...let's do this together!'

Phil Timson is HOPE Youth Director

Textify - Getting young people to use their mobile phones to start conversations about Jesus

Textify is a challenge from HOPE Revolution that encourages young people to kick-start conversations with friends about Jesus.

There are three simple steps:

Step One Choose: Make a choice and commit to praying for three of your mates for a week

Step Two Textify: At the end of the week text them a question or conversation starter

Step Three Talk: Go for it and speak boldly about Jesus.

The HOPE Revolution vision for Textify is to see conversations everywhere drenched in prayer, leading to young people coming to a deeper understanding of Jesus, and youth empowered to engage wholeheartedly in mission and have confidence in the gospel.

For more information and further tools that could be used to support this challenge please go to www.hope-revolution.com/textify

Resource

Street Dance Crew

YFC have a touring Street Dance Crew available to hire who use dance to connect with young people in a dynamic way. They offer a wide range of workshops and performances which are excellent for schools, churches, community days, festivals and events and they are passionate about inspiring and encouraging young people to use their skills and talents.

Contact info@yfc.co.uk to find out more.

Grants available see www.cinnamonnetwork.co.uk for details

Romance Academy

ONE

'Romance Academy helped me to see that I don't have to do whatever a guy wants; I have a right to say no. For the first time in my life I realised that I am precious and worth more than I previously thought of myself.'

16 year old girl

'Romance Academy is an essential tool for Youth Workers! It has equipped us to address and talk about these hot topics with young people with confidence, knowledge and understanding. Romance Academy has taught us what it means to really love and support the young people we work with and what a fantastic difference that has made in their lives.'

Zoe (Romance Academy Leader, Wirral)

Vision

Romance Academy seeks to break the cycle of damaging relationships by giving young people the tools to make positive choices around their sexual and relational health.

Through structured weekly sessions, team-building activities and a shared pledge, young people gain a supportive community that allows them to set healthy goals, grow in self-esteem and confidence to critique the sex-negative attitudes of their peer groups and wider culture.

The project began life as part of a BBC2 documentary mini-series called, *No Sex Please We're Teenagers* in 2005. The programmes (and subsequently the Romance Academy intervention project) were created to address the underlying causes of risky youth behaviour such as poor self-esteem, low aspirations and lack of positive family/community life. Through a unique 14-week intervention project, 12 young people explored, amongst other things, the value of healthy relationships.

Romance Academy is now a national charity that trains youth workers to run their own Romance Academies, empowering young people with the tools to make intelligent choices; thus helping them to avoid the negative impact that early and risky sexual behaviour could have on the rest of their lives and wider society.

Benefits

Comprehensive and Youth Centred

The Romance Academy material addresses the whole of life and relationships and is flexible, giving young people the space to be heard and to raise the issues they want discussed. Access to accurate information is essential and Romance Academy encourage input where required from local experts on topics such as drugs and alcohol as well as sexual health.

ROMANCE ACADEMY SEEKS TO BREAK THE CYCLE OF DAMAGING RELATIONSHIPS BY GIVING YOUNG PEOPLE THE TOOLS TO MAKE POSITIVE CHOICES AROUND THEIR SEXUAL AND RELATIONAL HEALTH.

Character development

Unlike traditional SRE lessons, the project is not a taught programme but focuses on nurturing self-discovery. The Romance Academy approach prioritises the growth of mature individuals as well as increasing knowledge.

Inspirational leadership

The programme gives young people access to positive role models ('wisdom-sharers') who are committed to journeying with young people for 14-weeks and beyond.

How easy is it to replicate this idea?

The Romance Academy project is incredibly easy to replicate. By attending a one day training course and buying into a three-year licence (£300), Romance Academy equips youth workers/organisations to deliver the 14-week intervention programme in their region, as many times as they like. All you need to run a basic academy is a male and a female leader, a line manager, a venue, young people and the downloadable toolkit.

Tips

- A lot of academies use this project to build relationships with local services within the community – sexual health clinics, the police etc
- Young people can be referred/recruited to your project from sexual clinics, doctors, the police, youth action teams and schools
- Academies run well when they have a mixture of young people from different backgrounds
- Local councils often have pots of money for projects like this
- Try to do a weekend/day away with your group early on. Building a positive community helps to foster a sense of intimacy, which is essential for this project.

Getting started

Find out when the next training day is at www.romanceacademy.org or contact Romance Academy.

Contact details

E: info@romanceacademy.org
T: 0208 416 7344
www.romanceacademy.org

'I've had a load of one night stands and they left me feeling bad. I would go for it all at once and then have nothing. When I heard about the Romance Academy I thought I was ready for it. I now have a girlfriend. I didn't do relationships before 'cos I was scared. I am taking it slowly with my girlfriend and we haven't had sex yet; we have a relationship and it's good.'

Luke, 16

'I was in a long term relationship when I began Romance Academy. During the first four sessions I started to discover what I really wanted and needed from a relationship and it was nothing like the one I was in. I was just going through the motions. I broke up from my boyfriend and I started to make decisions based on what was best for me. Romance Academy helped me discover the person I wanted to be and what I needed to build a great relationship."

15 year old girl

'By the end of the Romance Academy, 2/3 of young people who originally said they would have sex even if they weren't ready, had changed their minds.'

Evaluate

Young people asked to evaluate relationships

'This is the world our teenagers live in, where sex is as casual and as throwaway as fast food. Bombarded by images of sex 24/7, today's teenagers are having more sex, more often and at an earlier age.' So says a BBC documentary film clip used during one of the four multimedia presentations that make up CARE's relationship and sex education programme: evaluate...informing choice.

Media influence is taking its toll on impressionable young people regarding image and sexuality. Sex sells and all around us the pressure of advertising with its airbrushed magazine images, the TV soap storylines and the movies, all contribute to the relentless drive to lose one's virginity and look like the models, celebrities and latest X-Factor stars. Alongside these pressures, it's not surprising that the UK has the highest rates of teenage binge drinking, multi-drug consumption, unwanted teenage pregnancy and sexually transmitted infections in Europe.

It is against this backdrop that the evaluate programme was created and since its launch in 2004, teams of trained volunteer educators have been taking the material into schools and encouraging young people that they are valuable, significant and unique individuals and that their choices matter because they matter.

Over 140,000 young people have already been visited by evaluate teams and the results are promising. Where students are visited every other year with the programme, there is a steady drop in the percentage of sexually active year 11 students. It is clear evidence that the message given in years 7 and 9 is effective in encouraging students to delay and save sex for a committed relationship.

With the understanding that most problems currently hitting young people in the UK stem from low self-esteem, evaluate gets to the heart of this issue by constant affirmation and encouragement throughout the lively sessions, while at the same time tackling some serious subjects such as issues around pornography and grooming for sexual exploitation. Myths about pregnancy and STIs are dispelled and young people are shown where they can go for help.

'Why would young people make healthy choices if they do not value themselves?' asks Sue Lindars, Project Manager for evaluate. She drew attention to one topic where evaluate hopes to make a difference; 'Much of sex education in schools has assumed that young people will have sex under age and promotes 'safe sex' in response to this, meaning condom use. But although condoms make sex safer they aren't 100% effective even when used correctly and consistently. Safe sex is a faithful relationship with an uninfected partner.'

> Young people are encouraged to make a fresh start and make new choices for their own health and well-being in the future.

By bringing a fresh, modern and direct edge to relationship education and lifestyle choices, evaluate volunteers hope to enable healthy decisions that will not lead to future regret. There is a desperate need among young people for accurate and reliable information so that they can make informed choices about when they are ready to have sex and understand the media and peer pressures that are all around them. Those students who regret having sex are assured that there is a real possibility of a new decision. Described as 'secondary virginity' young people are encouraged to make a fresh start and make new choices for their own health and well-being in the future.

Developed to enable Christians to impact society with a positive and healthy message about relationships and sex, the evaluate programme, although not overtly Christian in approach, presents godly principles in a 'non-threatening, non-preachy' way. The heart of this project lies in the belief that every young person is a unique and valuable individual, capable of making and maintaining healthy choices if suitably equipped and supported. 'We believe that our educators will be like a breath of fresh air as they take this affirming message into schools' said Sue. 'We want to show young people that they matter; that they are unique and important, that their opinions and what they say is valued.'

The vision is for the evaluate programme to one day be available to every school across England, Scotland and Wales. Although this will take time to achieve, Christians who are recruited and trained as evaluate educators will be fulfilling the call to: 'Go into the world uncorrupted, a breath of fresh air in this squalid and polluted society. Provide people with a glimpse of good living and of the living God.' Philippians 2:15 (The Message)

For more information and to get involved please see www.evaluate.org.uk.

XL-Mentoring (XLM)

Vision

XL-Mentoring works with young people referred by local schools, pupil referral units, youth services and the Police, who are at risk of exclusion from school, or who have been excluded, and consequently look to anti-social behaviour, criminality and gangs for a sense of belonging, recreation and 'employment'.

Volunteer mentors meet with a young person for two or three hours every week for at least a year. They also contact and encourage them in-between meetings to help them achieve goals that they set together. Mentors are matched with young people through a Mentor Co-ordinator who also provides on-going support.

Home visits are made with families to explain the project and gain approval for the young person to participate, and often a residential weekend of activities for a group of mentors and young people can be used to establish trusted relationships quickly.

LOCAL COMMUNITY MEMBERS WHO BECOME TRAINED MENTORS FIND THEMSELVES BETTER EQUIPPED TO HELP THEIR OWN COMMUNITIES DEAL WITH OTHER LOCAL ISSUES.

Benefits

The young people benefit from a supportive, stable and nurturing role model relationship with their mentor and are encouraged to:

- ***Avoid educational failure*** – stay in (or return to) mainstream school, do their homework and complete their education.
- ***Develop positive attitudes and behaviours*** – improve communications and life skills enabling them to relate better to their peers, family and the local community.
- ***Set fresh goals and work hard to achieve them*** – having a direction in life and a plan of action, and to broaden their horizons and aspirations.
- ***Make wise life choices*** and choose not to become involved with (or to exit from) gangs, crime and anti-social behaviour.

Often families of the young people being mentored also benefit from the project, as the mentor frequently becomes involved in helping the family learn how to deal with the challenges and issues they face. Indirect beneficiaries include the positive impact upon teachers, Police and local communities due to the changes made in the lives of these young people. In addition, the local community members who become trained mentors find themselves better equipped to help their own communities deal with other local issues.

How to replicate this idea

XL Mentoring are training 1,000 mentor coordinators to work with 5,000 mentors across the country. If would like to be a co-ordinator or a mentor you can take part in their two-day training course which covers communication skills, safeguarding, project initiation, monitoring and supervision, and the ups and downs of mentoring relationships.

Each delegate will receive a Coordinator's Manual and five Mentor Manuals for them to use in the field along with other resources. Trained Coordinators and Mentors can also become part of the XLM Network with access to further training, information and support.

Find out about the next training course at www.xlp.org.uk/nationalxlm

Tip

Mentoring can be hard work and there are always challenges to overcome, however, the stories of transformed lives and futures are remarkable and they provide the fuel that feeds the vision for this project.

Contact details

www.xlp.org.uk
E: info@xlp.org.uk
T: 020 8297 8284

Sarah's story

At the age of 13, Sarah had experienced bullying for most of her school life. It began due to her being overweight, and has taken its toll over the years resulting in regular non-attendance at school. As a direct result she was underachieving academically, had very poor self-esteem, and became involved in fights when she retaliated against her tormentors.

Sarah's school referred her to XLP's mentoring project. As part of her induction into the project, she attended a residential weekend where she got to meet her mentor and the other mentees and mentors. During these few days away from her home and school environment she made new friends and enjoyed being part of the team-building activities. This was her first time away overnight out of London.

She has developed a trusting relationship with her mentor and now confides in her mentor about her struggles and how she feels. When she still finds herself bullied she is able to share and discuss it with her mentor. The mentor liaises with the school concerning any issues that arise that are affecting Sarah. So far, Sarah has achieved two out of three goals that she has set herself with her mentor, and has also moved up a set in maths. Her attendance has significantly improved and she is now reading more at home with her mother.

MENTORING CAN BE HARD WORK AND THERE ARE ALWAYS CHALLENGES TO OVERCOME, HOWEVER, THE STORIES OF TRANSFORMED LIVES AND FUTURES ARE REMARKABLE.

Sarah has also begun to work hard towards losing weight. With the support of her mentor she is now exercising regularly and has learned to eat more healthily. The resulting loss of weight has improved her self-confidence and self-esteem hugely. Sarah has told us that having a mentor has meant that there is someone who she can talk to, who encourages and motivates and supports her, and who understands her and cares about her wellbeing.

Youth club

ONE

Highway of Holiness in Tottenham, London, run a youth club to provide young people with a safe environment to come and interact, play, learn and develop their skills. They work with mainly disaffected young people in their community who are involved with gun and knife crime and anti-social behaviour.

The club caters for youth aged 11-19 from all sections of the community including young people from the travellers' community. Young people come to the youth club after school and are given subsidised food from the Highway Youth Café. The Highway Youth Café is a part of the youth club, and gives the young people the opportunity to develop entrepreneurial skills by running the café under adult supervision for a period of time. Each group is responsible for choosing what food to serve or sell, the pricing for food, advertising it amongst their peers, taking orders, serving the food, staffing the tills and doing the washing up. This is designed to give the young people the opportunity to develop their entrepreneurial skills and is judged as a competition by a panel including a local Chief Executive, an adult volunteer, and the customers.

Young people at the youth club also participate in recreational activities such as pool, table tennis, TV and interactive games, football and basketball. Each evening is divided into two parts with the second half of the evening dedicated to personal development and training in areas such as music production, dance, gardening and wrestling.

The youth club helps children who struggle to feel part of a wider community, or have been disadvantaged by an adverse family situation or a lack of opportunities. These children are often hurt, isolated and unhappy but the youth centre can give them renewed confidence and a real sense of well-being.

Yasmin, a 15 year old girl who regularly attends the youth club, turned up early one day and one of the youth workers discovered she had run away from home. After talking the issues through, Yasmin realised she had been in the wrong and agreed to return home. The youth worker took her back and spoke with her family to help them see where Yasmin was coming from. The youth worker kept in touch with Yasmin in order to counsel her and help her build a relationship with her step-father. Through this encouragement, Yasmin started to have a better relationship with her family and paid close attention to her studies. She was even allowed to take her GCSEs a year early and passed with As and Bs.

Find out more about the youth club at www.highwayofholiness.co.uk

One young man came to us as he wanted to leave his gang lifestyle. He was a feared gun man who dealt in drugs; he wanted to change but he didn't know what to do.

Working with gangs

T.A.G. (Targeted Against Gangs Response Team) seeks to build relationships with young men and women caught in the grip of a destructive gang culture. They provide a confidential telephone helpline (Gangsline), manned by trained specialists providing practical advice, support and prayer if requested. They also offer a 'gang exit programme' for those gang members ready to change, and they equip ex-gang members with the emotional, physical, financial and spiritual tools to break free from the downward spiral associated with gang culture.

T.A.G. is developing a website and training to help equip other churches who would like to undertake a similar outreach. See www.gangsline.co.uk for more information.

A life transformed

One young man came to us as he wanted to leave his gang lifestyle. He was a feared gun man who dealt in drugs; he wanted to change but he didn't know what to do. He enrolled at university and got a 2:1 but felt like he was slipping back into the gang lifestyle. He had met with Jesus and felt God told him to come to T.A.G. and took part in our mentoring programme. He excelled and became one of our mentors, going back to the area where he used to be a gun man to help others in a similar situation. At the same time a businessman approached us saying he wanted to train up ex-gang members, so this young man was his first trial. He completed the eight month training programme and became a fulltime employee. His mindset was changed; he was no longer lost but had a real purpose and drive.

TLG: The Education Charity

Vision

TLG is a charity with a Christian ethos enabling churches to work with children and young people at risk of exclusion from school or in crisis in their education. They work in primary and secondary schools with those showing behavioural difficulties and with pupils who have been excluded from mainstream education.

Approximately 370,000 fixed term exclusions are given to children each year; 37,000 of these fixed term exclusions are given to primary school children. These children and young people can end up in negative peer groups, become known to the Police and social services, get sucked into the criminal justice system and ultimately end up in prison. Statistics suggest two thirds of the prison population where excluded from school.

Primary schools (ages 7-11)

Prevention is better than cure so TLG trains groups of between two and 10 volunteer behaviour coaches from congregations to work in their local primary schools using the Early Intervention Programme. These behaviour coaches, led by a co-ordinator, offer coaching one hour a week during term time to children who may be struggling with their behaviour. During the hour the children work on design projects that are curriculum based as well as activities that cultivate strategies for behaviour management. The room and art materials are provided by the school and all the resources for the programme are included in the training given by TLG. The Early Intervention Programme offers a structure that brings school, church and family together in a way that ensures improvement for the children who are struggling in class.

Grants available see www.cinnamonnetwork.co.uk for details

How to replicate this idea

You will need volunteers who can commit to one hour a week during term time and who have some experience of working with children.

TLG will commit to funding half of the costs for each church partner who starts the Early Intervention Programme, meaning costs to your church will be:

Year 1: £1800 or £150 pcm

Year 2 onwards: £1200 or £100 pcm

We adopted Ben when he was 18 months old. It was very stressful from the start. Psychologists said his problems stemmed from deep-seated issues he had before he was adopted. When he hit other children, it wasn't because he wanted to hurt them; he wanted to be noticed. Ben ran away a lot and was very badly behaved. He was unaware of dangerous situations and would often run out in front of cars. He started nursery at three and was always fighting with other children. When it was time for me to pick Ben up at the end of school, I would feel physically sick. Teachers would call me in to explain what he'd been doing wrong. Parents would even shout abuse at me across the playground because of what Ben had done to their children.

When Ben was in reception class, the school threatened to exclude him. I was devastated and heartbroken. I'd waited so long to have a child and assumed he'd be perfect. I just had no idea how to change his behaviour.

Last October, at a parent's evening, we were asked if we wanted Carolyn to help give him some one-to-one support with his anger problems. We absolutely jumped at the chance! Early Intervention coaching has been a godsend; an absolute miracle. Carolyn is lovely and very calming. She calls me weekly about

Ben's progress and Pastor Mark from the church also visits us regularly. Ben has learnt how to deal with his anger, to think about good and bad choices and about consequences to his actions. He's changed a lot; he's matured. His teacher who has seen him the longest - and at his worst - said to me Ben's a completely different child. He is one of the most polite boys in the school.' He has even started approaching other children in the playground when they're fighting, and acting as a mediator!

I have a lot more sympathy for parents in the same situation now. When I see a child kicking off with their mother, I just go over to the mum. I touch her arm and say 'it won't always be like this. It will get easier'. Ben has completely changed and I can finally see a light at the end of the tunnel.

Lisa

Secondary schools (11-16 year olds)

At secondary school level TLG can partner with your church to set up an alternative education centre in a church hall or community centre. You will need to employ a staff team to work with vulnerable young people in an environment that resembles a hybrid of an education centre and a youth centre. The Education Centre will engage the young people for a term or more, working on their learning and behaviour difficulties and seeking to integrate them back into mainstream school. After-school activities and family support are an opportunity for the church to engage the young people and their families.

How to replicate this idea

Becoming a Secondary Alternative Education provider with TLG

You will need to employ a Centre Manager and a number of Learning Mentors to work with small groups of 6 -10 young people. Each day involves four lessons focusing on Maths, English, ICT and Key Skills, helping to prepare the young people for the next steps in their journey. The classroom environment incorporates formal and informal aspects of education so an IT suite and group work tables are alongside a coffee bar, pool table and games station. Referrals will come to the centre from local schools and the local authority who will pay to place a young person at the centre on a term by term basis. The aim is to help the young people overcome their learning and behavioural difficulties, engage with the youth programme put on by your church and see them reintegrated into mainstream school.

I DIDN'T USED TO GIVE NO-ONE A CHANCE AND I WAS ALWAYS ARGUING OVER SOMETHING. I'VE REALLY CHANGED.

Education Centres are more complicated to set up than Primary Early Intervention Centres and equipping a centre normally costs between £12,000 and £18,000 while modifications to an existing building normally cost between £10,000 and £30,000. The fees received from referrals should cover the costs of staffing the centre. TLG can provide the all the support necessary to run the school, including project management, support in opening the centre, fundraising, Line Management support, and Learning and Development Support including Continuous Professional Development.

Costs

TLG works on a Community Franchise basis with the church taking 70% of the fees and TLG taking 30% of the fees from the income received from referrals. TLG does not take any fees for its services until the first child has been referred to the centre.

Dillon's story

Dillon came to TLG having been previously excluded from a number of different schools and alternative provisions. He had spent time in a young offender's prison for robbery and had been arrested on a number of occasions. In his first week at TLG he was involved in a number of aggressive situations, leading to questions as to whether he could continue the programme. However, with ongoing support and guidance from the staff team, Dillon's behaviour changed dramatically within a short space of time. He became a lot calmer, constantly checking his behaviour and refusing to rise to other students' comments or taunts. The change seen in both his academic work and his attitude has been remarkable and family and teachers have both noticed the difference. Dillon himself comments:

'My biggest achievement since being at TLG is that I've learnt how to get on with everyone. I'm more polite- my mum says "how come you talk so nice!" That's the biggest change in me. I didn't used to give no-one a chance and I was always arguing over something. I've really changed.'

Dillon recently undertook a work experience placement and left with the glowing praise of his supervisor who described him as 'a model student with a hunger for knowledge'. Since leaving TLG, Dillon has enrolled on a full-time college course where he has completed a number of IT, English and maths qualifications with 100% attendance. He is now studying to be an IT practitioner.

Contact details

For those who are interested in finding out more TLG have regular Church Leader Days that will give you all the information you need. You can find out when the next day is at www.tlg.org.uk or by contacting the National Partnership Manager on 0845 5083242.

Redeeming Our Communities

Redeeming Our Communities (ROC) is a national charity founded in 2004 with over 35 projects throughout the UK. The charity's main aim is to bring about community transformation by creating strategic partnerships which open up opportunities for improved community life. They work with people of goodwill to create safer, kinder communities. The ROC model has seen crime and anti-social behaviour fall and fresh hope brought to some of the most deprived and challenging areas of the UK, urban and rural alike.

ROC brings together community groups, churches, the Police, the Fire & Rescue service, local authorities, probation, schools and other agencies to encourage them to work together in positive partnerships for practical 'on the ground' change. Projects are based on a proven social need like loneliness, drug abuse, domestic violence, lack of youth provision, troubled families, unemployment, repeat offending, low self-esteem, illiteracy and so on.

The ROC Café, a multi-agency youth club, has been one particularly successful project which has a proven track record in reducing crime and improving confidence and skills. Young people love the ROC Café; one young boy from a home where his mum has to work all hours to make ends meet described it as 'the living room I don't have at home'. The Police and other partners also love the ROC Café, reporting between 25% and 55% reduction in anti-social behaviour where the Cafés are located.

ROC is a tried and tested model which has been adopted in a large number of cities, towns and villages and has a proven track record. If you would like to use the ROC model to run a project in your community please visit www.roc.uk.com or call 0161-946-2373.

ONE YOUNG BOY FROM A HOME WHERE HIS MUM HAS TO WORK ALL HOURS TO MAKE ENDS MEET DESCRIBED IT AS 'THE LIVING ROOM I DON'T HAVE AT HOME'.

Working with Students

Rich Wilson

The greatest hope for our universities being impacted with the love of God is for Christian young adults to be fully prepared for the university experience. This means that the millions of pounds spent employing youth workers is an investment that can see a huge return as Christian youth become Christian adults. According to research[2] only 27% of Christian students attend church regularly at uni leaving a massive 73% disengaged. With better preparation our students could be making a much bigger impact for God at university.

Ripple effect

When Anna turned up to university in 2004, she was prepared. She committed to a local church; she gave herself to being discipled and to discipling others; she led friends to Jesus and encouraged many others to start their journey. With the support and backing of the local church she initiated outreach to clubbers on the Student Union's busiest night of the week. She was effective whilst being a student and sowed seeds that meant the church is still reaping from her work. Today the club mission which she started is a partnership between the Student Union and local church, ministering to up to 3,000 students in a single night. When a Christian turns up to university prepared the ripple effect can be massive.

Imagine more

Imagine that it isn't just a handful of new Christian students that are prepared for university, but a whole generation. Imagine that they go to university ready and excited about facing the challenges and opportunities. Imagine that they are now ready to be part of local church as an adult with a robust theology for what that means. Imagine that they can answer questions on sex, drink and faith with confidence and sensitivity. Imagine that they will join clubs and societies that are full of students who aren't yet Christians and be willing to take on leadership responsibility. Imagine what a whole generation could do who were prepared, linked to churches, prayed for and sent.

We don't send missionaries abroad without the right preparation, so why would we send 18 year olds into Freshers Week without any?

Preparation

We don't send missionaries abroad without the right preparation, so why would we send 18 year olds into Freshers Week without any? University campuses are mission fields with one of the most clearly-defined, unreached people groups in the UK. It is essential that Christians are prepared for the university experience.

Preparing your young people

Be resourced

Get hold of some resources – don't reinvent the wheel. The latest resources give an up to date account of university life. Whilst it is fun to reminisce about your university years, the culture and student mission moves on quickly so our preparation needs to reflect that.

Be intentional

Preparation takes time. Plan an evening or a series of evenings where school leavers from your church or churches across the town can talk through the breadth of issues related to being a student. Topics to cover could include:

[2] *Conducted in 2011 by the Christianity and University Experience*

- How to prepare for the transition from school to university.
- How to make the most of the opportunities and navigate the pitfalls.
- Discuss what university life is like and what to expect.
- Talk about what it means to make new friends and push through loneliness.
- How to find a church you can serve.
- Talk about boundaries with money, sex, drink, porn and dealing with hard times.
- Brainstorm ways to make a permanent impact for God on the lives of those people that students meet.
- Plan what students can do to strengthen their faith and become more of the person God intends them to be during their time at university.

Link to local church

Connecting and committing to a local church has the biggest impact on a student's faith during and after university. The majority of student mission is now being pioneered out of local churches and so it is mission critical that students connect, commit and serve churches.

Action

Be proactive

Tens of thousands of people have benefitted from Student Linkup, a Fusion initiative to connect students and churches. Visit the website www.fusion.uk.com and download the 'Student Linkup App' to find out more.

'Student Linkup connects student to church and church to student. You can find resources and be linked to a church online.'

The website lets you browse a comprehensive list of over 1,000 churches who are cheering on students, read summarised profiles online and their key message to students. This isn't about consumerism, it is about linking students in to churches who will support and encourage them. If your church isn't listed you can connect at http://www.fusion.uk.com/churches

Sending students

The old story

'A couple of the young people are just about to go on a gap year. They are being interviewed and prayed for at the front of church. Rob, Sam, Esther and Emma are half listening. They are distracted, aware this is their last Sunday and they are about to enter Fresher's Week in two days' time. No one has prayed for them and they don't feel prepared for some of the things they have heard happen at university. It is likely only one of them will connect with a church at uni.'

The new story

Introduce a Student Linkup Sunday. Take 10 minutes during a Sunday service each September to stand with Christian students as they make their home among the UK's largest and clearly defined unreached people group.

Pray

In small groups or front-led intercession pray for the thousands of Christian students starting uni this month that they will:

- Find a church and integrate quickly.
- Feel supported by friends and family.
- Make new friends and be a friend to others.
- Make a difference as they love God and the university.

Send

Interview any students you know who are about to start uni. Pray for them and commission them to be good news to the student world.

Interview any students you know who are about to start uni. Pray for them and commission them to be good news to the student world

Give

Give them a present of a Student Linkup School Leaver Pack. This collection of resources is designed for an individual student heading to uni, and provides the best possible start to uni life. It offers insights and encouragement, top tips and discipleship material, to help new students make the most of their time at university.

Welcome back

Your student missionaries will benefit from regular encouragement and prayer throughout their first term and even a visit from a trusted leader. Coming back at Christmas and Easter isn't always easy; they have changed, grown up and need points of reconnection. If you commissioned them, find out how the first term has gone. Invite them to be part of a small group for young adults for the vacation time. Create a group if necessary.

Receiving students

When students are 'Linked up' and are committed to a local church it is time to empower them to reach their peers.

The loveyouruni project is serving thousands of churches to love millions of students

Over the next decade the loveyouruni project aims to resource and encourage thousands of churches to love their colleges and universities. To see a generation of Christian students live with purpose, compassion and conviction, in order that thousands more students would encounter and respond to Jesus. Local church needs to be at the heart of student mission and students at the heart of local church.

Missional small groups

Whether you call them cells, clusters, life groups or small groups, we're talking about small to medium sized missional communities centred on Jesus and making disciples. They form the basis for sustained and effective mission as part of local church ministry among students. These missional small groups are the foundation of the loveyouruni project.

The project has many expressions; sharing stories of how God is moving amongst students and commissioning them to reveal his Kingdom on campus; linking new students to churches; strengthening students and student workers with training and equipping; fresh and innovative mission ideas and action; working together to disciple a generation as they are challenged to be followers of Jesus in their universities and beyond.

Rich Wilson is the National Team Leader for Fusion

Contact details

www.fusion.uk.com
E: hello@fusion.uk.com
T: 01509 268505

Today's students, tomorrow's culture makers, influencers and leaders

In a recent lecture, world evangelist, Os Guinness[3] described how, if we want to see culture influenced by the gospel, the university is a key environment. By the time students become culture makers, influencers and leaders, their world view is already set by the ideas they learnt at university ; therefore, the university represents both a strategic mission field and a unique opportunity.

Students are open to new ideas as they form their identity and world-view away from home and live and work in close proximity to each other. University is normally the first realistic chance unbelievers have ever had to meet a vibrant community of Christians (Christian Union/CU group in halls of residence or the main CU on campus) and to be able to attend well run, attractive events hosted by their peers.

[3] *Os Guinness address given at the Newfrontiers Everything Conference 17/03/2012*

THE UNIVERSITY REPRESENTS BOTH A STRATEGIC MISSION FIELD AND A UNIQUE OPPORTUNITY.

Mission ideas for students

Uncover the Bible

TWO THREE

Uncover is a Christian Union campaign to help students engage with the gospel. It's a series of six Seeker Bible Studies written by international evangelist and author Rebecca Manley Pippert, designed to be read with friends in a one-to-one or small group setting in a coffee shop or bar. The aim is to empower ordinary students to share the gospel with friends who perhaps would not come to church or join a course like Alpha. The campaign has already seen hundreds of students come to faith in Christ and joining their local churches.

Calum Taylor, a geography student at Hull University, talks about the impact Uncover has had in his university context: 'Our CU is passionate about seeing the students at Hull discover Jesus. A number of us have gone through Uncover with our friends. Through using it, I am able to say to my friends: "Have a look with me at this guy called Jesus – I think he is so awesome that I want to live for him, let's see what you think!" It is important to have a warm and honest atmosphere that our friends are comfortable to open up in – and Uncover is ideal for this. As I went through the studies with both of my friends, each time they discovered more about Jesus and became more and more excited about the relationship they can have with him.'

Find out more at www.uccf.org.uk/uncover or take a look at UCCF's apologetics website www.bethinking.org.

Healing on the Streets

What is it?

Healing on the Streets (HOTS) is an opportunity to offer prayer to passers-by in your town, village or city. It usually happens in a place where there is a large footfall and a team hand out flyers, chat to people, and ask if they would like prayer for healing. It enables you to connect with your community every week, powerfully expressing God's love outside of the church walls. Over time you may find you build relationships, create stepping stones for people to come to Jesus, and see them healed along the way.

How to get involved

This idea was started in Coleraine, Northern Ireland, by the Causeway Coast Vineyard and has spread across the globe with new ministries springing up in North America, Africa and Australia. Many churches from various denominations are running Healing on the Streets and seeing many people healed and coming to faith.

If you'd like to run one in our area we suggest you visit an existing HOTS ministry before you start, visit a HOTS training launch, or hear about the ministry personally from one of the recognised HOTS leaders. This will help you decide if it is the right ministry for your church to sustain. If you decide it is HOTS will offer you training and resources and an ongoing partnership.

Please contact HOTS via their website to find out about training.

A story from Canterbury

A lady shuffled towards the chairs and sat down and we went over to her. She had an infection in her chest and had had it for a month. Every time she breathed in it really hurt. We prayed for her and after two or three minutes we asked how she felt and she said she still had the pain so we asked if we could continue praying for her, reaffirming that God loves her. We prayed again and she said, 'It's gone! The pain is gone!' She breathed in really deeply and there was no pain.

We prayed again and she said, 'It's gone! The pain is gone!' She breathed in really deeply and there was no pain.

A story from Winchester

A lady came for prayer with curvature of the spine in both the lower back and between the shoulder blades. Three vertebrae were fused in the lumber region, and her hips were tipped at an angle which gave her restricted movement. After we prayed her hips seemed to relax and the left leg moved down in line with the right leg. She reported that she spent a long afternoon walking round Winchester with no pain, no tiredness or aching in her back, and after a lively evening service she had an incredibly comfortable two hour ride home to the North Cotswolds. Normally, car journeys are uncomfortable. Each day she realises that there is something she can do that she couldn't do before. Praise God!

Resources

DVDs and CDs of Healing on the Streets

This set includes full recordings of all the HOTS training (three discs) and one evening session by Mark Marx.

Training Manual for Healing on the Streets This includes all the teaching on HOTS. You can order via email: healing@causewaycoastvineyard.com

Contact details

www.healingonthestreets.com
E: healing@causewaycoastvineyard.com
T: 0044 (0)28 7032 6161

Creative Arts

Saltmine

In our constantly advancing, creative, media-centric world, many churches still revert to a spoken word-based style of communication with few creative visuals, participation and interaction. Sir Ken Robinson is a renowned expert in the field of creativity and innovation in education. He is passionate about using a language that is accessible, involves participation, ownership and interaction and says that 'Creativity is as important as words'.

We worship the Awesome Creator and are made in his image, therefore we have diverse creative capacities that can bring energy, colour, surprise and excitement into our churches. We have God-given creative strengths that need to be discovered and grown if we are going to really connect and communicate in new and fresh ways - ways that enable accessibility, participation, ownership and interaction.

At Saltmine we are passionate about supporting churches and inspiring all generations through creativity using theatre, media and interactive teaching. We aim to tell God's story and values with grace, truth and an inclusive heart to all. We believe that throughout history, humanity has always loved a story, and a story has the power to engage, equip and bring hope.

One Hope

One Hope is a whistle-stop tour of the Bible, telling the story of the world from creation to the life and work of Jesus (originally written in partnership with UCB). It is valued as an educational tool to support the teaching of Christianity where children learn about the Bible and engage with questions about faith. During a recent workshop following the One Hope performance, two boys from different schools asked our team 'why did you become Christians?' For us this question and many similar inquiries, confirms the value of this visual way of communication.

WE WORSHIP THE AWESOME CREATOR AND ARE MADE IN HIS IMAGE, THEREFORE WE HAVE DIVERSE CREATIVE CAPACITIES THAT CAN BRING ENERGY, COLOUR, SURPRISE AND EXCITEMENT INTO OUR CHURCHES.

One of Saltmine's goals is to enable the Church to transform mission through the creative arts. To this end we produce seeker-friendly plays throughout the year, especially at Christmas and Easter. Experience reveals that unchurched people are more open to come into the church building for a theatre performance than a church meeting.

Mission is also about the church working outside its own building and so every year we write new plays, often inspired by a biblical character or story, for churches to offer to local primary schools. This gift of a performance is a wonderful way to bless a school and develop closer links. One annual partner said in a report: 'Our mission week with Saltmine reached over 4,500 primary aged children and was generously funded by seven local churches working together - what a mission field on our doorstep!'

Creative outreach using a theatre performance is a great missional opportunity for churches to work together to reach all ages. At a recent event a Police officer said he would invite his whole Police team to a future performance... 'as it was inclusive and non-threatening but inspiringly thought provoking and opened people's eyes to the life and person of Jesus'.

Resources

If you'd like to find out more about Saltmine resources or book them to perform at your church, visit www.saltminetrust.org.uk

Musicals for young people

TWO Composer Sheila Wilson has written over 40 musicals suitable for children and young people that you can put on in church or in local schools. A number can be run any time of year with special musicals explaining the stories and themes of Easter, Christmas and Harvest. All the resources you need (including backing music if you're short on musicians) can be found at www.redheadmusic.co.uk.

ONE TWO **Pure Creative Arts** is a dynamic and multi-faceted company who work through music, theatre in education and workshops to challenge young people to discover their individual worth and potential. For more information on their theatre productions, dance and drama workshops, teaching and evangelistic dramas, how to book the PURE band for performances and leading worship contact info@pure-potential.org.

TWO **Springs Dance Company** offers inspiring performances for churches and schools to suit all tastes and contexts. They also offer workshops for all ages in churches, and in schools will provide tailor-made workshops to link with the curriculum, whether RE, Dance, PSHE or Citizenship. For further details please contact info@springsdancecompany.org.uk or visit www.springsdancecompany.org.uk.

Starting a choir is a fantastic opportunity to work with other churches cross-culturally, demonstrating that we are committed to working together.

Idea for young people

Flash Mob Creatives

ONE Want to draw a crowd in order to raise awareness of an event you're holding? Get your young people to create a Flash Mob. Genetik is the Message Trusts year out training ground for missional leadership, and they have found this simple idea has been fantastic in drawing a crowd in the centre of a village, town or city, and then inviting those people to an event or using it as an opportunity to share the gospel.

The students practised a routine in advance that started off small, adding more and more people as it went on. Alternatively you could use a drama, mime to music, or have a band playing with each instrument seemingly joining in from nowhere until the whole group is playing.

Once over, one person should explain why they did it and then share the gospel or invite people to an event such as a carol service, guest service or fun day. Others can also circulate round the gathered crowd, either during the performance or at the end, handing out flyers or other give-aways that explain why they are there. Flash Mobs can be repeated again and again at intervals in the same place or in multiple places around the town on the same day in order to make a noise and draw a crowd.

Choirs

ONE Gareth Malone has demonstrated the power of bringing groups of people together to sing. We've seen the impact on the workplace and the military, watching in fascination as the process of being in the choir has changed the singers and those that hear their music.

Starting a choir is a fantastic opportunity to work with other churches cross-culturally, demonstrating that we are committed to working together to learn from one another and to see our communities impacted by HOPE. We can sing music from several traditions, harnessing the power of gospel music, as well as traditional and modern hymns.

Music is a part of all traditions, denominations and groupings and Gareth has shown us that this is a moment in our culture for choirs to have new impact. There are many opportunities to showcase the talents of your choir, whether in shopping centres, local schools or specially-run musical events, so let's work together to demonstrate our unity and to bless our communities with the power of music.

Ashford Vineyard

Chris and Nic Kimmance

Having watched TV show, The Choir *with Gareth Malone we wondered if we could take on a similar venture when we moved to plant a church in Ashford, Kent. After some deliberation, we decided that a choir would provide a fantastic opportunity to get to know people in the local area and, as a new church, to give something to the community.*

We started with a website and a Facebook page, then the local newspaper ran an article on us and the local radio picked up the story, giving daily announcements about the choir in the run-up to our first rehearsals. On our opening night we had 80 people there and Ashford Sings! had been born. We completed our first two gigs in local shopping centres in the run up to Christmas and, as we have some people in the choir who work at the local hospice, we've since partnered with them to raise around £8,000 for their work.

So, what of missional opportunities? Firstly, it is important to say that the choir is not a clandestine fishing trip, music in one hand and a concealed barbed hook and bait in the other. We believe that by spending time with people, there will be chances to be a signpost to a relationship with Jesus that will change someone's life. Many people aren't interested at worst, or, at best, are very slow to start asking questions. This has to be OK. In the meantime, we have a community of people to whom we can model love. People pay a small amount each week to come along, but really that covers costs and helps some people out with choir T-shirts or the chance to come on tour. We've made a couple of trips so far – one to Germany and one to France as these are great opportunity to spend time together and get to know each other. There are many in-depth conversations that happen when all the activity has finished.

AN IMPORTANT ELEMENT OF THE CHOIR IS MAKING PEOPLE FEEL SPECIAL AND THAT THEY MATTER. ONE OF THE KEY WAYS WE TRY TO DO THIS IS BY STAYING IN TOUCH WITH PEOPLE.

An important element of the choir is making people feel special and that they matter. One of the key ways we try to do this is by staying in touch with people. Emails are sent to people who miss a couple of rehearsals and flowers are often taken round to people who have been ill. Making people feel welcome when they are there, matters. Ensuring people feel missed when they're not there, also matters.

Community is formed, we believe, through process and crisis. In short, our process is our weekly rehearsals, where we intentionally put a break in proceedings, to give people the chance to talk and drink (decent) coffee. Crisis points are our performances. These two combined, help to gel people together as 'a singing community' as our strap line says.

As Ashford Sings! *has continued we've seen nearly 300 people pass through the doors. In this thriving community that has become a key part of many people's lives, there is a lot of laughter and fun shared. People only look for signposts when they realise they're lost and in much the same way, as we build relationship with people, so we are able to give them the chance to be introduced to Jesus.*

Sports

Barry Mason

Sport, as a ministry, has enabled churches across Britain to share who they are with those who live around them in relevant ways.

The main understanding of how to engage in sport ministry for local churches has been identified in three key areas - namely those of IN SPORT, AROUND SPORT, and THROUGH SPORT. These are very distinctive areas of ministry, yet all important aspects of how the Christian community can use sport as a strategic element of their wider vision for mission.

IN SPORT addresses the needs of those people who identify themselves as sports people and what role church has to play in meeting those needs. On an individual level, this is about churches valuing the members of their congregation and wider community who have a passion for participating in sport, at any level, and supporting them in how they live out their faith in the world of sport.

On a larger scale, this is about churches hosting events that appeal to those who are sporty.

The Christians in Sport Quiz night is a great way to reach people with a love of sport and they can also supply speakers to help host (and to give an evangelistic talk) if required. This provides a great pub quiz atmosphere with high quality, up to date questions and a friendly setting within your church or a local social centre. See www.christiansinsport.org.uk for more details.

AROUND SPORT is probably the area of ministry which was most widely experienced in our country most recently with the Olympics & Paralympics opening the nation's eyes to just how much a major sporting event can capture public interest. We still have further opportunities around Rugby World Cups, the Commonwealth Games being held in Glasgow in 2014, The Ashes, and future football

IN SPORT ADDRESSES THE NEEDS OF THOSE PEOPLE WHO IDENTIFY THEMSELVES AS SPORTS PEOPLE AND WHAT ROLE CHURCH HAS TO PLAY IN MEETING THOSE NEEDS.

World Cups and Euro tournaments. Churches have a great opportunity to put themselves at the heart of their community through these national sporting events.

Consider a festival around these activities, providing a community atmosphere to experience sporting events, when often the only option has been the local pub for the adults, or stay at home for the family. Large screens and a welcoming atmosphere are two simple criteria to act as an invitation to enjoy events ranging from Champions League matches, International Tournaments through to Awards evenings and annual events like Wimbledon or the Six Nations.

Fusion Youth & Community has created a full pack based on their global experience being applied in the UK - explaining everything that would be needed to deliver a festival. The pack gives a step by step guide from start to finish of setting up a festival of any size in your community, covering the basics of setting up team and gathering required equipment through to the trickier aspects of council permissions and preparing for long term follow up. Downloaded it from www.fusionyac.org.

Café in a Box is a great resource for inspiring churches to run a youth focussed café, using any sporting event as a catalyst to gather and welcome their friends. Aylesbury Vale YFC have taken the experiences they have gained in setting up over 20 youth cafes through local churches and council and poured it all into a complete guide pack which can be downloaded from www.cafeinabox.info.

Whilst the major sporting events are the obvious headliners, local events are just as key an opportunity for the local church to engage with. Providing refreshments and hosting for the Salford 10K, the Suffolk Sevens or the North

Shore Surf Tournament will relate much more directly with those participating and watching for whom the event is a major commitment.

THROUGH SPORT is a much wider remit when it comes to ministry opportunities. This considers the use of sport as an activity to join with the wider public community who will happily engage in such events. Whilst this can include football leagues and golf days as an overlap with IN SPORT, it also means running tournament days and teaching within schools.

The likes of YFC's Nomad team (who use a panna football cage) or Daniel Cutting (Professional Freestyle Footballer) are able to use sport to connect with an audience, be it in a structured sense (classrooms, event days) or unstructured (start performing in the local high street). Such performances create an atmosphere where people can chat and ask why the church is serving the community in this way.

We're excited to see the church plan to integrate these young people into their existing youth work.

The Nomad team share, "We partnered with Plymouth Christian Centre as they launched their football youth ministry. A large number of new contacts were made around the cage (including getting to know two Nepalese lads who only moved to the UK a month ago). We're excited to see the church plan to integrate these young people into their existing youth work."

Barry Mason is sports advisor for YFC and chaplain at Salford City Reds

Community Sports Ministry

ONE One of the best ways to get started on any of these areas of ministry is to set up a Community Sports Team (CST). This begins with identifying the people in your church who have an interest in sport and commissioning them to consider what could work for your church(es). Most churches have members who have a passion for sport, but they are not seen as people with ministry potential. If these people are encouraged and supported they can open the doors of the church to many of the local community who may not have even considered coming in otherwise.

Develop a 'Community Sports Team' and you can connect with people through the powerful tool of sport; specifically through:

1. **Community Sports Camps** - weekend or school holiday activities for children or youth
2. **Community Sports Tournaments** - evening or weekend sports specific events for children, youth or adults
3. **Community Sports Festivals** - 'try it and play' events for the whole family at night or during weekends.
4. **School Sports Ministry** - one day 'Games' missions, PE teaching, after school coaching clubs, assemblies and themed RE lessons.

For access to free training and resources to help stage the above ministry activities (or others as you so choose) and to develop a multi church 'Community Sports Team' to ensure ongoing ministry legacy and sustainability please visit www. worldsportministries.com

World Sports Ministries (WSM) Director, Grant Shepherd says, 'WSM Newham is the latest CST and the first of many in London Boroughs. In partnership with other sports ministries, Transform Newham and many churches within the borough, WSM has begun to partner and serve within the area. The Newham team have organised and hosted Under 16 football tournaments, the CrossBar Challenge Sports quiz and partnered in family fun festivals and match screenings.'

To get started in this direction, email reception@ yfc.co.uk and request further info on sports ministry, where we can connect you to the resources or opportunities that will suit your needs.

For delivery of sports ministry in your local church there are a range of events which are relevant depending on the demographics of your church congregation and the target group within your community. Football teams, Golf days, sports

> A COMMUNITY SPORTS TEAM IN YOUR CHURCH COULD EMPOWER PEOPLE TO CONSIDER WHAT WOULD BE MOST EFFECTIVE IN YOUR COMMUNITY.

coaching, activity/fitness classes, day trips to events, big screen viewings are all possibilities to explore how sport can be a relevant way of connecting with your community. If it's on the back pages of the newspaper (local or national) then people are talking about it; if it's active and participatory then people can experience community through it; if there is more than one taking part then people can improve themselves through friendly competition. A CST in your church could empower people to consider what would be most effective in your community.

Nomad

ONE

Nomad are YFC's high energy touring team focused on using a dynamic blend of cage football and relational youth work in order to engage young people with the good news.

The Dutch style 'panna' football utilised by Nomad is a highly effective, versatile tool for sports ministry. The 3 metre high steel cage allows Nomad to connect with young people in a wide variety of settings whilst remaining relevant and absorbing. In schools Nomad deliver a range of cross-curricular lessons focusing on the values and

lifestyle of Christianity. The lessons make use of a varied mix of learning styles in order to provide an interactive and enjoyable learning experience.

Nomad can be a brilliant addition to any detached youth work programme, relevantly engaging with young people where they are. The team regularly run tournaments and cage days at festivals, community days, park events, churches and more. All Nomad coaches are FA qualified, fully trained youth workers. The team are always willing to adapt and meet the specific needs of the area in which they are working and aim to serve you as best they can in your location.

For more information or to book please visit http://www.yfc.co.uk/what-we-do/mission-teams-and-artists

Whatever the size and demographics of your church and the community it is in, there is a place for sports ministry as a strategic part of your outreach.

Step 1 – gather those in your church who could be interested in making it happen

Step 2 – contact those who have done it before and gained some experience (see above)

Step 3 – allow God to use you.

Love Running

Love Running started in Bristol in 2009. It began with a simple idea: wouldn't it be great if we could get our church to run the Bristol 10k en masse? We could demonstrate love in action to those around us. We could raise money for the poor, the oppressed and the needy. We could invite our friends to participate with us in something self-evidently good. We could capture the imagination of our whole city. And we could get fit doing it.

Our initial goal was to have 100 runners and raise £25,000. In the event, we had 300 runners and raised £72,000. We've done it twice since and brought our totals up to 1,400 runners and over £300,000. It's been utterly revolutionary and has now spread to other churches, cities and countries. There's Love Running now in Wales, the north of England, London and the Home Counties, as well as South Africa and Australia.

We've seen Love Running have an incredible impact in engaging Christians with social action and non-Christians with the church

The secret to Love Running is that it is not for those that 'love running'. Rather it is about those who want to see Love running - running to where it's needed the most, running to where it can do most good. That means that we're not aiming at the hard core sports enthusiast, but the person who's never done anything like this before. It's running for the rest of us. That makes 10k a challenge - a challenge that will inspire friends and sponsors, but a challenge that is doable.

We've seen Love Running have an incredible impact in engaging Christians with social action and non-Christians with the church. It's something that's good wherever you look. It's good for you physically, it's good for you socially, it's good for the poor, it's good for the city and, with a series of spiritual training exercises to go alongside the physical ones, it's good for you spiritually.

As a result of the initial successes in Bristol, Manchester and Cardiff, we've now partnered with Tearfund and World Vision to produce a free resource pack for churches who want to do Love Running themselves. The pack contains step-by-step instructions and advice, as well as publicity, booklets and a fully customisable 'intelligent website', complete with training guides, videos, meditations and everything you need to attract, engage and register runners.

It's an idea that is too good to keep to ourselves and we want to give it away to the whole church. To find out more and get your own resource pack and website, visit www.loverunning.org

Resources

For information on many sports ministries in the UK visit www.uksportsministries.org.

Working with Elderly People

James Mumford

A recent poll by the Centre for Social Justice (CSJ) found that almost a quarter of a million over-75s were planning to spend Christmas day alone. Even worse, the poll found that 370,000 over-75s have no regular daily contact with other people. Many of the responses reduced the pollsters to tears. One 90 year old woman from Yorkshire, when asked how much time she spends with others, replied, 'Does the TV count?'

With the breakdown of community life, loneliness has become the most profound problem facing the poorest older people in our country. Whether in a rural context or in the inner city, elderly isolation is by its very nature a hidden problem. It does not spill out onto the streets like youth crime. On the contrary, it happens behind closed doors, afflicting those who are out of sight and out of mind. The World Health Organisation (WHO) rates loneliness as a higher health risk than smoking. The impact of chronic isolation on an individual's resilience cannot be exaggerated.

The church's response

Despite the scale of the isolation problem there are, however, grounds for hope. For while many isolated older people are hidden from society they are often known to many statutory authorities such as Police officers on the beat, fire services who cross the threshold to install smoke detectors, hospital doctors and GPs. These professionals can help your church make contact with lonely and vulnerable older people.

With the breakdown of community life, loneliness has become the most profound problem facing the poorest older people in our country.

Care homes

Surprisingly there are also high levels of loneliness among Britain's 400,000 care home residents. At one nursing home I visited I came across a 99 year old gentleman who said this to me, 'the outside world never comes in here'. All too often care homes are places where the community fears to tread. Indeed, care home managers often report the declining visits even from family members.

The good news here is that finding opportunities to serve older men and women living in care homes is often easier than in the community. A couple of years ago my wife, Holly, and I went to meet with our local care home and set about exploring with them the possibility of taking a group of our friends from our church small group to put on themed teas once a month. The home were receptive to this idea and we began to visit.

We made mistakes; we underestimated things – the challenge of dementia, for instance; and we learnt lessons. Not least that serving in this kind of way requires teamwork and you can only reach/ engage with as many people as you take in (i.e. you need a high number of volunteers), because communication is challenging. But it has been a huge honour.

James Mumford is Senior Policy Researcher at the Centre for Social Justice

Ideas from Fusion

Outings and holidays

ONE Organise day trips to near or far places of interest as an opportunity to socialise and perhaps when you have done a few of these, organise a long weekend or even a week away together.

Meeting needs

ONE Seniors are often concerned with finances, health and death so consider inviting experts in these fields to come and give guidance on these issues (such as how to handle your finances, health advice, funeral arrangements etc). Before you set anything up, ask a few people what would be of most interest and help to them.

Eating together

ONE With many seniors living alone, they often don't bother to cook proper meals for themselves. Get church members to provide a dinner for the elderly people in your community, or organise a trip to an eatery that will provide the group with a low cost lunch. For simple and low cost alternatives you could have a coffee and desserts evening or an afternoon tea.

Encourage church members to befriend elderly people and invite them over for weekly meals.

> OFFER TO PRAY FOR AND WITH ELDERLY PEOPLE WHO ARE SUFFERING PHYSICALLY OR EMOTIONALLY.

Interest groups

ONE As you get to know the elderly people in your community you may find they would like events based around special interests such as arts and crafts, gentle exercise, photography, technology, indoor bowls or board games.

Special events

ONE Holidays can be a particularly painful and lonely time, so try to arrange Christmas, Easter and summer activities such as special meals, film viewings, day trips and social activities.

Daytime Alpha

THREE Hold a special Alpha or Christianity Explored group and arrange transportation to and from the venue for elderly participants.

Prayer

THREE Offer to pray for and with elderly people who are suffering physically or emotionally and give opportunities where they can tell you of friends or family members they would like you to pray for too.

Three times a year a team in the Upper Wylye Valley holds an event for more than 50 senior citizens who may be housebound, unable to afford a holiday, or who have no family. Between 10.30am and 3.30pm they play games, do crossword puzzles, play bingo, and sing popular old songs. Before they all sit to eat a hot lunch together, there is a prayer and thought for the day. Each person is picked up and dropped home by someone on the team, and at Christmas and Easter everyone leaves with a small gift.

Kings Community Church (KCC) near Southampton has been working with the elderly people in its community for a number of years and has seen some amazing results. Once a week they run HALO (Have A Lunch Out) and they currently have 115 members, with around 70 also attending the weekly Sunday afternoon gospel service with an afternoon tea.

As needs grew they started a group for dementia sufferers with themed days, handicrafts, games, singing and outings, as well as lunch. They include in the programme a simple gospel message, hymn singing and they offer individual prayer.

To encourage more men to get involved, KCC ran a men's day trip to a submarine museum and then started a men's group called The Shed which offers alternate weeks of outings and a drop-in coffee time. They regularly invite Christian speakers to give testimony as part of these events. They also run a Holiday at Home every August providing three days of activity during a month when almost all community activities stop for older people.

Since starting this outreach to the elderly, KCC have seen 60 people attend their Alpha course and have five cell groups running (including two in a local sheltered housing complex) and take services once a month in two nursing homes. Several members have been baptised, the eldest being 85! They have seen many put their faith in Jesus and, having taken a number of funerals, have also been able to speak to the families of elderly people about Jesus. They said:

Over the years God has done exceedingly, abundantly more than we could ever ask or think. We've seen that old age, poor sight, hearing, memory or mental ability are no barrier to the power of the gospel to save. One of our over 90 year olds had been widowed and was quite lonely. She had been visited regularly but seemed indifferent to the gospel. The breakthrough happened when one of the team went the extra mile with her by taking her to a hospital appointment and she started asking questions, reading Christian books and started coming to a cell group. The team member had the joy of leading her to the Lord and Loreen was coming regularly to church until she was moved into a nursing home this year.

THEY HAVE SEEN MANY PUT THEIR FAITH IN JESUS AND, HAVING TAKEN A NUMBER OF FUNERALS, HAVE ALSO BEEN ABLE TO SPEAK TO THE FAMILIES OF ELDERLY PEOPLE ABOUT JESUS.

Parche – pastoral action in care homes

All those in residential care have suffered loss of various kinds. Many will have lost their spouse and all of them have had to give up their home and most of their precious possessions. They will probably have lost physical or mental faculties and all these losses cause pain and sadness.

This generation of elderly people have mostly been brought up in the Christian faith, but once they move into residential care, they are often cut off from Church life. Parche – Pastoral Action in Residential Care Homes for the Elderly – was set up to bring pastoral care to older people at this most vulnerable time in their lives by linking local churches with older people living in residential care.

Parche team members find that, if given the opportunity to talk, elderly folk will often ask questions about death and the value of life, whether or not they have been active members of a church in their younger days.

In Eastbourne, East Sussex, where the project was set up, teams from 30 local churches are linked with 73 local care homes. Each month the team of volunteers visits their care home to lead a short Christian service and to chat with residents.

Parche provides training for the teams and resources including CDs of favourite hymn tunes, Bible studies and service guides.

If you would like to explore the possibilities of establishing Parche in your area please contact Parche.

Contact details

www.parche.org.uk
T: 01323 438527
E: parcheenquiries@hotmail.co.uk

Link Visiting Scheme

'I no longer feel trapped inside my house. I feel like I'm living again.'

'It's a life-line. Thank you.'

'Even when I first met my volunteer I felt so much better. I felt someone cares for me for a change!'

The Link Visiting Scheme is a befriending service based in the Borough of Wokingham aiming to combat social isolation among older people primarily through home visits carried out by volunteers once a week for between one and two hours. This contact is often a lifeline to those receiving visits as they may not have contact with the outside world throughout the rest of the week.

Link also now offers weekly 'Understanding Computers' courses to enable older people to access all the internet has to offer, allowing them to communicate regularly with relatives and investigate local activities available to them. They also hold regular 'Pie and Pint Clubs', Singing Groups, Bowls Clubs and various outings and special events, supporting over 250 older people through a team of over 130 volunteers.

Benefits

There is growing evidence of the detrimental effect that isolation and loneliness can have on the health, well-being and life expectancy of people of all ages. The model of The Link Visiting Scheme provides a crucial social point of contact which, in itself, helps to build self-confidence and self-esteem and often leads to improved mental health and independence. Consequently, Link friends can gain improvements in their mobility and explore options to visit local clubs, church activities and events leading to the establishment of a wider circle of friends.

Even when I first met my volunteer I felt so much better. I felt someone cares for me for a change!

Grants available see www.cinnamonnetwork.co.uk for details

Volunteer visitors also gain from the experience of sharing in the life of an older person leading to a greater understanding of life in earlier times. Volunteers often report a sense of achievement and mutual benefit by having contact with a member of the community who appreciates them.

Challenges

Finding a suitable visitor for a particular person can be a challenge, particularly where there are specific interests or hobbies to try and match. Older people themselves will at times require more specialised knowledge or experience, either because of particular character traits or memory loss etc. We provide necessary training enabling volunteers to respond to these situations effectively, and ensure that there is appropriate support in place.

How easy is it to replicate this idea?

This model works well in both rural and urban settings and can be set up with minimal resources. The primary need is for a team of Christians with a heart for older people and an enthusiasm to work with various churches and other agencies. A period of around six months is required to plan and prepare for the launch of a project during which time networks are developed, relationships built with key agencies, volunteers recruited, office space obtained and funds raised. This process will be supported and guided by those with experience within The Link Visiting Scheme. An initial sum of around £3,500 would enable a small scale project to start followed by a further £3,000 per year to run the project on a voluntary basis. An annual sum of around £13,000 would be required if employing a staff member for two days per week.

The model works best if run as a partnership between local churches.

Tips

- As with any community project, we recommend assessing the local need prior to embarking on the planning process. Many local communities now have increasing numbers of older people who are often living alone, however the need for a befriending project should be established as part of the planning process.
- Make contact with the Adult Services Department at the local authority as well as voluntary organisations involved in supporting older people.

Contact details

www.linkvisiting.org
E: Individual email address available from website
T: 0118 9798019

Carol's story

When we first met Carol she was quiet and withdrawn. She felt nervous at the thought of being with people she didn't know and didn't have the confidence to go outside on her own. She had a few health worries and her son lived a distance away. She was spending many days alone and speaking to no one. Like many of the older people we meet she was in desperate need of seeing a friendly face - someone willing to spend some quality time with her and show a real interest.

After meeting her we introduced her to a volunteer who shared her love of gardening and wildlife. Some weeks they would take a trip to a local garden centre then pot plants together. The simple act of visiting began to transform her life and it didn't take long to see the results. Her volunteer encouraged her to join a local club doing gentle exercise. We arranged for the library to visit regularly and deliver books for her to read. We enrolled her in a club that took her out once a month on an outing and she came to our monthly pub lunch. Her mobility improved too and she began to take short walks in her neighbourhood and joined her local church!

My role as a volunteer visitor has taught me a lot about what older people have to offer.

Sheila started visiting in 2009 and immediately realised that this was what she wanted to do. She had always cared about older people and was concerned about their need to get out more. She quickly realised that the regular visits made a significant impact in the life of her Link friend and this in turn enabled her to gain a sense of satisfaction. Sheila said, 'My role as a volunteer visitor has taught me a lot about what older people have to offer. Once we get through the small talk it is wonderful to be able to hear all about the wide experiences of my Link friend. I do not find the visits at all boring – it is a blessing to spend time with her.' Sheila was moved to have been told by one of the friends she visits 'you have become the daughter that I never had'.

Sheila, Link volunteer

Working with the Media

Working with the media provides a great opportunity for the Church to raise awareness about all the things it's up to. The more people who know about the projects on offer – and the heart behind them – the more people may want to get involved in your activity and/or come to church! In the past, churches have often been wary of the media, worrying that they will twist things we say and that they have a hidden agenda to make us look bad. The truth is that most local journalists are just looking for a good story that will interest their readers – something that no doubt all your activities in the church can provide!

The Evangelical Alliance has put together these helpful tips for effective communication with the media:

1. Put together a list of local media contacts and be rigorous about keeping their details up-to-date. Many journalists can be easily contacted via Twitter and Facebook too.
2. Look at how your local press report things and write your press release in that style, not forgetting that journalists don't like attachments so send the release in the body of the email. Review the local press for relevant articles to establish an understanding of the outlook and style. Remember that a news story always tries to answer six questions - what, where, when, how, why and who – so make sure your press release does that. The journalist will appreciate it.
3. Decide on your message and repeat it in different ways throughout your press release. Repetition can work well if done right.

> THE TRUTH IS THAT MOST LOCAL JOURNALISTS ARE JUST LOOKING FOR A GOOD STORY THAT WILL INTEREST THEIR READERS – SOMETHING THAT NO DOUBT ALL YOUR ACTIVITIES IN THE CHURCH CAN PROVIDE!

4. Arrange a meeting with the editor or a senior journalist of your local newspaper. Good relationships will help your press releases be viewed more favourably. This is vitally important.
5. Take a number of good, high quality, high-resolution photos to go with your press release – sometimes having a good image can determine whether your story gets used. Also, if they are needed to support the story, make sure that you have clear, understandable statistics at hand.
6. Contact local radio stations – BBC stations have regular religious programmes each Sunday (see news.bbc.co.uk/local for details) and independent stations are keen to hear good local news stories (find a directory of stations on www.radio-now.co.uk)
7. Issue press releases regularly, especially when you have a local angle on a story that is appearing in the national press.
8. Invite the local press to an appropriate event such as a community barbecue and to an event where they can meet a number of local church leaders together.
9. Try to have the same spokesperson all the time and make sure all your communications such as your website are saying the same things for consistency.
10. Read up on it. Suggested reading:

Public Relations - a practical guide to the basics by Philip Henslowe (Kogan Page)

Public Relations in Practice Edited by Ann Gregory (Kogan Page)

How to write a press release

Format – Use a single A4 page, double space the lines and use size 11 or 12 font. If, when you have written the press release, it is longer than you thought cut it back to one page by using 1.5 spacing for the lines and/or using a smaller font (don't be tempted to simply reduce the text size to fit it all in).

Date – State the date clearly at the top of the page.

Heading – At the top of the page write a VERY short and punchy heading for the story. The heading should be underlined in bold and in UPPER CASE.

First paragraph – An introduction clearly and concisely describing the 'who, what, where, when and why' of the story.

Further paragraphs – You may include up to three or four further paragraphs, depending on length, which can quote someone involved, describe facts, tell a brief story and/or quote a leader.

Words – Use language that is used in our culture avoiding jargon words that you might only hear in the church community.

Contact – At the bottom of the page include the name, telephone number and email of a nominated media spokesperson and a web address for the relevant organisations if available.

Photograph – For press contacts do provide a quality digital photograph which can be attached to the press release email.

Set up a photo opportunity for the local media that involves an interesting group of people, in an interesting place, doing something interesting.

Publicity ideas

- ***Make your story about local people*** – Demonstrate the benefit your project brings for a particular group of local people, such as young people, the elderly or single parents.
- **Celebrities** – Involve a local celebrity or public figure such as a Member of Parliament in your project or programme's event, as this will provide the media with another point of interest in your story.
- **Photocalls** – Set up a photo opportunity for the local media that involves an interesting group of people, in an interesting place, doing something interesting.
- **Statistics** – Link in your story to any local or regional statistics that demonstrate the community need you are addressing, such as the fact that youth crime rates are high as kids are bored in the holidays so you're running a youth initiative for them.
- **Community questionnaire** – You could run a very simple community questionnaire in order to gain some figures on what people think about particular issues or situations. For example 77% of local people are concerned about the lack of activities for young people.

Resources

The Evangelical Alliance has a helpful section on their website covering working with the media, writing letters to editors, an example press release and information on local media. Visit the Media Resources section of www.eauk.org for more information.

VIDEOSCHOOL

Hosted by BBC presenter Cherrie Healey, VIDEOSCHOOL is a DVD training resource and reference manual that aims to equip the Church with the skills it needs to tell its stories using visual media.

VIDEOSCHOOL started as a series of courses aiming to give delegates from churches, charities, NGOs and youth organisations the opportunity to learn from professional producers, directors, camera operators, presenters and editors from the world of TV and film. It provides a unique opportunity to have hands-on learning, mixed with expert guidance from industry professionals, with just a dash of real-world pressure all in the space of a few days.

VIDEOSCHOOL has now been captured into six programmes that each focus on a different part of short film production including camera basics, presenting, editing, and production.

VIDEOSCHOOL is partnering with HOPE to make this available at a subsidised rate and will be providing training events to compliment the VIDEOSCHOOL resource. Whether you are an enthusiastic amateur looking to sharpen your story-telling skills or a youth group looking for a new challenge, this course offers a unique opportunity to go on a fun and inspiring journey into the world of film making.

For more info please visit www.videoschool.org

Working with Victims of Violence

Imagine living a life forced to serve men daily in any way they choose. Imagine living in fear of violence and abuse.

This was the reality for Zoe, who was trafficked into the UK for the purposes of sexual exploitation; she was repeatedly raped for profit.

Zoe was asked to come to the UK from Eastern Europe by a friend who told her she could arrange a job for her in a hotel. On her arrival Zoe was picked up by a man and a woman and taken to a hotel. Then she was handed some underwear and told to put it on. She was then violently abused, raped on multiple occasions and forced to work as a prostitute. Zoe realised with increasing horror that she had been trafficked. She was moved from town to town in the UK and then sold to another trafficker. She was too terrified to escape. At one point a police officer even spoke to her but she was too scared to tell him what was really happening; her trafficker had told her they owned the police. After months of investigation Hope for Justice found Zoe and rescued her from this devastating situation. One of the investigators told her, 'Zoe, you're a princess. You're a daughter of the King.' As she sobbed, the investigator heard her whispering, 'I'm a princess, I'm a princess.' Zoe was immediately placed into aftercare to allow her to recover and she's now rebuilding her life.

This is just one of the heart-breaking stories involving trafficking victims that Hope for Justice regularly deal with.

Human trafficking is modern day slavery. It's a serious, organised crime and it's a big business. Drugs and guns can only be sold once by a criminal but criminals can sell a victim's services again and again.

The easiest way to understand human trafficking is to break it down into three simple parts.

Act - HOW criminals do it e.g. recruitment, transportation, transfer or harbouring.

Means - The WAY criminals do it e.g. threat or use of force, abduction, fraud, deception, abuse of power or position of vulnerability.

Exploitation - WHAT criminals do it for e.g. prostitution, sexual exploitation, forced labour or services, slavery or removal of organs from a person without their consent.

Hope for Justice's vision is to assist the police practically through intelligence-gathering and rescuing trafficked victims within the UK. They build bridges of trust between police and victim, and act as a conduit for intelligence that would otherwise never see the light of day. They then move rescued victims into aftercare, offer protection and rehabilitation, and help rebuild the lives of the children, men and women who have been robbed of a life we take for granted.

Through all of this, their key role is ensuring that perpetrators are held responsible for their crimes via prosecution. The Hope for Justice legal team focuses on evidence and intelligence-gathering to generate prosecution cases and develop strong, professional relationships with law enforcement.

You can get involved! **ACTFORJUSTICE** is a network of over 100 groups in the UK that support the rescue mission of Hope for Justice. Each ACTFORJUSTICE group is made up of like-minded people who take their passion for ending human trafficking to the next level and act. Groups are mainly based around church communities and meet once a month to pray, fundraise, campaign and spread the word in their local community.

For more information visit www.hopeforjustice.org.uk

Human trafficking is modern day slavery. It's a serious, organised crime and it's a big business.

Small Groups that Empower Mission

Getting our small groups excited about mission provides an amazing resource for churches to sustain mission on a long-term basis. Give each small group in your church access to a copy of this resource and encourage them to spend an evening talking, praying and planning together about what they could commit to as a group.

Resources

Matt Garvin from Fusion has written a book called ***6 Radical Decisions*** which comes with a free Small Group Leaders' guide. It provides an accessible and empowering pattern for equipping the members of your church to find their unique place in mission with Kingdom Cells at its core.

GETTING OUR SMALL GROUPS EXCITED ABOUT MISSION PROVIDES AN AMAZING RESOURCE FOR CHURCHES TO SUSTAIN MISSION ON A LONG-TERM BASIS.

Top five ideas for small groups:

1. ***Sacrificial giving during Lent***
2. ***Neighbourhood pancake party***
3. ***Love your street***
4. ***Harvest supper***
5. ***Random acts of kindness***

Cell UK has created a resource called ***40 Creative Missional Ideas for Small Groups*** which is a tin holding 40 cards, each with an idea for mission that take about five to ten minutes per small group meeting. This is a great way to get groups thinking about being missional and how their members can make a difference in the work place, where they live and in the context of the local church. Find more details at www.celluk.org.uk

final thoughts
'One of the aims of HOPE is to bring together the whole church to show we can work together for the sake of the Kingdom.'

United But Different

Encouraging and exploring greater unity across ethnic lines

Yemi Adedeji

One of the aims of HOPE is to bring together the whole Church to show we can work together for the sake of the Kingdom. Unity with believers from different backgrounds is crucial, for all believers are equal in God's sight. Yet whilst we must be willing to come together, we must remember that diversity can be celebrated too.

Throughout the New Testament we see that Christ's Kingdom brings belonging, membership, communion, equality, common purpose and familial bonds. Jesus' attitude to Samaritans is especially important in demonstrating the radical inclusiveness of his ministry and Kingdom in the face of the Jewish hatred of Samaritans. Luke refers to Samaritans for this purpose six times in his two books. Nevertheless, Jesus' own ministry was directed mostly to Jews. His mission to the Jews was expected to set the context for Gentile reception of the message.

Peter proclaimed 'I now realise how true it is that God does not show favouritism, but accepts from every nation the one who fears him and does what is right' (Acts 10:34-35). In Ephesians 2, Paul reminds his Gentile readers that at the cross Jesus made one new man out of Jews and Gentiles, by abolishing the dividing wall of the law. While the cross is where hostility between God and man ceases, Paul explains how it also put to death hostility between people who are part of 'the body'. This was a politically radical message.

In Revelation we have a wonderful picture of the Great Commission fulfilled, as people from every nation, tribe, people and language stand before the Lamb. The unity of humankind as seen in Genesis is redeemed, yet Revelation does not suggest that the differences are obliterated. These are still worshippers from different nations, tribes, peoples and languages and this diversity reflects God's glory even further; different people are united in a common act of worship.

WHILST WE MUST BE WILLING TO COME TOGETHER, WE MUST REMEMBER THAT DIVERSITY CAN BE CELEBRATED TOO.

The practice of unity

It is perhaps difficult to understand what it means to be a member of another ethnic group; it is particularly difficult for majority ethnicities to imagine how it feels to be in a minority. The influence of race on our thinking or our interaction with other people is often subconscious. Christians need to awaken their consciences in this area, and reflect on our thoughts, words and actions. Rather than denying that we often stereotype people on the basis of ethnicity, or subtly seek to disassociate ourselves from people of other ethnicities, we need to take positive and practical steps to appreciate the wonderful unity that is the one body of Christ.

As individual Christians we might make friends with believers and non-believers from other ethnicities – by inviting them to our church or home for lunch, or by making contact with ethnic minority parents at the local school. By talking to Christians with radically different backgrounds, it is possible to renew our faith and to become conscious of some of our failings and how culture has distorted the gospel. Too often Christians follow the world's model of friendship, seeking to get alongside those who are like them. This is natural, and yet in this increasingly globalised world, we have all the more opportunities to meet and befriend people from other backgrounds for the sake of the gospel.

As we befriend those of other ethnicities, there should still be opportunities for us to identify our own heritages, for instance, considering what it means to be a Nigerian Christian, or a white English Christian. This can involve an appreciation of the way God has formed our particular cultures – our history, music and language – and how this shapes how we apply our faith. There will also be areas, such as relationships with the wider community or family and particular forms of social interaction, which mean that we will feel more at home with believers who are like us. This should not be denied. The individual believer should thus seek to live out the twin principles by seeking after those unlike themselves, and also by finding comfort from those of a similar heritage. The local congregation of believers should seek to live within the tension of unity and diversity.

Corporate worship must involve the coming together of peoples from multiple backgrounds in terms of ethnicity, class and age, to glorify God and to help each other to follow him. Such gatherings will require sacrifices in terms of preferred styles of singing and preaching. Yet there will need to be other occasions where differences are recognised, such as in the organisation of small groups for fellowship. Each congregation will have to find a balance between the unity of the gospel and how God calls us as people with different identities.

The multiethnic church is a tremendous resource for evangelism. By drawing attention to the diversity of its members, the Church might present an attractive alternative to the cultural relativism so prevalent today. The multiethnic Church presents the gospel as something that holds for people everywhere, and which is visibly followed by all ethnicities.

Ultimately there is only one Church. As believers we should see ourselves as members of a global communion of Christians from multiple nations and backgrounds. Let's strive for a balance between unity and diversity. The time is soon coming when both will take their proper place. It is a glorious prospect to look forward to the multiple nations, tribes, peoples and languages of heaven!

Revd Yemi Adedeji is Associate Director of HOPE

A Big Vision

Roy Crowne

It's a big vision, a big dream, to mobilise the whole Church into mission, to see every village, town and city being good news; but that's the challenge. It's like when you have a piece, or many pieces of a jigsaw laid out on a table, it can look random and very confusing. However, once all those pieces, no matter how large or small, find their place in the jigsaw, what seemed confusing becomes an amazing picture.

We live in a country with many different churches of different sizes, shapes and groups of people. As long as we stand alone, people won't see the amazing picture that is there. But when we come together, whether in a village, town or a massive city, we see what Christ can do to reveal his Church in transforming our communities. We need to recognise that we're part of the family of God and that in working together, the Church can do extraordinary things. If we take a step of faith and invite people to be part of even the smallest coffee morning, lunch club or village social evening, within the rhythm of mission, very soon our churches could become the heartbeat of our communities.

I'm convinced the time is right for these things to happen. When we shared the vision of Hope08, to see churches in every village, town and city reach out with the good news of Jesus Christ, through word and actions, churches in Devon and Cornwall wanted to embrace that initiative but realised there were many villages spread across a wide geographical area. They dreamed up a cream tea initiative under the HOPE umbrella for every village to take part in during the summer. A very simple, achievable, mustard seed idea resulted in many villages coming together, sharing stories of faith around a cream tea and putting the Church at the heart of their village communities. Nothing is too small for God to breathe on and bless.

We need to recognise that we're part of the family of God and that in working together, the Church can do extraordinary things.

What has God placed in your hand that you could do, that he could breathe on and bless and could result in transforming lives and transforming communities? He is always working and the Church, this unique sleeping giant, has the opportunity to awaken and be all that God has called us to be.

So, the time is now, to pray, to see what God could do and what a great legacy could be left where churches find one another, realise they can work together, being and speaking good news in villages, towns and cities.

It's been impossible to put every idea and resource in this book and so if you're looking for more ideas, then do visit HOPE's website www.hopetogether.org.uk.

My prayer for you and for the Church is that we'll take hold of our God-given opportunities, take a step of faith, find people that will join with us together and do as Jesus has commanded us, in both words and actions to bring about changed communities.

Index

Acknowledgements

HOPE Executive Director:

Roy Crowne

HOPE Associate Director:

Yemi Adedeji

The HOPE Board of Directors:

Steve Clifford (Chairman)
Evangelical Alliance

Andy Hawthorne OBE
The Message Trust

Mike Pilavachi
Soul Survivor

Steve Price
HOPE

The HOPE Leadership Team:

Wendy Beech-Ward
Compassion

Matt Bird
Make It Happen*

Ian Bunce
Baptist Union of Great Britain

Gavin Calver
Youth for Christ

Joanne Cox
Methodist Church

Jane Holloway
World Prayer Centre

Ann Holt OBE
Bible Society

Rachel Jordan
Church of England

Wayne Malcolm
Christian Life City Church

Ade Omooba
Christian Concern/Christian Legal Centre

Keira Phyo
Tearfund

Laurence Singlehurst
Cell UK

David Westlake
Tearfund

Spring Harvest

Thank you to everyone who has contributed ideas, articles and help to this resource including:

Matt Bird, Craig Borlase, Rebekah Brettle, Catherine Butcher, Lyndall Bywater, Lucy Cooper, Ken Costa, Graham Cray, Steven Croft, Roy Crowne, Evangelical Alliance, Roger Forster, Fusion Youth and Community, Paula Gooder, James Featherby, Mark Greene, Michael Harvey, Adrian Holloway, Jane Holloway, Agu Irukwu, Christopher Jamison, Philip Jinadu, Andy Kennedy, Wayne Malcolm, Barry Mason, James Mumford, Simon Nicholls, Rachael Orrel, Andy Paterson, Kiera Phyo, Laurence Singlehurst, Dave Smith, Rt Hon Caroline Spelman MP, Rt Hon Stephen Timms, MP, Phil Timson, UCCF, Celeste Viggers, Rowan Williams, Rich Wilson, and to all the churches and charities who shared their stories and expertise.

Editorial team

Director - Roy Crowne

Associate Director - Yemi Adedeji

Commissioning Editor - Laurence Singlehurst

Editor and writer - Liza Hoeksma

Project manager - Steve Gee

Editorial Consultant - Catherine Butcher

Cover photography: Alex Baker
www.alexbakerphotography.com

Designed by Mike Thorpe:
www.design-chapel.com

Contact HOPE at:

8A Market Place

Rugby

Warwickshire

CV21 3DU

www.hopetogether.org.uk

T: 01788 542782

E: info@hopetogether.org.uk

Published by HOPE08 Ltd

New International Version - UK (NIVUK)